# India 2000:
# The Next
# Fifteen Years

# India 2000: The Next Fifteen Years

*The papers of a symposium conducted by the Center for Asian Studies of the University of Texas at Austin as part of the 1985-86 Festival of India in the United States*

James R. Roach, editor

The Riverdale Company, Inc., Publishers
Riverdale, Maryland, USA

Published in India by
Allied Publishers Private Limited
New Delhi   Bombay   Calcutta   Madras
Bangalore   Hyderabad   Ahmedabad

Library of Congress Card No. 85 63423
ISBN 0-913215-11-2


©The Riverdale Company

Published in the United States of America by
The Riverdale Company, Inc., Publishers
Suite 102, 5506 Kenilworth Avenue
Riverdale, Maryland 20737

Allied Publishers Private Limited
13/14 Asaf Ali Road
New Delhi 110002


Production and Manufacturing by
Publishers Resource Center
Reston, Virginia

# Preface

The essays in this volume were written for a seminar at The University of Texas at Austin, February 7–9, 1985. Originally planned as a small local enterprise, the seminar was enlarged by its inclusion as an event of the 1985–86 Festival of India in the United States. We are grateful for the assistance of the Indo-US Subcommission on Education and Culture, especially Maureen Liebl of the Subcommission's New York office, and for contributions in kind by Air India and Pan American World Airways.

To reviewers — if there be any — inclined to make familiar comments about difficulties in discerning a symposium's organizing theme, or about variegated topics, or even about the differing quality of papers: We thought of those in planning, but we wanted a subject that was current, would require participants to focus on the reasonably short term, would accommodate a number of disciplines, and would have appeal to a generally interested public. Those objectives were met, even if the price may have been the loss of some inner consistency between book covers. In any case, most of the essays can stand alone as informed and thoughtful contributions.

We note with sorrow the death in May 1985 of Professor Raj Krishna, a participant and contributor. His abilities as economist-provocateur enlivened many Indo-American exchanges and he will be missed. We are pleased that this collection includes some of his last thoughts and opinions about his country's economy — present and future.

The editor takes full responsibility and expresses his apologies to any author who may feel that undue liberties have been taken with his or her essay. He expresses his thanks to members of the Center for Asian Studies staff — Louise Flippin, Tracey Lee, and Elizabeth Andrews, and Elizabeth Brown in particular — and to Mary Power and John Adams of The Riverdale Company.

*Austin, Texas*                                                                 James R. Roach
*January 1986*

*v*

# Contents

# The Contributors

**LAWRENCE A. BABB** is Professor of Anthropology at Amherst College. His University of Rochester Ph.D. is based on research on popular Hinduism in the Chhattisgarh region of Madhya Pradesh. He has also done research on Hindu institutions in Singapore and on modern sectarian movements in urban North India. He is the author of *The Divine Hierarchy: Popular Hinduism in Central India* and has contributed numerous chapters and articles on aspects of Indian religion to books, journals, and reviews.

**CHIDANANDA DAS GUPTA** has been a professor of English, advertising executive, independent film producer, and editor of *SPAN* (published by USIA for Indian readers), and most recently a Fellow of the Woodrow Wilson Center at the Smithsonian Institution. He is the author of *Cinema of Satyajit Ray, Talking About Films*, and contributions to journals and newspapers. He has been a member of the board of directors of the Indian Film Finance Corporation and of juries of international film festivals. His best known film is *Dance of Shiva*, a documentary on the life and work of Coomaraswamy.

**SUSAN G. HADDEN** is Associate Professor at the LBJ School of Public Affairs at The University of Texas at Austin. Her recent research has centered on a variety of environmental and health issues, including hormones in cattle feed, siting of hazardous waste and radioactive waste disposal facilities, regulation of pesticides, and the state of the environment in India. Her book, *Read the Label: Providing Information to Control Risk*, describes regulation of food, drugs, consumer products, workplace safety, and the environment. Earlier, Hadden's work focused on agricultural policy in India and provision of rural infrastructure. She majored in Sanskrit as an undergraduate.

**ROBERT D. KING** is Dean, College of Liberal Arts, Rapoport Professor of Liberal Arts, and Professor of Linguistics at the University of Texas at Austin. His first field research in India was with the Munda Language Project sponsored by the University of Chicago in 1963, and he has made recent visits to India in 1982 and 1984. Dean King serves as a member of the Board of Trustees of the American Institute of Indian Studies.

**RAJ KRISHNA,** who died on May 20, 1985, was Professor of Economics in the University of Delhi School of Economics. Holder of a Chicago Ph.D. in agricultural econometrics, he taught at the University of Rajasthan and at Stanford, and was with the World Bank in Washington in 1969-70 and 1973-75. He served on many Indian government advisory bodies and committees, most prominently the Planning Commission, Agricultural Prices Commission, Seventh Finance Commission, and the Land Reforms Committee. His articles and papers have appeared in books and journals published worldwide. Several recent papers focused on the Indian economy, growth, investment, employment, and poverty.

**C. T. KURIEN** is Director of the Madras Institute of Development Studies, a post assumed in 1978 after fifteen years as Professor of Economics at Madras Christian College. He has a Stanford Ph.D. and did post-doctoral work at Yale. He is a member of the Panel of Economists of the Indian Planning Commission, and in 1983-84 served on a panel of experts preparing the UN World Food Council's document on **The World Food and Hunger Problem.** His publications include *Poverty and Development, Economic Change in Tamil Nadu,* and *Dynamics of Rural Transformation.*

**SWADESH M. MAHAJAN** is Senior Research Scientist and a member of the Institute of Fusion Studies at the University of Texas at Austin. His graduate work was done at Maryland and Princeton and he has been Visiting Professor at the Indian Institute of Plasma Physics in Ahmedabad. His work focuses on plasma physics and on quantum mechanics and relativity theory.

**V. K. NARAYANA MENON** is Chairman of the Sangeet Natak Akademi (the national acadamy of music, dance, and drama of India). Educated at Madras and Edinburgh, he worked for the BBC during World War II. He joined All-India Radio in 1948 and eventually became its Director General. From there he became the founding Executive Director of the National Centre for the Performing Arts in Bombay, a position he left to join the Akademi in 1982. His books include *Balasaraswati* and *The Communications Revolution.* He was awarded Padma Bhushan in 1969, and currently is a member of the Indo-US Subcommission on Education and Culture.

**GAIL MINAULT** is Associate Professor of History at The University of Texas at Austin, specializing in modern South Asian history. She has lived and worked in Pakistan and Bangladesh as well as India, and spent 1982-84 in India doing research and translations from Urdu texts. Her publications include *The Khilafat Movement, Voices of Silence* (forthcoming, translated from Urdu), and two edited volumes, *The Extended Family: Women and Political Participation in India* and *Separate Worlds: Studies of Purdah in South Asia.*

**M. N. SRINIVAS,** Honorary Professor of the Indian Institute of Management in Bangalore, is formerly a Homi Bhabha Senior Fellow and Joint Director and Senior Fellow of the Institute for Social and Economic Change. He has been a teacher or fellow at Oxford, Manchester, Baroda, Delhi, Stanford, Santa Cruz, Cornell, the Center for Advanced Study in the Behavioral Sciences, Australian National University, New England (Australia), and Singapore. He was awarded Padma Bhushan in 1976. His publications include *Religion and Society Among the Coorgs of South India, Social Change in Modern India,* and *The Remembered Village.*

**E. C. G. SUDARSHAN** is Co-Director of the Center for Particle Theory and Professor of Physics at The University of Texas at Austin. (Currently, he is also acting as Director of the Institute of Mathematical Science in Madras.) He holds a Rochester Ph.D. and was a Corporation Fellow at Harvard in 1957-59. He was awarded Padma Bhushan in 1976 and the Bose Medal from the Indian National Science Academy. He is the co-author of *Introduction to Elementary Particle Physics, Fundamentals of Quantum Optics,* and *Classical Dynamics.*

**PAUL WALLACE** is Chairman and Professor of Political Science at the University of Missouri at Columbia. He holds a Berkeley Ph.D. and has spent frequent periods of fieldwork and research in India, beginning in 1963. He has studied rural and peasant political movements, state politics, aspects of center-state relations and, increasingly, the Punjab. He is co-editor of *Political Dynamics of Punjab* and editor of *Region and Nation in India.*

**MYRON WEINER** is Ford International Professor of Political Science at MIT. His work in India started in 1953 and his many publications include *Politics of Scarcity; Sons of the Soil; State Politics in India;* and *India at the Polls, 1980.* Currently he is engaged in a comparative study of electoral politics in developing countries and at MIT is head of an interdepartmental study group on migration and development. He is a member of the American Academy of Arts and Sciences.

# India 2000:
# The Next
# Fifteen Years

# Introduction

JAMES R. ROACH

# I

The impact of a "successor generation" on life in the West has been much written and speculated about, as the presence and influence of 40-year-olds begin to become more apparent in politics, public service, the media, and business. In India that generation has not had to work its way up; it started at the top when a youthful Rajiv Gandhi became Prime Minister following the assassination of his mother in October 1984. He has also assumed the leadership of the Congress (I), the political party that has dominated the Indian scene since independence in 1947 and is still the only countrywide party. Rajiv Gandhi is the third generation of a family that, with two brief interruptions, has supplied India's Prime Ministers since 1947. Among heads of state in the democratic world today — indeed, in the world generally — he is surely *sui generis*.

By mid-summer of 1985, following highly successful parliamentary elections and somewhat less successful state assembly elections, and after state visits to Moscow and Washington, the first assessments of the new leader began to come in. These were mostly very tentative and mostly eschewed prediction. He is attractive, personable, surprisingly at ease for his years and limited public experience; forthright but not tendentious; pragmatic as — it is suggested — befits an engineer, airline pilot, and one concerned about science and technology and their potential in his country. He is not given to lecturing others, as his grandfather often did — albeit often with charm and wit. He does not reveal the ideology or suspicion that at times gave an abrasive edge to his mother's public behavior. And, of course, there are the early New Delhi reports and rumors of shifts in the inner circle, in the Cabinet, in the party hierarchy in favor of new, younger figures who, it is said, are more "attuned" to the new leader's informal yet impatient and experimental "style." We are advised to anticipate a "new era" in the politics and governing of India, with important consequences for the country's social and economic as well as political future.

The think pieces that appear, and the adjectives that are used, are not unfamiliar to those who have observed shifts of leadership in many parts of the world, including India. The initial enthusiasm and optimism are high, the new chief is wished well, but only the passage of time will show if the hopes and promises are realized — and, it is fearlessly predicted, some will not be. Anyone familiar with India will recognize this phenomenon, and that is why most first assessments wisely are tentative ones. Those who know India are sensitive to its diversity, complexity, traditions, and multiple problems and demands. They express admiration for the new Prime Minister, and do wish him well, but wait to see where he seeks to lead India and with what success, the different observers applying different criteria of "success."

The essays in this collection originally were written for a February 1985 seminar, and many were essentially complete before the changes that followed October 1984. Some are about topics little affected by politics. Others are about the very stuff of politics. Their authors made revisions in light of events and the violence of which Mrs. Gandhi's death was a part. But the striking fact is that these events, however deplorable or unexpected, had little effect on the validity of what had already been written. India goes on, the continuity is strong, and the conditions and problems confronting a new leadership remain much as before. Thus, an exercise planned to speculate about India in the next 15 years — to the year 2000 — became, if tragically, more relevant than it might have been. In these essays the reader encounters facts and opinions about much of what Rajiv Gandhi has inherited, as well as many suggestions about the agenda that confronts India's successor generation.

# II

From first to last, attention is drawn repeatedly in these essays to the divisions within India's population and society, and the increasing difficulty for government in simultaneously containing and responding to the activism and the demands arising among these elements. There is need for an Indian Madison to do a new treatise on factions in politics, for in India these have become deeper, sharper, and more self-conscious over time. While India is unlikely to fragment in ways that Selig Harrison once speculated about in the 1950s, Indian public life and political behavior reflect a heightened awareness among Indians of their separate identities, and a willingness to pursue selfish interests at considerable cost to others and to the nation at large.

Educational and employment reservations, and other forms of "protective discrimination," intensify the self-consciousness of those who are — and hope to remain — the beneficiaries, and of those who are not among the eligible. While many Indians have enjoyed the new opportunities and advantages arising from economic growth, many others have been excluded. There is more recognition of this condition on both sides of the divide. Independence and democratic government have, in fact, fed this divisive self-consciousness by providing new institutions and channels for the expression, pursuit, or protection of separate interests: central and state legislatures, federalism, public education, political parties, elections, and, on occasion, even the law enforcement agencies. Recently, the military has been used to supplement or to supersede inadequate or unreliable police forces.

Many Indians insist that foreigners, even knowledgeable ones, exaggerate the depth and seriousness of India's internal divisions. Contrary arguments state that these divisions have always existed. They fluctuate in intensity and seriousness, with no more than one or two ever becoming truly difficult at the same time. The authorities ultimately manage to cope. Further, it is asserted that political and economic changes ameliorate the friction and often lead formerly divided interests to join in pursuit of common causes. One might cite the burgeoning activity by and on behalf of women as a current example of line-crossing.

It would be easier to be sanguine about India's prospects if the economic and population projections were, respectively, higher and lower. Politics in India is largely about distribution and there are or will be too many seeking or expecting, and there is not enough and will not be enough with which to respond to all that is desired. Professor Kurien writes of the "paradox" of development that has brought many into the economic mainstream but has left so many behind, some even farther behind than before. Professor Raj Krishna's forecasts to the year 2000 suggest the probable worsening of this situation.

The optimist will find India's glass half full, the pessimist will find it half empty. Certainly the accomplishments since independence, and the accelerated pace of change in many sectors in the last decade, should not be denigrated. India's problem of numbers versus its resources is a constant — even an acceptable fact of life if one is not personally suffering the consequences.

India has paid a price for overcentralization of development planning and administration. Its large and rigid bureaucracy has a self-interest in perpetuating the status quo. Its political party system has never presented the Indian public with genuine national and viable policy and leadership alternatives to those of the Congress party. This situation has precluded a national debate about "distributive justice." Distributing poverty is not an acceptable option; some resources have gone untapped; some sectors have been too much encouraged, others given little attention. Many now have significantly more, while the numbers on the other side of the poverty line are growing more self-conscious and impatient.

Marxists call this economic class struggle. Their analysis is not wrong but is incomplete since on both sides of the line there are many other diversities that characterize Indian society. Boundaries and barriers exist vertically as well as horizontally. The demands are sometimes economic but as often they are about something else. The result is a bewildering and fascinating complexity, beloved of social scientists but the despair of Indians who would like to move quickly. But present political arrangements — a constitutional system neither federal nor unitary, and a system of dispirited parties that neither broker nor present national alternatives — do not provide the means to move. Nor do they provide the means to cope with the intensified division of Indians into combative groups pursuing their diverse interests. The freedom movement succeeded too well. The new generation no longer worries about its independence, but the national vision that helped to found and unite modern India has been eroded by the new politics and economics that heighten multiple group awareness and provide means for the expression and pursuit of the groups' conflicting interests.

The argument has been pushed too far here, except that it reflects the concerns of many of those who write in the following pages about the next 15 years in India. It may be well to exaggerate India's divisions so that a government, more highly conscious of its inheritance, will remember that commissions on national unity and a preoccupation with an upward GNP curve are not enough to underwrite optimistic expectations about India in the year 2000.

# III

These remarks have been mostly about politics and economics, and they have dwelt more on diversity than on unity because the diversities probably pose the greatest difficulties for those who must think about India's future. Yet, India's diversity is moderated by strong cultural traditions. Hinduism, with its tolerance, flexibility, and many streams, provides reassurance for many of India's otherwise separate groups. Still, a confident, resurgent Hinduism may feed a reaction by religious minorities who do not equate India and Hinduism. Sikh demands are a dramatic and current case in point, and there is never a month without some form of Hindu-Muslim confrontation. Such episodes are likely to be increased in frequency by an Islamic revival.

India ranks second in the world in the production of motion pictures. This popular entertainment has a uniting effect by increasing familiarity with Hindi and by its embrace of the old myths, values, and traditions. Yet many films are in regional languages, not Hindi, and in real life the old values and traditions are seen to be eroding and irrelevant to new problems and demands. In contrast, the "new cinema," with its attention to inequality and injustice is heightening the awareness of those who imagine themselves victims, and may encourage their political action. This suggests that this widely accessible modern source of popular ideas may be a nationalizing vehicle, but may also encourage or reinforce division and contention.

The great performing arts of India, and their slowly changing classical traditions, will persist whatever the political tendencies. They are a potent, long-lived nationalizing force, especially as they accommodate what was once dismissed as regional or even folk music, dance, and drama. They are now, as Dr. Menon points out, far more familiar and available, thanks to film, radio, and television. The status of the artist, too, has improved so that he or she now is treated as a professional: educated, more independent financially, and no longer bound to the "court." This improved status not only enhances reputation, but encourages and permits adaptation and experiment. Whatever the political and economic forecasts, in the years ahead one may predict a flowering across the entire diverse spectrum of Indian art.

Religion, tradition, and the arts do not always prevail, and sometimes are themselves the cause of controversy; but their influence in knitting and holding a country together, and as symbols to be evoked or appealed to by leaders, are of singular importance to India. That is the reason an attempt to think about the year 2000 has of necessity included a cultural component.

# IV

And where does the whole exercise come out? There is no "either-or" conclusion, there is no balance sheet, and there are still mostly questions. But they are questions that have to do with the richness of India, its unparalleled complexity, its new leaders and their generation, its public institutions, and its material base. The questions, too, deal with human beings who are inheritors of an overarching tradition westerners can scarcely imagine, human beings who are intensely wed to beliefs, values, and ideas of status that sort them into stubborn and often violent self-conscious groups that find great difficulty in compromising.

Every Indian and every foreigner sees India a bit differently. Many Indians think foreigners are too fascinated by the traditions. Many foreigners think Indians are not sufficiently aware of how alive and forceful those are. For many Indians modernization and development and change are desirable. Many foreigners deplore the rapid pace of change and some of its consequences, and wish India could somehow develop without so much modernization. On both sides one finds sentimentality, impracticality, skepticism, qualified hopes, enthusiasm, and great expectations. Priorities differ. So do projected timetables. And who knows what completely unexpected event, within or without, may upset all reasonable judgments?

Yet no one doubts that the year 2000 will be reached, that India still will be there, and that — probably — in 15 years the changes will not be beyond measure, the problems will not be unrecognizable, and an effort to look to the next quarter-century may again be an appropriate subject for an international seminar. The organizers could do worse than to begin by studying the essays in this volume: How prescient were their authors? How many of their topics still belong on an agenda that speaks to the year 2025?

# Part One

# An Overview

Chapter One

# On Living
# in a Revolution

M. N. SRINIVAS

# I

Predicting for a small and relatively homogeneous country is not so hazardous a task as predicting for a vast, diverse, and highly stratified country such as India. But even for India, predictions for particular items such as population, food, clothing, shelter, education, or employment are not only feasible, but form the basis of national planning. "Total" scenarios for the future, however, present a different level of complexity, and involve such imponderables as the part played by leading personalities, choice between different courses of action, and historical accidents which, by definition, are unpredictable.

Having stated these perhaps apparent but necessary cautions, I shall try to examine a few of the important problems facing the Government of India today, which need to be solved during the next 15 to 20 years. It will be obvious that my disciplinary bias as well as my personal limitations have influenced both my selection of problems and the manner of their treatment.

# II

The title of this essay, "On Living in a Revolution," calls for a word of explanation. Indians *are* actually living in a revolution, although it is not always recognized by many of them nor, for that matter, by the outside world. This is because India's revolution is a novel one, brought about by the adoption of a new Constitution in 1950. While the Constitution as a whole is responsible for setting in motion many forces of radical change, one particular feature of it has been crucial — the decision to introduce universal adult franchise. That decision was made when over 80 percent of the population lived in 550,000 villages and when the literacy rate was 17 percent. Until recently the revolution has been relatively bloodless, but it appears that the country may be entering an increasingly violent phase of social change. I shall only suggest here that such violent change is attributable, directly or indirectly, to the Constitution. India is thus the somewhat unusual case of a country that adopted a complex and sophisticated Constitution which *opened* the way to increasingly violent social change. A more familiar pattern is the one in which an old regime is overthrown by massive collective violence and *then* a new Constitution is drawn up, laying down the principles on which the polity and society are to be reconstructed.

The adoption in the Constitution of a policy of "protective discrimination" towards "the weaker sections of the society," comprising primarily the Scheduled Castes and Scheduled Tribes, and secondarily the Other Backward Classes, hastened this Indian revolution. As, at each election, an increasing number of the poor and underprivileged were politically mobilized, the revolution became more encompassing and serious, although often it has been sidetracked by the political pursuit of unabashed populism. Yet another factor aiding and abetting the revolution has been rapid population growth, and that, too, from India's large pre-independence base. There is the constant danger that if the country's food supply does not increase fast enough to feed its ever-growing millions, and if its anti-poverty and family planning programs do not succeed, then widespread misery and chaos will follow. That will not only signal the failure of the present revolution but is likely to give birth to one of the more orthodox variety.

Adult franchise made it necessary for political parties and candidates to reach out to voters scattered in more than 500,000 villages and in the many towns and cities. This seemingly impossible task was achieved by putting to new uses such traditional institutions as caste and ethnicity, patron-and-client relations, kinship, and locality. Key individuals in each constituency acted as brokers for political parties and candidates, and as vote banks. In the process, even isolated and backward groups became politically mobilized, and learned the crucial lesson that just as important leaders came to seek their votes at elections, they in turn could ask them for favors once they were in office.

The abolition of untouchability in all its forms, and subsequently making its practice a cognizable offense, were primary steps in the fight against inequality. Only an indigenous government could have made such a far-reaching move. Of course, the legal abolition of untouchability needs to be distinguished from its actual disappearance, especially in the villages. It is a matter of common knowledge that even though the scheduled castes have the legal right to enter high caste temples, that right is not generally exercised. Any move on their part to enter these temples will bring down the wrath of the high, particularly the dominant castes. The scheduled castes also do not have access to the wells of the high castes. Officials and politicians find it more convenient to have separate wells dug for the scheduled castes. In rural teashops the latter are now served tea and snacks but usually in vessels meant exclusively for them. In other words, inequality continues, but the scheduled castes have access to facilities which they did not have before; and I must add that since independence pollution ideas have become weaker everywhere, particularly in the urban areas, and this has made social relations far less difficult than in the past.

The abolition of untouchability is backed up by certain positive measures devised for the more rapid advancement of the scheduled castes and tribes. Scheduled castes are treated on a par with the scheduled tribes for purposes of the various benefits and concessions subsumed under the term "protective discrimination" (also called "positive discrimination" or "discrimination in reverse"). The problems of the scheduled castes are, however, very different from those of the scheduled tribes, untouchability being peculiar to the former. Further, since the latter generally live in compact blocks while the former are scattered in the myriad villages and towns in India, it is far more difficult for development programs to reach them.

There is a lesser level of preference available to the other backward classes (also termed "socially and educationally backward classes"), and during the last 35 years there have been two attempts by the national government to identify these classes. The first attempt, the Kalelkar Commission in the 1950s, proved unsuccessful; the second came in the 1970s during Janata rule, when a commission was appointed under the late Mr. B. P. Mandal, former Chief Minister of Bihar. The commission took three years to submit a report and when, two years later in 1982 it was placed before Parliament, it was heavily criticized.[1] The Mandal Commission recommended that 27 percent of all jobs in government and seats in educational institutions be reserved for the backward classes, which it interpreted as backward castes. It estimated that these constituted 52 percent of the total population of the country, including 8.4 percent in minority communities. The reservation recommended by the Mandal Commission was in addition to those already existing for the scheduled castes (15 percent) and scheduled tribes (three percent). Thus, had the Mandal Commission report been implemented total reservations would have amounted to 45 percent.

While the Government of India has yet to implement these recommendations, several state governments have prepared their own lists of socially and educationally backward classes, and reserved for them a share of jobs in government and seats in educational institutions. The concern for reducing inequalities is serious, and protective discrimination is seen as a principal means of achieving that goal. The political compulsion to pursue a policy of protective discrimination arises from the fact that the poor and low-status groups greatly outnumber the rich and high-status groups. Political survival depends on winning the votes of the former.

The Constitution provides for reservation of seats for scheduled castes and scheduled tribes in the lower houses of legislatures. The number reserved for each group is directly related to its portion of the total population. The Constitution thus made certain that the needs, grievances, and concerns of these two groups would find expression in the legislatures. The other backward classes do not enjoy such a reservation. The national government also issued administrative orders to ensure reservation of government jobs and seats in educational institutions for the scheduled castes and tribes, whereas any reservation presently enjoyed by the backward classes is the result of initiatives by certain state governments in response to local pressures.

Reservation of positions for scheduled castes and tribes has been extended to all elective bodies and government-appointed committees. Reservation of jobs has been extended to the many public sector factories and other government-owned enterprises. India's commitment to a socialist pattern and to a continually expanding public sector has been strengthened by the reservations policy. A vast section of the Indian people has come to have a stake in the public sector, a condition that seems to have gone largely unnoticed.

There are various programs intended to benefit the weaker sections of society and, in all such programs, the scheduled castes and tribes enjoy a preference over other components of the weaker sections. In the grant of free house sites to the poor, in the allotment of surplus land obtained by imposing ceilings on rich farmers, in the grant of loans by the nationalized banks to promote self-employment and so on, the scheduled castes and tribes are accorded priority. It is not surprising that envious members of the high castes sometimes refer derisively to the scheduled castes as "new Brahmins" or "government Brahmins."

The benefits and concessions devised for the scheduled castes have had some beneficial effects, and the impact would have been even greater but for corruption and the influence of local patrons who interpose themselves between government and the people. In different parts of the country, a few sub-castes and kin-groups among scheduled castes (e.g., Mahars and Chamars) now include many individuals who are educated, comparatively well-off, and in positions of influence. In a number of cases their economic position is probably better than that of some of the rural artisan and service castes.

# III

As noted earlier, the level of benefits and concessions in force for the scheduled castes and tribes is higher than that for the socially and educationally backward classes. In 1950, for instance, the President of India promulgated a "Scheduled Castes Order" listing scheduled castes in various parts of the country entitled to the benefits of protective discrimination. No such list exists for the backward classes. Both the

Kalelkar Commission and Mandal Commission reports included long lists of castes considered backward. The Kalelkar report was plainly unsatisfactory, as it contained five minutes of dissent — including one from the Chairman, while the Mandal report seems not to have found favor with the government of the late Mrs. Gandhi. In the absence of a central list it has been left to each state to prepare its own, and there are considerable differences among the states in the earnestness with which they promote the interests of the backward classes; this again is related to the political clout which the latter wield. The south Indian states are far more active than their north Indian counterparts in providing reservations for backward classes, while West Bengal does not recognize the existence of any backward classes.

The criteria for determining "backwardness," as well as the quantum of reservation for backward classes, have been the subjects of widespread debate. These are matters about which there are strong feelings, and intense political pressure has been applied to decision-makers on this subject. Persons have gone to court when decisions on reservation rules or their application in any particular situation have affected them adversely. A considerable body of case law now exists on the subject.

It is significant that the phrases used in the Constitution, "other backward classes" and "socially and educationally backward classes," have been widely interpreted by state governments, and the commissions appointed by them, as referring to castes or sub-castes. In other words, classes have been equated to sub-castes, ignoring totally the phenomenon of intra-caste heterogeneity. Admittedly, this is minimal in the case of very small artisan, service, or laboring castes in backward rural areas, but it is noticeable — if not striking — elsewhere and in other castes. Heterogeneity is especially noticeable in dominant, land owning castes spread over a region. Many dominant castes have been included among the backward classes, and once included they are reluctant to shed the privilege; there is a vested interest in backwardness.

Leaving aside the question of reservation for the scheduled castes and tribes, there is a sharp difference of opinion between those who argue that castes or sub-castes are the natural units for the application of backwardness criteria, and those who think that backwardness can only be decided by applying socioeconomic criteria to individuals. The former argue that the caste system is the source of the backwardness of historically oppressed low-status groups and, therefore, sub-castes must be the units of consideration. But once castes are taken as units, there seems to be little hesitation in applying socioeconomic criteria to its individual members in order to exclude the better off.

Those who favor applying socioeconomic criteria to individuals point to the heterogeneity prevalent within sub-castes, and in particular to the existence of some very poor among "advanced" castes. This argument stresses the crucial role of poverty in the determination of backwardness. It criticizes the opposition by pointing out that after three decades or more of reservations for backward castes, the number of such castes appears to be on the rise. Every group seeks to be classified as backward in order to have access to government jobs and seats in medical, engineering, and technical colleges. In some states it is not unknown for members of the advanced castes to bribe officials to obtain certificates declaring that they belong to one or another backward caste, and that the income of their parents is below the prescribed ceiling.

The proportion of benefits to be set apart for the weaker sections as a whole, and the proportions to be set apart for merit as decided by performance in examinations, have been the subject of debate as well as judicial decision. In Karnataka today, for example, while 53 percent of the jobs and seats are reserved for the weaker section as a whole (including scheduled castes and tribes), an additional 15 percent is reserved for the poor without reference to caste. This reduces the percentage allotted to the "general merit" pool to 32 percent, but even here there are deductions of one percent for each of the following categories: offspring of "freedom fighters" and of "defence personnel," physically handicapped candidates, National Cadet Corps candidates, and, finally, sportsmen and athletes! The net result is that the percentage for merit alone is reduced to 27 percent.

By and large the southern states have energetically pursued a policy of providing benefits and concessions to the other backward classes. Without going into great detail, it is a fact that the origins of this practice go back to the early nineteenth century when some artisan castes in Madras Presidency, objecting to Brahmin domination, made a representation to the Board of Revenue to the effect that all men should be appointed to public offices without distinction.[2] A non-Brahmin movement, as such, was launched only in 1916-17 when the Justice Party was founded. In the huge, multilingual Madras Presidency, Brahmins represented only 3.2 percent of the population, but dominated higher education, the bureaucracy, and the professions.[3] Their displacement was essential for the progress of the non-Brahmin groups, an extremely heterogeneous lot that came together to demand the introduction of what may be called "caste quotas" for government jobs and seats in educational institutions.

To cut a long and complicated story short, by the late 1920s there existed in different parts of peninsular India a system of caste quotas that became stronger and more complex as time went by. Reservation of seats in legislatures for the scheduled castes and tribes was provided for in the Government of India Act, 1935, and this was carried over into the Constitution of India. In other areas reservation was provided by administrative orders, while backward class reservation was left to the states.

South India, thus, has been accustomed to caste quotas in education and jobs for nearly 60 years; in north India reservation for backward classes is relatively recent. In the absence of systematic studies the reasons for this are speculative, but certainly Brahmins are not so small a minority in the Hindi region as they are in the south, nor have they been so dominant in education, bureaucracy, and the professions. Other groups were at least as prominent: *kayasthas*, some Muslim groups, and immigrant Bengalis who settled in parts of north India following the establishment of British rule. In other words, there was no small minority whose prominence provoked all the others to combine against them.

The relatively long experience of caste-based reservations in the south and its absence in the north is significant. It probably means that inter-caste inequalities will persist for a longer time in the north. A few years ago, when Mr. Karpoori Thakur was Chief Minister of Bihar, he tried to introduce reservation of government jobs for backward classes, i.e., castes; this immediately resulted in violent outbursts all over the state and the reservation was withdrawn. In early 1985 two northern states, Madhya Pradesh and Gujarat, in the face of violent higher caste opposition, also had to withdraw or postpone enhanced reservation for backward castes. In both cases the enhanced reservations were announced before elections in order to attract backward caste votes. In Madhya Pradesh the quantum of reservation for the combined categories of scheduled castes and tribes and the backward castes was raised to 78 percent, leaving only 22 percent for merit; in Gujarat the reservation for backward castes was raised from 10 percent to 28 percent. The Gujarat government acted in the face of its own recent Rane Commission report, recommending occupation and income rather than caste as criteria of backwardness. There were violent and protracted riots in the state, many lives were lost, public and private property was destroyed, and in the end army units were required to restore order.

The riots in Madhya Pradesh and Gujarat have had the effect of bringing the national government into the picture. The Home Minister has expressed his desire for a national consensus on the issue of reservation for the socially and economically backward classes, but he has hastened to assure the scheduled castes and tribes that reservation for them will continue. Parliament will have to act by 1990 when present reservations are due to expire.

Caste quotas for jobs and seats in educational institutions, though meant for designated classes, in the last analysis benefit only individuals and their families. The beneficiaries often display an eagerness to distance themselves from their fellow castemen, and to be identified with professional colleagues and the new middle classes. But even a bloated public sector cannot provide employment for more than a tiny fraction, so the pursuit of employment-oriented development, and of anti-poverty programs aimed at meeting the basic needs of large numbers of the very poor, assumes a high priority.

Anti-poverty programs are difficult to implement and cannot be done quickly. Land reforms, with all their limitations and distortions in implementation, belong to this category, but the effects of land reforms vary from state to state, depending on the determination with which they are implemented. Even so, reforms have removed from the scene holders of concessional tenures such as *zamindars, jagirdars,* and *inamdars,* and have made it very difficult for absentee landowners to keep their land except when they belong to the dominant castes. Reforms have also benefited actual tenants and cultivators in some states; this is indeed a step forward. Yet another positive measure is the package of programs devised for small and marginal farmers, following the Green Revolution of the 1960s which largely benefited rich farmers.

The food-for-work programs, which appear to have caught on, enable landless laborers to find work during lean periods of the agricultural year. Some states have modest housing schemes for the weaker sections; the importance of such schemes is not only in the quantum of relief provided but in suggesting to people that other opportunities may be forthcoming. The same may be said of attempts to provide free lunches for school children in villages, low-interest bank loans to the poor to help them become self-employed, and very modest pensions to poor widows and old men. The abolition of the institution of bonded labor is also important, although the institution still lurks in more backward areas and many of those who have been freed remain unemployed. Some state governments are actively trying to provide electricity and pure drinking water to villages. In sum, the quality of life in villages is beginning to change.

# IV

India's population is now nearly 750 million, and is expected to reach one billion by the end of the century. India's planners need constantly to remember this as they juxtapose plans for increasing productivity in many areas with efforts to reduce the rate of population growth.

The decade from 1950 to 1960 was substantially frittered away, insofar as any serious efforts at family planning were concerned. Today few will remember that there was strong ideological opposition to family planning from several quarters. Marxists regarded it as a western effort to hold down the population of developing countries. Some economists thought the surplus labor of a fast-growing population would be required in the construction of big dams and other labor-intensive projects; such a view was too facile, if only for ignoring the difficulties involved in moving large numbers of people among project sites. Family planning was opposed by Catholics, Muslims, very orthodox Hindus, and Gandhians. The minister in charge of Health and Family Planning was a staunch Gandhian and the only method of family planning acceptable to her was the so-called "natural" method. Thus was born the "rhythm" system, according to which cohabitation was limited to certain "safe" days. The specialists in charge devised a necklace of colored beads on which one had to be moved every day, the appearance of red beads indicating "unsafe" days. The peasants who had been given the necklaces often forgot to move the beads regularly; a few deposited the beads where they belonged, around the heads of the images they worshipped or over the lithographs of deities.

The problems of meeting the basic needs of a population of 750 million are awesome, made more so by the awareness that numbers are constantly rising. Luckily for India, its food production increased from about 50 million tons in 1950 to over 150 million tons in 1983, but food and other resources cannot expand indefinitely. Effective population control is a necessity, and efforts to limit population must take place on all fronts. As part of that effort it is essential to work for the rapid alleviation of mass poverty, and for the provision of health services that will reduce infant, child, and maternal mortality.

The removal of mass poverty, stupendous as is that task, is only a part of the struggle to control population growth. In fact, the initial effect of the reduction of poverty may be to increase greatly the population that needs to be managed. Thus, disincentives will have to be introduced into the family planning effort, instead of relying only on incentives as has so far been the case. One obvious suggestion is to restrict benefits and concessions available to the other backward classes to the first two children only. This may appear harsh, but the alternative to effective population control is a breakdown of the economic and social fabric; this message must be carried with force and urgency to the weaker sections.

# V

The family planning push is likely to feel the positive effect of changes
that are taking place in the position of Indian women. It is well known
that among urban, educated women the average family is small, a tendency even more marked when the woman is employed. In such families
there is more participation by the husband-father in household chores,
including childrearing, and conjugal relationships are less inegalitarian.
Such a family may have a nuclear-like appearance, but it is not nuclear
in the western sense. It has active links with the husband's and wife's
natal families, and frequently the husband makes a regular monetary
contribution to his natal family. Also, relatives on either side may spend
long periods of time with the family, either for education, medical treatment, or employment.

It is not unlikely that this type of family will become a model for emulation by upwardly mobile members of the urban working classes, and
by educated immigrants from rural areas. It happens that Hindu high
castes form a substantial element in the urban middle classes, so that
when industrial workers and immigrants from rural areas emulate those
classes they are continuing a traditional tendency to emulate the higher
castes. Nowadays upper caste culture, particularly among the urban-
educated, is increasingly secularized and westernized.

There are the beginnings of a women's liberation movement in India,
also more conspicuous in urban than in rural areas.[4] The leadership is
provided largely by highly educated and articulate middle class women.
Apart from seminars and conferences which they periodically organize,
women's organizations are engaged in collecting data on the status and
working and living conditions of very poor women, particularly those
in villages. Women are being organized in different parts of the country,
one of the best known efforts being that of Mrs. Ela Bhatt, organizer
of the Self-Employed Women's Association (SEWA) of Ahmedabad.

The dowry, and the havoc it wreaks in different sections of the society, is an issue around which a number of urban women are now organizing. Large sums of money and goods are often transferred to the
groom's family from the bride's family, which also bears the frequently
very costly wedding expenses. Several women's groups have sprung
up to combat dowry. They investigate cases of cruelty inflicted on the
wife because of unmet dowry demands, initiate legal action where
necessary, publicize events, stage protest marches, and enact street

plays. Dowry does not come down with increased education. On the
contrary, it frequently increases with the greater education of the parties concerned, and the incidence of dowry is increasing in India as it
spreads to new caste groups and regions. Combating dowry, along with
other conditions affecting women's rights, will become increasingly important in the next decades. Substantial gains are likely to be made by
Hindu and Christian women in the near future, but that may only widen
the distance between them and Muslim women.

# VI

Let us now briefly consider changes that are occurring in the relationship between patrons and clients. The institution of patronage is not
confined to rural India, but I shall consider only its rural manifestation
since its urban manifestations are too numerous for brief discussion.

Rural society is hierarchical in more than one way, although it is usual
to refer only to caste. There is also a hierarchy based on land ownership.
Anyone who owns a sizeable piece of land is a patron, and patrons usually come from the high or dominant castes. When the members of a
dominant caste own the bulk of arable land in a village or a local area,
the collective power of the caste increases over non-landowning members of artisan, service, and laboring castes. Traditionally (that is, in
pre-British times) it was not land that was scarce but labor, and a land-
owner had to look after his laborers well in order to retain them. But
the enormous rise in India's population, from about 120 million in 1830
to about 750 million in 1984, has crowded the arable land and sharply
intensified competition for access to it. This has seriously affected the
power of clients to hold their own.

Traditionally, the patron-client relationship was a multistranded one,
the patron being employer, creditor, arbitrator and, generally, friend
and protector, while the client was bonded laborer, tenant, sharecrop-
per, debtor, and general servant. The client was expected to serve his
master loyally and to have his master's interest at heart. In rural India
several groups of patrons and clients often come together to form factions, and a village is usually split into two or more. While the personnel
of factions shifts over time, and some members of one faction go off to
join another, an outside threat usually leads to a closing of village ranks.
Factionalism, like caste, is a part of the rural social structure, and there
is often insufficient appreciation of this.

A patron's clients traditionally included members and families of the artisan and service castes who worked for him. They were paid fixed amounts of grain at harvest. They had roles in the patron's house during life cycle rituals and were paid separately for this. All in all the relationship was close; at one time, in the course of my fieldwork in Rampura in 1948, I came across an ancestral graveyard which included a faithful retainer's grave.

A radical transformation is occurring in relations between patron and client. The latter are now increasingly paid cash, and this is particularly true in agriculturally prosperous areas. Not infrequently outside laborers are employed in preference to traditional clients, as they are more hard-working and cheaper. The rules of noblesse oblige are giving way to considerations of profit, to the disadvantage of clients. Patrons would like to get maximum service for minimum payment, while clients prefer to do the minimum for as much as they can get. In my village fieldwork, as far back as 1948, patrons were complaining of a general decline in the loyalty of clients, and how this was reflected in the quantity and quality of their work. At the same time, clients were beginning to see patrons as their exploiters.

These changes affect and reflect rural migrations. In the last 25 years agriculturally prosperous regions have attracted labor from far and near. Laborers from dry and unirrigated areas gravitate to more prosperous areas. In this sense, immigrant labor acts as a depressor of wages, but it is also a means to an income for some of the poorest people. Many poor immigrants would have gone to the wall but for the new work opportunities available in the richer agricultural regions.[5]

There now occur mass migrations of seasonal workers from Orissa and eastern Uttar Pradesh to the agriculturally prosperous states of Haryana and Punjab. Similarly, Marathi-speakers in the northwestern regions of Maharashtra migrate to neighboring Gujarat for seasonal work. In addition to such interstate seasonal migration, there is much movement within states. This is welcomed by landowners, who would not otherwise be able to transplant, weed, or harvest their crops, but while landowners may welcome immigrants the indigenous laborers do not. Immigrants bring down wages and they may be used to discipline indigenous labor, and since a good part of the latter are members of the scheduled castes they become antagonistic both to their high caste employers and to the immigrants. This may yield a high caste versus scheduled caste conflict, or a conflict between indigenes and outsiders.

# VII

A depressing scenario for the future concerns the conflict between dominant, landowning castes and scheduled castes. This is likely to become increasingly violent and bitter, and will be a primary arena for the struggle for equality in India.

As is widely known, the scheduled castes traditionally have performed certain essential village tasks, some of which — sweeping and scavenging, removal of dead animals, leather work — were considered polluting as well as degrading. Scheduled castes were a very important source of agricultural labor. They suffered a number of collective disabilities and were often punished for failure to show deference in speech and gesture to the higher castes. But the scheduled castes' position is changing, and the pace of change is accelerating. Thanks to protective discrimination, there is now access to education and jobs in government and the public sector, and as a result — all over India — some members of the scheduled castes are in white-collar and professional jobs, and have higher living standards than members of the high castes. Again, thanks to reservation, some members of the scheduled castes have been elected to legislatures at both state and national levels, and a much smaller number have become ministers. Not only do high caste candidates seeking election have to solicit scheduled castes' votes, but members of high castes now have to approach scheduled caste ministers for a variety of favors. These events are happening for the first time in Indian history.

In spite of the changes occurring in the relations between high castes and scheduled castes, large numbers of the latter are dissatisfied with the slow pace of change. Young and educated members of the scheduled castes are particularly dissatisfied and angry. Open defiance of the authority of high castes is increasingly encountered, especially among groups such as the Mahars in urban Maharashtra. During the early 1970s, the Mahars formed the Dalit Panthers, deriving inspiration from the Black Panthers and committed to the promotion of the cause of scheduled castes through violent revolution.[6] The Panthers were responsible for producing a body of protest literature called *dalit sahitya*, rejecting caste, inequality, and exploitation. Now *dalit sahitya* exists in other Indian languages, encouraging the militancy of the scheduled castes and the weaker sections.

While the scheduled castes have made substantial gains, and pollution ideas have weakened generally, the fact remains that large numbers of people — particularly those in rural areas — do not accept the idea that the scheduled castes are their equals. The progress achieved by some scheduled caste members has only aroused the anger and envy of others, who attribute the former's success to reservation and reverse discrimination. The refusal of some scheduled castes any longer to perform some of the traditional and degrading duties is seen as an affront to dominant caste dignity. These castes think that government is pampering the scheduled castes and encouraging them to defy traditional authority. It is deplorable but not surprising that violent clashes frequently occur, and that people are beaten up, huts set afire, and women raped. Such clashes are not confined to rural areas although there they are far more common. They seem to be more frequent in Hindi-speaking regions, but other parts of the country are not free of them.

It is likely that these clashes will continue to increase. As more and more members of the scheduled castes become educated and assert themselves, resentment against them is likely to grow. The fact that even in the year 2000 about 70 percent of the population will be rural, will mean that many Indian villages will become mini-battlefields for inter-caste fights; and since resentment at scheduled castes' progress is not confined to the dominant castes, some conflict may bring all caste Hindus together — including those just above the untouchability line — against scheduled castes. Under the circumstances, some of the latter may look to conversion to another religion as a solution to their problems, and as a way of scoring against caste Hindus for their hostility. But such a step might only worsen the situation, inviting the wrath of the Hindus of an entire region.[7]

The benefits and concessions which the scheduled castes are enjoying will expire in 1990 unless further renewed by act of Parliament, and their renewal will very likely be an issue in the 1989 general elections. Political parties, anxious to secure the votes of scheduled castes, will probably propose to extend concessions for another decade. This will antagonize other sections of the population, particularly the numerically small artisan and service castes, who lag behind the scheduled castes who have benefited from reservations. A strong backlash against the policy of protective discrimination is likely to build up, and such a policy is not likely to survive into the next century; but it is probable that the ending of protective discrimination will be preceded by widespread violence.

There is a positive aspect to the conflict between the dominant and high castes and the scheduled castes, which is important and must be noted. Bloodshed, incendiarism, death, and rape have to be seen as integral parts of the process of translating into reality the rights which the Constitution of India grants to scheduled castes and tribes. To say this is not to condone the savage attacks, but to acknowledge that the conflicts are part of a process of social, economic, and political change. When violence is perpetrated on scheduled castes by dominant castes, it attracts much media attention. Questions are asked in Parliament and in state legislatures, voluntary bodies visit the scene, and the police (who are generally reluctant to take action against powerful village leaders) are forced to move. More importantly, there is a general raising of consciousness about the rights of scheduled castes, and the latter become aware of the fact that they have supporters and friends in the world outside their village. If conflict is indispensable to improving permanently the lot of scheduled castes, then its presence cannot be entirely deplored.

# VIII

Two Hindi terms, *dalit* and *kisan*, are being used increasingly in a political context. This usage is indicative of changes that may come about in the pattern of political alignments. *Dalit* refers to the poor, oppressed, and exploited classes of society, and as such it includes scheduled castes, scheduled tribes, artisan and service castes, and agricultural laborers. Since the poor greatly outnumber the well-off, and oppression and exploitation are widespread — particularly in rural society — the *dalits* are potentially a powerful force. It is not surprising that political parties vie with one other as champions of the vote-rich *dalits*. A striking example of this is provided by the Bharatiya Lok Dal, headed by the Jat leader of Uttar Pradesh, Charan Singh, which altered its name almost overnight to the Dalit Mazdoor Kisan Party. (Very recently the party reverted to its old name.) Charan Singh wanted his party to be considered as representative of all *dalits* in the country; ironically, leftist opinion regarded him as a symbol of the *kulaks* in rural India.

Attempts to unite classes of people on the basis of the secular criteria of poverty, exploitation, and oppression raise the question of whether the very poor among caste Hindus are prepared to align themselves with scheduled castes in order to advance economic interests. There are two obstacles. One is that caste Hindus may believe they will suffer a loss in status if they align themselves with scheduled castes; this is not likely to be a serious obstacle even though vested interests may try to exploit the cleavage. But the fact that scheduled castes enjoy benefits and concessions which other *dalits* do not may prove to be an obstacle to cooperation in a struggle against their oppressors. The division of the weaker sections into two tiers, one more "forward" than the other, may have unforeseen consequences for the struggle for class equality that is occurring in the country.

The terms *kisan* and *ryot* refer to peasants, and are like *dalit* in that they are labels cutting across traditional alignments such as caste, sect, religion, and ethnicity, and group people on the basis of their actual occupations. Since the 1970s farmers have shown an increasing ability to organize and are now recognized as a powerful pressure group. The erstwhile Bharatiya Lok Dal was essentially a peasant's party, and so is the Agriculturists' and Toilers' Party of Tamil Nadu. The Shetkari Sanghatan, a peasant organization of Maharashtra, has shown a disinclination to become a political party, while the Karnataka Ryatara Sangha has stopped short of becoming a party — although in recent elections it supported eleven candidates. Peasants' organizations periodically stage massive rallies and processions in support of their demands, including higher support prices from government for major crops, debt relief, lower power charges, and so on. Governments, both national and state, show increased sensitivity to the demands of peasant organizations.

Leftists generally regard these organizations as essentially representative of the interests of rich peasants, and therefore unworthy of support. To say the least, this seems an odd point of view. A strong farmers' organization may be helpful in the modernization of agriculture, including the increase of production. Without increased production that keeps up with population growth the entire economy will falter. And even if it is true that farmers' organizations represent only the interests of the rich, the contradictions inherent in such organizations should lead sooner or later to poorer peasants forming their own separate bodies. The fact that *dalit* organizations are already in existence is a sign of this.

*Mazdoor*, also a comprehensive term like *dalit* and *kisan*, has been used freely in the organization of industrial labor in a number of towns and cities. Its acceptance has not ended caste and other cleavages among workers nor has the existence of such cleavages come in the way of organizing urban workers on the basis of their common occupational interests.

# IX

What may be termed "runaway ethnicity" generates a tough set of problems for the Indian nation-builder. In runaway ethnicity, race is compounded by such other factors as language, religion, economic backwardness, and physical isolation. Runaway ethnicity is hard enough to cope with, but when to it is added the continuous immigration of outside groups which threaten to swamp—numerically and culturally—the indigenes, the situation is likely to become explosive. This is the situation in the northeastern state of Assam, but before considering Assam a general comment about the tribal northeast is necessary.

The northeastern region is divided between mountains and plains, the former inhabited by such tribes as Nagas, Mizos, Khasis, and Daflas. In the 1950s and 1960s both Nagas and Mizos wanted to be independent, and in each area there were armed bands waging guerrilla warfare against the Indian government. Today some Mizos, the Nagas in a part of Manipur, and a section of the population of Tripura still are not reconciled to their respective governments. Although the national government has rejected all demands for independence, large sums have been invested in the development of the tribal areas. A university was established in Shillong to serve the northeastern hill region, and legislation was enacted giving statehood to Meghalaya, Nagaland, Manipur, and Tripura, and Union Territory status to Arunachal Pradesh and Mizoram.

Tribal separatism in the northeast is accentuated by the tribals' profession of a religion distinct from that of the people living in the Assam plains. Historically, foreign missionary influence was strong in the tribal areas, and while the missionaries did a great deal for the tribes they did not encourage them to think of themselves as Indians. On the other side, Indian nationalism was not friendly to foreign missionary enterprise, particularly in the tribal areas. There have also been instances of tribal separatism encouraged by outside forces unfriendly to India.

The integration of all the tribes into the national mainstream will take time, no doubt well beyond this century. It is not unlikely, however, that open insurgency is at an end, unless some special and unforeseen circumstances resuscitate it. The facts that Nagas, Mizos, Khasis, and others govern their own regions, that their representatives sit in the national Parliament, that at least a few tribals have achieved power and prestige in the country, and that qualified and able tribal youth can get well-paid jobs in government service, help to lesson the sense of separatism and give the tribes a stake in the entire country's development and prosperity.

Educated Indians now regard tribal crafts and textiles, and the rich variety of tribal dance, as part of the national cultural heritage. This assists the integration of the tribes into the national mainstream, but there are other aspects of tribal life which need to be fully accepted by other Indians — particularly the plains Hindus. The tribes of the northeast region, for instance, are used to eating all kinds of meat, including beef and pork, and consumption of liquor is part of their way of life. Their sex mores are unlike those of the high caste, puritanical Hindus. Each tribe has its own distinctive culture and ritual. All this may encourage a view that tribals are aliens when, in fact, they are part of an India that always has been and will remain multicultural, multilingual, and multireligious. A secular India can accommodate all religions, including that of the tribes. And the idea that upper castes, living in the more accessible parts of the country, somehow constitute a "mainstream" which others are expected to join by shedding their particular cultures, is a dangerous view that works against national integration. The great liberalization in diet, dress, and general lifestyle that is occurring in the lives of urban Indians must be welcomed, for it facilitates the accommodation of groups which may regard themselves or be regarded as peripheral.

During the last five years the plains of Assam have emerged as a major problem area. The Assamese have demanded the revision of the state's electoral rolls on the basis of 1967 records in order to make certain that "foreigners" — who migrated to Assam during and since the 1971 Bangladesh war — do not succeed in becoming citizens. The Assamese fear that the immigrants, along with Bengalis who settled there earlier, are altering the ethnic if not the religious composition of the state. Large numbers of middle class Bengalis spread over north India, including Assam, during the colonial period, filling white-collar and professional jobs. These Bengalis were proud of their culture and literature, and were regarded by many educated Indians throughout the country as among the most advanced. Present day Assamese, however, have a strong sense of cultural identity and they do not want to be swamped by more powerful influences from outside. They also believe that the resources of their state, which include oil, tea, and forest produce, are being exploited by outsiders.

Feelings against outsiders are not confined to the northeast. In the 1950s and 1960s the Shiv Sena movement grew to power in Bombay, and while it opposed outsider appointments to jobs in preference to the indigenes, it singled out south Indians for attack. The Shiv Sena is the self-appointed guardian of Maharashtrian interest and, among other things, it agitates periodically for redrawing the boundary between Maharashtra and Karnataka, so that Belgaum city and some adjoining areas will be transferred to Maharashtra. It takes its name from the great Maratha leader, Shivaji, who was a champion of Hinduism. The Shiv Sena played a prominent part in the Hindu-Muslim riots in Bombay late in 1984. In the subsequent elections to the Bombay Municipality in 1985 the Shiv Sena emerged as the dominant party, and it proposed to expel all those who migrated to Bombay after 1974 and to restrict future immigration by a system of permits.

A "sons of the soil" movement has been a feature of Karnataka, the Kannada Chaluvaligaras heading a movement to "protect" the interests of Kannadigas against outsiders. The Chaluvaligara movement has links with the Kannada film industry, and cinema theaters preferring to exhibit Hindi and Tamil films in preference to Kannada films occasionally have been subjected to stone-throwing and vandalism. In the last few years, strong links have been formed between the local film industry and the advocates of a militant pro-Kannada stance. Kannadigas complain that they have been discriminated against for employment in the big industrial projects located in Bangalore by the national government. They declare that Tamilians and Malayalees from neighboring states have been preferred, and attribute this to the fact that Tamilians and Malayalees headed the factories when they were started. They demand that a majority of posts in factories in the state should go to indigenes, and general feelings against outsiders have grown in Karnataka in the last decade.

The Sikhs of the Punjab are well known for their farming abilities and have played a key role in making India self-sufficient in foodgrains. They are prominent in industry and trade. Twenty-two percent of the officers in the armed forces are Sikh, while Sikh soldiers number 120,000.[8] But in their home state of Punjab they are under-represented and Hindus over-represented in most urban and modern occupations.[9]

Many Sikhs insist that they have been denied a proper Punjabi-speaking state, as the Hindus of the region profess to be Hindi-speakers even when Punjabi is their real mother-tongue. Sikhs lay claim to some areas in Haryana and Rajasthan, and to a greater share of the waters of the Ravi-Beas rivers. They also want Chandigarh as the exclusive capital of the Punjab, rather than as a Union Territory serving as joint capital for both Punjab and Haryana.

Space does not permit a full consideration of the tangled politics of the Punjab. The killings and the trauma of partition forced a strong sense of self-identity on the Sikhs, and this has grown since 1947. A powerful voice of Sikh interests and aspirations is the Akali Dal, and it and the Congress (I) have been contending for primacy in the politics of Punjab. In recent years the Akalis have militarily championed many Sikh claims, and have demanded much greater powers for the state vis-à-vis the national government. Extremist Sikhs want an independent state called Khalistan, and in pursuit of this have killed many Hindus and members of the deviant Sikh sect, the Nirankaris. Some of the extremists, along with their leader, Sant Bhindranwale, claimed sanctuary and took shelter in the Sikh holy-of-holies, the Golden Temple at Amritsar. Eventually, government forces stormed the temple in June 1984 to clear it of the extremists and their considerable cache of arms, a happening that led in the end to the assassination of the Prime Minister, Mrs. Indira Gandhi, on October 31, 1984. This was followed by the killing in Delhi of hundreds of innocent Sikhs at the hands of organized Hindu mobs, and the violence and counter-violence continued.

The events of the last few years have led to the alienation of large numbers of Sikhs, and it is the difficult task of statesmanship to bring them back into the mainstream. No responsible Indian government can concede the demand for independence, but it cannot forget that the Sikhs are a brave and self-respecting people, inhabiting a sensitive border area, and that effort must be made to meet their just grievances expeditiously. The Sikhs in the Punjab are aware that one-third of their number live outside the Punjab and that there is no alternative to coexistence with Hindus. The fact that during recent anti-Sikh riots, thousands of ordinary Hindus risked their lives to protect Sikh neighbors, is a fact neither side should forget.

Fundamentalism is not peculiar to the Sikhs. Islam is experiencing a fundamentalist surge everywhere, and in Pakistan President Zia has campaigned for an "Islamic State." If Pakistan grows increasingly fundamentalist, this is likely to stimulate a Muslim revival in India, in turn feeding Hindu communalism. It is not widely realized that many Hindus have a grievance against their government for radically altering laws governing their marriage, divorce, inheritance, adoption, and guardianship while refusing to touch similar laws of the Muslims, even though the changes in Hindu laws were introduced in pursuit of the aim of a common civil code. Many Hindus think that the government's sensitivity to, and respect for, the culture and institutions of minorities contrasts sharply with its attitude to Hindu culture and institutions.

For two centuries Hinduism has been under attack from foreign missionaries, an attack which has led to its gradual transformation. Hinduism today is radically different from that of 1800 A.D., for instance, and this needs to be stressed. To mention but one example, Hinduism no longer relies almost entirely on caste and sect for its perpetuation. Voluntary, neighborhood, and professional associations play an increasingly important part in the lives of Hindus. For the first time in a millennium Hindus have access to political power at a national level. This may tempt them to flex their muscles, but that would be a mistake.

India, then, has a long way to go before its myriad castes, communities, and ethnic groups are transformed into an integrated nation. But an integrated India will not result in cultural homogenization, for it must be repeated that India is and remains a multilingual, multireligious, multiethnic, and multicultural country, far more like western Europe than any of its constituent states.

India's nation-building problems will pursue her well beyond this century. During this period, crises are bound to surface — the present is a time of acute crisis — threatening at times to rend the fabric of the

Indian nation. But chances are good that this will not happen, and that competing or conflicting parties will back away from the precipice, as they have done before. This is as much a hope as a prediction, for the social scientist knows, or ought to know, that his discipline does not enable him to predict what the future holds. He is at best able only to predict broad trends, and trends are only one set of determinants of the actual course of the future.

## NOTES

I thank my friend and former colleague, Mr. V. S. Parthasarathy, for critically reading drafts of this essay, and for helpful suggestions. Needless to say, the responsibility for the views is entirely mine.

1. S. Viswam, "The Reservation Conundrum," *Deccan Herald*, April 19, 1985.

2. G. S. Ghurye, *Caste and Class in India*, Bombay, Popular Book Depot, 1957, p. 179.

3. E. F. Irschik, *Political and Social Conflict in South India*, Berkeley and Los Angeles, University of California Press, 1969, pp. 14, 18.

4. See the essay by Gail Minault in this volume.

5. T. S. Epstein, *South India, Yesterday, Today and Tomorrow*, London, Macmillan and Company, 1978, p. 139.

6. Arun Sandhu, "The Dalits," *Seminar*, May 1974, pp. 29-31.

7. In this connection see Mumtaz Ali Khan, *Mass Conversion of Meenakshipuram*, Madras, The Christian Literature Society, 1983, pp. 65-67.

8. Romesh Thapar, "When the State Collapses . . ." *Illustrated Weekly of India*, December 23-29, 1984, p. 12.

9. S. S. Gill and K. C. Singhal, "The Punjab Problem," *Economic and Political Weekly*, April 7, 1984, p. 606.

# Part Two

# Traditional Culture
# and
# Popular Culture

Chapter Two

# Traditional Culture, New Mediums, Interaction, and Diffusion

NARAYANA MENON

# I

The main disciplines in my life have been music and literature, with dance and theater close behind. While dealing with culture, it is therefore inevitable that there will be a bias towards my main interests where I feel confident and at home; but I shall certainly not overlook the other components of culture. I have been talking and writing about this "composite" culture for a long time, so I cannot help dipping into some earlier statements in preparing this essay.

Well before the second millenium B.C., even before the advent of the Aryans, India had a high civilization of its own, usually and popularly described as Dravidian. We have evidence of an even earlier state of culture than the Dravidian, but what we now call the classical civilization of India is a fusion of Dravidian and Aryan, a fusion which took centuries to achieve and which was by no means a smooth or easy one. To start with, the advent of the Aryans, in the words of Ananda Coomaraswamy, "meant a severe cultural decline, which lasted for many centuries. Only when Aryan culture was fertilized by the indigenous culture did it begin to advance to form the classical civilization of India." Culturally speaking it was like "the victory of the conquered over the conquerors."

Coomaraswamy has described the subtle fusion of the two cultures in its widest and most meaningful emanations:

> Indian art and culture . . . are a joint creation of the Dravidian and the Aryan genius, a welding together of the symbolic and the representative, the abstract and the explicit, of language and thought. Already at Bharhut and Sanchi the Aryan symbol is yielding to its environment and passing into decoration; Kushana art, with the fact of imagery and its roots in *bhakti*, is essentially Dravidian. Already, however, the Indra-Shanti figure at Bodhgaya shows Aryan affecting Dravidian modes of expression, anticipating the essential qualities of all later satvik images. The Gupta Buddhas, Elephanta Maheshvara, Pallava lingams, and later Natarajas, are all products of the crossing of two spiritual natures; there is an originally realistic intention, but accommodated to the terms of pure design.
>
> Every icon is thus at once a symbol and a representation; the worshipper, though he knows that the deity takes the forms that are imagined by his worshippers, is nevertheless persuaded that the form is like the deity. Just in the same way the ascetic and the sensual, opposed in primitive thought, and all other parts of opposites, are theoretically and emotionally reconciled in medieval philosophy and faith. This in a real sense was a marriage of the East and West, of North and South, consummated, as the donors of an image would say, for the good of all sentient beings; a result, not of a superficial blending of Hellenistic and Indian techniques, but of the crossing of spiritual tendencies, racial samskaras (preoccupations), that may well have been determined before the use of metals was known.

But within the framework of this fusion and the cultural pattern it set, there are quite discernible colorations which give Dravidian creativity, particularly in literature and music, a consciousness of its own.

Language must have played a significant role in this context. The Dravidian languages continued to be cherished and cultivated in the south, notwithstanding the gentle pressures of the Aryan immigrants. Words and music have a special relationship, particularly in vocal music. Words affect the melodic line, even the rhythmic structures. The inflections of a language leave their imprint on melody and rhythm, on style and phrasing. We know of the immense richness of Tamil classics, dating back to the pre-Christian era, of the many epics, "anthologies" of lyrics, long poems, of the wealth and beauty of Sangham literature, all of which represent the consciousness of a community independent of the mainstream of the Aryan cultural pattern, and fully aware of the difference.

The Dravidian sphere of influence, as early as the third century B.C., stretched right across the Deccan from east to west, south to Kanyakumari and spilling into Sri Lanka. There was the Andhra empire in the north, the powerful Pandyan Kingdom to the south. Trade flourished. So did the arts. There is evidence of a high level of poetry, drama, and music. The colorful interaction of poetry and music was important and meaningful. Cross-references are significant. Even a work like *Tolkappiyam* (circa second century B.C.), one of the oldest classics, which is really a grammar of Tamil, has references to music which give us valuable information on the state of the art. Other classics, which use Tamil phraseology, describe instruments, melodies, musical theory, and practices. The Sangham literature is full of it.

In the middle of it all stand out one or two works which give us clear and detailed pictures of a composite culture. *Silappadikaram* by Ilango Adigal is a moving story, or a "romance" if we prefer to call it that, in verse interspersed with prose. It was written towards the end of the second century A.D. or the beginning of the third. Ilango was a Jain, and the brother of King Shenguttuvan of the Cera dynasty who ruled over the western coast of southern India. One of the key characters in the story is the beautiful courtesan Madhavi, a fine musician and dancer, and in Ilango's descriptions of her performances we get a clear picture of music and dancing as practiced in his day.

I quote from Alain Danielou's translation of *Silappadikaram:*

> Madhavi's music teacher was an expert performer on the harp and
> the flute. He could vocalise and could draw from the drums
> well-rounded sounds, mellow and deep. He could adapt the music to
> the dance, and understood which style best suited each technique of
> expression. He had a profound knowledge of the subtle intricacies of

the classical melodies, yet he could invent new variations. He taught
the various styles of dance and of music, and brought out the most
subtle shades of the composer's intentions . . . .

The young drummer who accompanied Madhavi . . . was familiar
with all the types of dance, *musical notation* and singing. He knew
prosody, modes and rhythms, the blend of beats and counter beats,
and the defects that may arise from their contrast. He was
well-acquainted with popular tunes, and he could firmly establish the
required rhythm patterns of his drum, using an artful double-stroke
to mark important beats. He intertwined his rhythmic fantasies with
the plucking of the lute, the lament of the flute, and the soft accents
of the songs. He controlled the voice of his drum so that the more
delicate instruments could be heard, though, at proper times, he
would drown out all music under the deafening thunder of brilliant
strokes.

The flute player of the group was also a scholar who knew all the
rules of diction and the way hard consonants are softened to please the
ear. He knew four kinds of trills, possessed the science of modes and
adjusted his pitch to the deep sound of the *mulavu* timbal. He took
care that the drums be tuned to the fifth note of the flutes. He artfully
followed the singers, improvising new variations within the bounds of
modal forms, and showed his art of melody by setting off each note so
that it might be clearly distinguished.

Then there was the harp master who played a fourteen-stringed
instrument. To establish the mode *(palai)*, he first plucked the two
central strings, which gave the tonic *(kural)*, and the octave *(taram)*.
From these, he tuned the third *(kaikkilai)*, then the low strings from
the octave and the high strings from the tonic. After tuning the sixth
*(vilari)*, he played all the fourteen strings, showing all the notes of the
mode from the low fourth *(ulai)* to the high third *(kaikkilai)*. The
sequences that form the modes appeared in succession. Starting from
the third, the scale of the mode *(palai)*, known as *padumalai* was
obtained. From the second *(tuttam)*, he started the *Shevali* mode,
from the seventh *(taram)* the *Kodi* mode, from the sixth *(Vilari)* the
Vilari mode, and from the fifth *(ili)* the *Mershem* mode. Thus the
various groups of intervals were arranged. On the harp, the low
sounds are to the left. It is the opposite with flutes. A good harp player
is able to blend low and high tones with median ones in a manner
pleasing to hear . . . ."

Madhavi herself was an accomplished performer on the harp.

Madhavi then carefully followed the eight rules of perfect music: the
tuning of the instrument *(pannal)*, the caress of the strings to indicate
the mode *(parivattani)*, the exact pitch of each note *(araidal)*, the du-
ration of the pauses *(taivaral)*, the grave *adagio (shelavri)*, the easy
blend of the words of the song *(vilaivattu)*, the sentiment *(kaivul)* and
the elegant design of the vocalisation *(kurumpokku)*.

Her fingers, wandering on the strings with plectra carved in emeralds, evoked a buzzing swarm of bees when she practised the eight ways of touching instruments; the isolated pluck *(vardal)*, the caress *(vadittal)*, the hard stroke to bring out the resonance *(undal)*, the presentation of a theme *(uruttal)*, the pull on the string to reach the note from above *(teruttal)*, the chords *(allal)* and arpeggios *(pattadai)*.

There are passages like this throughout this moving "romance." These are lucid statements on music, musical instruments, style of playing, subtleties of tuning, and finesse in performance that the academic scholarly treatises hardly ever provide. One has only to try to read chapters 28 to 33 of the *Natya Shastra*, which deal with music, in contrast to passages of the type above. I doubt if there is any literature, poetry or prose, which describes musical theory and practice with such skill, in language so clear, meaningful, and communicative, as passages in the *Silappadikaram*, written about 1700 years ago and of such relevance even today. I do not mean only Indian music; I am saying this of all music, and what we know of it in the second and third centuries A.D.

*Silappadikaram* had a sequel, *Manimekhalai*. This is not so rewarding, though even here there are hints and promises of the arts of the period. Both works are really secular in character; if the author of *Silappadikaram* was a Jain, *Manimekhalai* is like a Buddhist work. What is important and should be of great relevance to us today is the fact that Hinduism, Jainism, and Buddhism coexisted easily and naturally at a time when faith and dogma were spelt with capital letters.

There are close parallels in the growth and development of music and the dance. I cannot think of any major culture or civilization in the world in which the relationship of music and the dance is closer, and few in which music, dance, and drama are so closely linked. The word *Sangita* once meant more than "music" in the narrow sense in which we use it today. It implied a close relationship to dance and to the theater. The line of demarcation between music and dance, dance and drama, was a thin one. Every traditional dramatic performance had something of the character of what is today described as dance-drama. Is *Koodiyattam* a dance form or a theatrical form? Is *Kathakali* dance or drama? In the Indian tradition, every *nata* had to be, and in fact was, an actor, dancer, and musician as in *Koodiyattam* even today. This says something of the training and the discipline required of an artist.

There are two important attributes of this composite culture. One is its continuity. Take, for instance, the Vedic period, nearly coeval with the high civilization of Egypt. Vedic texts are still recited in India, not just mechanically as something from the past, but with an awareness of their relevance as a living force. (I am told that in Egypt today, hardly any Egyptian priest or layman knows of the prayers spoken in the Pharaonic temples.) This continuity is not just linear. It represents the essence of many phases of knowledge and wisdom, renewing itself all the time — *parivartana* — and revitalizing itself in the process, interlinking feelings and experiences of all kinds.

There is a popular misconception that this represents an unchanging way of life and thought. This is nonsense. It represents four millennia of struggle and growth during which dynasties rose, declined, and fell; religious faiths were accepted, absorbed, and set aside, and various schools of philosophy provoked intellectual speculation of the highest sophistication. Architecture and sculpture, music and the dance, drama and poetry flourished in abundant variety. There have been, and are still, islands of orthodoxy and primitive, narrow concepts. There have been periods of war and pestilence, and despair alternating with triumph; through it all runs a strong and clearly recognizable thread of continuity.

The second aspect of this composite culture is its interdisciplinary character; music, dance, the visual arts, and literature are all governed by the same attitudes. In all of these the stress is on emotional rather than intellectual sincerity, on the lyrical impulse rather than the dramatic, on concord rather than discord, on intuition rather than argument, on contemplation as much as on action. The result is an inwardness, a subjectivism rather than the objectivism of the West. Let me illustrate this from the dance.

The fundamental difference between Indian dancing and western ballet is in the way in which a given idea is realized in performance. In Indian dancing, the dancer (like the musician in Indian music) is the center, the figurehead of the idea, and the dance, as it were, emanates from him. In European ballet, the idea of the dance is projected onto the dancers. It is an objective realization of the idea by the creator of the dance, the choreographer, who uses the dancers as a vehicle for the expression of his ideas. This makes the Indian dancer (like the Indian musician), within a strictly traditional code, a creative artist, whereas in European ballet the dancer's role is an interpretative one, to infuse and bring life to the choreographer's conception. This also makes Indian dancing essentially a solo affair. Even when there is a group of dancers, as in the more dramatic forms of Indian dancing like the *Kathakali* of Malabar, the dancing takes the form of a series of solo performances. Groupings are unimportant. The dancers are related purely by the continuity of their narration. The wide sweeping lines of the ballet are absent. Minute gestures become important.

These gestures *(mudras)* are the essence of Indian dancing. They are a comprehensive language, and any story, incident, or shade of emotion can be satisfactorily expressed. (Two well-trained *Kathakali* dancers, by using these gestures, can carry on a conversation on almost any topic in everyday life.) Their eloquence is the eloquence of poetry, not the realistic eloquence of prose; they suggest but never imitate; they evoke a mood but never state it. In western ballet, conventional movements such as an arabesque or entrechat or pirouette are freely used by a choreographer to express certain ideas or types, not to mention the clever and dramatic use of the mime. But there convention often becomes an embarrassment, even an impediment. Even in such a poetic ballet as *Les Sylphides* the male dancer looks slightly ridiculous. (It is this hidebound convention which has led to new growths in the dance styles of Europe and America — movements led by such dancers as Mary Wigman, Martha Graham, Kurt Jooss, Merce Cunningham, and their pupils — completely outside the traditional conventions of classical ballet.) The traditional language of the Indian dance is so rich and so complete that it helps the creative artist rather than hampering him. This is the highest form in which tradition should operate, and it is the severest test of any tradition.

And so to the theater. Here I have to be careful; dates are bandied about, sentiment often gets the better of reason, and age is sometimes thought a criterion of greatness. Artistic validity is the test of any art form. What are the criteria here? To me, personally, the structure, the style, the nobility of a play are among the values that matter — qualities which enhance our awareness of life. Kalidasa's *Abhignana Sakuntalam* is one of the great poetic-dramatic creations in all literature. *Oedipus Rex* is "the supreme height of dramatic concentration and intensity" on the stage. A profound sense of the value and sacredness of life can be seen in both. To think that the flowering of Kalidasa's genius meant only three plays for us; that of the 100 plays that Sophocles wrote, we are left with only seven. It is our good fortune that we can see even today the theater at Epidaurus: what proportions, what acoustical excellence, what dimensions; what care and love must have gone into its building; and what an audience the plays would have had 2,300 years ago! Bharata has left us detailed descriptions of the theater as he envisaged it, but from that to the Koothambalams of Kerala is a far cry, though the few left to us are little gems of theater architecture.

And there are the great names among the dramatists — Bhasa, King Sudraka, Kalidasa, Bana (author of *Harishchandra*) and Bhavabhuti (author of *Malati Madhava*) — whose creativity helped to make the third to the eighth centuries A.D. the pinnacle of our early culture. This was the age of Bhasa, Kalidasa, Bhavabhuti; of the magnificent murals, of which Ajanta is the best known and most admired; of the great bronze sculptures of the south; of Sanchi, and of the bas reliefs at Mamallapuram and other places. This was the age of Aryabhatta and Brahmagupta, great mathematicians and astronomers. This was the period when theories and concepts of the dance as expounded in the *Natya Sastra* were developed and put into practice, and when the *ragas* of our music acquired a form and personality which made them unique in musical history.

The years following the eighth century saw the flowering of the *bhakti* cult in the south. The great philosopher-teachers Sankara and Ramanuja dominated the movement, which saw a resurgence of Hinduism after the gentle strains of Buddhism and Jainism in the centuries immediately preceding. Then came Islam; young, vital with its attendant culture from Iran and Samarkand, and its fusion with the life and culture of the Indo-Gangetic plain. And, finally, the traumatic experience of western colonialism which created dents in the edifice of this continuing Indian culture. But that culture was strong and resilient enough to withstand the onslaught, and evolved into a new phase where tradition and modernity meet without detriment to either.

# II

Rabindranath Tagore is a good example of the link between tradition and modernity. He is the most important figure in modern Indian arts and letters. Though it is as a poet that Tagore will be judged by posterity, he was also a novelist, short story writer, dramatist, painter, musician, and educator. No modern writer has given utterance to uniquely Indian traditions and traditional values in more eloquent or moving language, whether in poetry, music, or drama. His great ability to work music, dance, and drama into a unified whole, and to meld ancient truths, fables, and legends with contemporary experience, reflected the unity of his being and of his art.

And where are we now? Creativity is tempered by social, political, philosophical, and artistic forces. These forces strengthen one another and enrich, or occasionally debase, creativity. But the arts do have a role to play in the development process, and total development is possible only when literature, art, philosophy, and the sciences interact.

Is this possible in a divisive world of narrow-minded parochialism, false pride and "holier-than-thou" attitudes? That is where those two oft-repeated, self-conscious words "national integration" come in. My feeling is that if we do not emphasize and push too much, the process of national integration will slowly but inevitably work its way. Language has a special role, but it is the Hindi of that much-maligned medium, commercial cinema, rather than of All India Radio, that will make Hindi the Indian *lingua franca*. Aggressive postures will not work. Common sense will.

The point I make is that we should let the things happening around us take root naturally and not hurry to label them as exemplary cases of national integration. Take, for example, the painter M. F. Husain's participation in the Sao Paulo exhibition a few years ago. Husain was an invitee and honored guest at this prestigious exhibition, and his contribution was a whole section of the gallery illustrating the *Mahabharata*. When in a press interview he was asked whether he was not a Muslim he said, "Yes, but I am an Indian and my roots are deeper and older than Islam." Chinna Maulana Saheb, a well known Muslim *nagaswaram* player, plays his instrument regularly at the Thanjavur temple. Hyder Ali, a good Muslim, is one of the leading singers in the *Kathakali* programs at Kalamandalam. I have vivid memories of the late Rahimuddin Khan, the great *Dhrupad* singer, singing Saraswati Vandana in chaste Sanskrit and the late Abdul Karim Khan singing Thyagaraja's *Rama, nisamana mevaru?* (Rama, who is there to equal you?). The number of painters, sculptors, musicians, actors, and film stars who are married to a spouse of another religion or region is large and the language they use is slowly becoming the *lingua franca* of India. There are many such happenings in spite of the pressures of fundamentalists and terrorists.

Let us try not to underline the obvious. The moment there is a prize for a film on "national integration" there will be self-conscious and embarrassing creations, but you will not get a *Garam Hawa* or an *Achut Kanya*. There was a recent press report headlined "Integration through Idli." It included the names of well known commercial directors planning to launch films to help national integration, with the most obvious titles and even more obvious intentions. God help them. And their audience!

# III

We often overlook the role of the arts in the developmental process, but they have political and ideological implications. The recognition and restoration of human dignity are prerequisites of freedom, and in this we are motivated and inspired by the arts. Full freedom is not possible without cultural identity. We need to fulfill ourselves in our own environment against our own background if the arts are to continue to bloom.

Today in India there is a growing realization of this. On the cultural scene tradition and modernity do meet. They are no longer treated as inimical. One is not destructive of the other. There is a fuller, more meaningful awareness of "tradition." We have shed or are shedding our sentimental association with such words as well as with associations of divinity or invulnerability. As T. S. Eliot has said:

> It is dangerous to cling to an old tradition, to confuse the vital with the unessential, the real with the sentimental. Tradition does not mean a return to some previous conditions so as to preserve it in perpetuity. It should stimulate our living and our thinking. What may have been a legitimate healthy belief or practice yesterday may well be a pernicious belief today. . . . What we can do is to use our minds, remembering that a tradition without intelligence is not worth having, to discover what is the best life for us . . . as a particular people in a particular place; what in the past is worth preserving and what should be rejected; and what conditions, with our power to bring about, would foster the society that we desire.

There is certainly an awareness of this, as can be seen if we examine and analyze the cultural scene in India. If it were not so, our arts would appear an anachronism. We are very conscious of the world we live in: atomic energy, guided missiles, "sputniks," industrial psychology, vitamins, sulpha drugs, and international finance. We are a modern nation acquiring rapidly a modern international outlook and consciousness. The expression of this consciousness would need new techniques, new idioms, new styles. Our most significant painters, sculptors, architects, poets, and dramatists realize that art and life are not things apart.

In the visual arts, Bombay, Baroda, and Delhi are the most significant areas of creativity. Of course there have been bitter controversies, clashes of interests and of attitudes and of ideologies, and even the Lalit Kala Akademi has often been the center of passionate exchanges. But these should be seen primarily as a striving for excellence, as signs of impatience and dissatisfaction of angry young men with the establishment. Conflict is energy; it is particularly so with creative arts. The paths of true artists never run smooth.

Today our painters are making their presence felt at international exhibitions all over the world. Some are living abroad. Krishna Reddy, one of the leading figures in graphics, lives in New York. So do Newton Souza and Samant. Raza lives in Paris. Styles and ideas and temperaments vary. Some stand committed, others are detached observers. The scene is a lively one. The Gallery of Modern Art in New Delhi is a good index of the quality and achievement of our painters. Delhi's modern art show, the Triennale, after its teething troubles and heartburns, has come to stay, and whatever the cynics might say, it has placed India once again in the mainstream of the visual arts.

As for music, there is more good classical music heard today and performed publicly than perhaps at any other time in our history. There are better and larger audiences, and listening is more intelligent and more critical. There is a great deal of creative activity going on at all levels, and there is a new type of musician growing up: musicians who have had a fairly liberal education, who are of an independent turn of mind, who have a scientific approach to techniques of performance, who understand the psychology of listeners. Among these are musicians like Ravi Shankar, Ali Akbar, Vilayat Khan, Gyan Prakash Ghosh, Mushtaq Ali Khan, Nikhil Bannerji, Amjad Ali Khan, Ram Narayan, Debu Chaudhuri, Brij Narayan, Zakir Hussain, Budhaditya Mukerji, N. Rajam in the north, and musicians like K. S. Narayanaswami, S. Balachander, Doraiswami Iyengar, T. N. Krishnan, Palghat Raghu, Umayalpuram Sivaraman, T. Viswanathan, Lalgudi Jayaraman, M. S. Gopalakrishnan, Maharajapuram Santhanam, T. V. Gopalakrishnan in the south. There are more; I have picked at random.

Some of them, like Raghu, Sivaraman, Viswanathan, Gopalakrishnan, Rajam, Debu, Budhaditya, and Doraiswami Iyengar are university graduates. They have travelled widely in India and abroad, learning and giving at every opportunity. Some have left their mark at international music conferences in Europe and America, opening the ears of the West to the hidden and unsuspected beauties of our musical system. This is a new type of musician, better equipped musically and intellectually than his forefathers. These are men proud of their profession, respected in society, economically well-off, capable of discussing musical and professional problems, ridding music of pointless conventions and superstitions, who are full-fledged citizens of the world, unlike their forefathers who were treated with scant respect and who, for all their technical wizardry, were uneducated and often could not sign their own names.

This new generation is neither unaware of nor disrespectful to the classical tradition, but their awareness is a new awareness. They look forward, unafraid of change or experiment. They are aware of the new tempo of living. This is a big change, a change for the better, and a preparation for more significant changes to come, and it has happened in just a few decades. It is not unconnected with the attainment of political freedom, because it is the beginning of the expression of a new consciousness both in the musician and in his art.

If we pause to think, it is astonishing what has happened in, say, 15 years. Princely patronage disappeared overnight with independence. Music has taken a big leap from the chamber to the concert platform. Time honored conventions like the time-theory of music are slowly fading, and have in fact disappeared in some areas of south India. The leisurely techniques of all night sessions, and *ragas* spread thinly over hours, are giving way to new discipline, greater precision, more economy of statement.

A word must be said about "film music."

Popular music in India is becoming serious business. The best of it represents a serious search for new idioms and techniques, and through it all is emerging a new genre. The popular commercial Indian film—not the warm, human, sensitive work of Satyajit Ray or the purposeful, socially-conscious work of our young film-makers—is made to a formula. It must have at least half a dozen songs, two or three dance sequences, and the inevitable fight sequences. The hero and the heroine burst into song on the slightest provocation.

Originally this music was sentimental, sweet, nostalgic, and the smooth voice of the singers, the touching lyrics, and the slick accompaniment made it a new kind of experience. The emotional impact of the music with the screen images was fantastic. In course of time the musical style began to develop, and it enveloped sex and violence, love and war, bittersweet happenings, stark tragedy. Then the folk element began to enter; film companies and groups travelled all over rural areas, collecting, documenting, working on folk material. This is a positive aspect of the situation, because this new genre of music is becoming a mirror of social problems and a power to reckon with. It is a form of such immense popularity and prevalence that it becomes a matter of concern for poets and lyricists, even for serious musicians. Classical musicians like Ravi Shankar, Ali Akbar Khan, Vilayat Khan, Ram Narayan, Hariprasas Chaurasia, and Shiv Kumar Sharma have all tried their hands at film music, bringing to it new attributes and creating new concepts of incidental music.

Perhaps I have overemphasized what should be described as an aberration of the mainstream, but it is as much a part of the musical scene in India as pop is of the musical scene in Europe and America. It dominates the recording industry, it has youth in its grip, and we have to be on our guard; an aberration can get out of control. Fortunately it has not made any incursions into serious music, diluting it or debasing it in any way. It has so far remained an exotic weed in the many-splendored garden of our traditional music.

What of the films themselves? The film in India has a kind of Janusfaced profile. The standard commercial film — with its fixed formulas of songs, dances, fights, sex, violence — is rarely a work of art. Censorship is strict and inflexible, but there are ways and means of getting around it. An art form which in many parts of the world has played a significant role in restoring and rehabilitating national dignity has become in India a caricature, if not degradation, of many cherished qualities and values. The "new cinema," however, is a ray of hope. It was Satyajit Ray who showed us on celluloid the quality of life in India, with his wide sympathies, this gentle humanism, and his artistry. It was he who pointed out to his younger compatriots that compassion can be as dramatic and moving as anything else; that life without the tinsel and the hollow glamour of the studios can be deeply moving; that fine films can be made on small budgets if one is resourceful. To the warmth and humanism, the refinement and sophistication of Ray, angry young men like Govind Nihalani have now added the exposure of corruption and brutality, and the fight for social justice. So the banalities and crudities of the commercial cinema are on trial and we see a film like *Gandhi*, without conventional lovemaking or songs or dances or staged fights, holding our attention for over three hours and bringing a lump to the throats of the toughest and most hardbitten.

The electronic media are making the biggest impact. Radio and television have taken classical music, opera, and ballet to the homes of millions of people the world over, who never before had a chance to hear or see such things. The nature and magnitude of this impact on the public mind is still difficult to assess, and poses both challenge and responsibility.

Obviously the situation calls for the greatest catholicity of tastes. There is the noble heritage of "classical" music, the mainstream of every tradition and the accumulated heritage of centuries. This has to be preserved and enriched, its hidden beauties revealed to the public. There is the rich and variegated treasure house of folk music. This has to be discovered, resuscitated, and placed in its correct perspective. There are the new types of creative impulses and experimental music. These are to be encouraged. There is the vast and growing repertoire of light music, jazz, and other types designed primarily to please and sometimes to titillate the sense. Here, cheap and debasing vulgarizations have to be set aside in favor of clean styles and genuine craftsmanship. But who is to decide? Good taste is an indefinable attribute, of which custodianship is both a tricky and thankless job. Still one must act, following liberal human values without losing a sense of proportion.

If music is primarily an "aural" art, then the dance and the theater are visual "spectacles." And now it is television that can play an effective role in the projection of the visual arts. Just imagine what programs like *Civilization* or *Roots* were able to achieve. There is an important point to be borne in mind. Marshall McLuhan has drawn our attention to it: "Any understanding of social and cultural change is impossible without a knowledge of the way media work as environments."

Traditional cultural forms *do* change through dissemination by mass media. Arrangements of folk music and adaptations of folk theater lose their real and basic qualities unless we are very careful. In the long run cultural values are affected. For better or worse? I do not know, but the characteristics of the media make such changes inevitable.

And so it continues. There are still islands of orthodoxy side by side with scientists who hold their own in the councils of advanced technology. Bullock carts, primitive ploughs, and oil lamps sit alongside nuclear reactors. It is an exciting period of transition and we have not yet adjusted. Our arts, to borrow an expression from Walter Kerr, are struggling to give birth to themselves all over again on a dozen fronts, fronts charged with an air of expectancy. The wave of westernization of the colonial era has now charged into a wave of modernization. Westernization implies borrowing and imitating, modernization means creativity as an integral part in the growth of a great tradition. It is difficult for a cultivated Indian brought up in his traditional background to get into the spirit of *"Death Of a Salesman,"* or *"Who's Afraid of Virginia Woolf?"* We have to function in our own environment, in our own social milieu, within the constraints of our economy, as *we* think and react, if we are to fulfill ourselves.

Chapter Three

# The "Indian Scientist:"
# Some Reflections

SWADESH M. MAHAJAN and E. C. G. SUDARSHAN

## Introduction

The role of science-based technology as a strong and effective force for development and its capacity to improve the living standard of the Indian people were clearly appreciated by the builders of modern India. Jawaharlal Nehru, a seer of science-based humanism, lent his enormous prestige and power to the cause of building, encouraging, and sustaining institutions for technological research and development and institutions devoted to the pursuit of the pure sciences. He had the courage to dream about a new India "whose temples were to be the universities and research laboratories." The message to the youthful scientists was that over and above the intrinsic adventure of participating in the scientific quest, they were also contributing to nation-building. It was heady and infectious. India committed itself to the task of implementing an ambitious scientific research program. Over the years the program was to grow into an enormous scientific-technical service which spurred the next generation of students into the pursuit of science and technology. In addition to the various national laboratories and major research institutes and a few distinguished universities, the new institutes of technology entered into the propagation of technical expertise with a vengeance. While many students from these institutions felt they should go abroad for higher learning, the level of advanced studies in science and technology in the country had already reached a new high. India's scientific manpower is awesome; by some counts its manpower is the third largest in the world, surpassed only by that of the two superpowers.

Thus, there appeared on the Indian scene a new type of person, a symbol and product of a new national orientation, heir to the university heritage of "truth unto its innermost parts," to go "where no man has reached," to follow "knowledge like a shining star." On this person is pinned the nation's hope to leapfrog into the prosperity associated with a technological industrial society. This new person, the harbinger of a new era, is the object of our study.

## The Indian Scientist

This essay deals with the "Indian Scientist," a person of Indian origin involved in scientific research. Although most such people are found in their natural habitat — Indian laboratories, research institutes, and universities — a very substantial number are associated with foreign institutions, mostly in the West and particularly in the universities and industrial laboratories of the United States. The American pool has been increasing rather rapidly, with a large steady flow from major Indian universities, including the institutes of technology. For our purpose, we shall take this phenomenon, the existence of a large group of Indian scientists in America, as a "given" of the system. We do not propose to discuss either the dynamics or the consequences of this migration but limit ourselves solely to an analysis of the scientist's condition and a little bit of his science, sociology, and psychology. We do, however, suppose that this community is important enough to warrant such an examination. No statistics will be given, and we plan to cover the broad subject by concentrating on scientists working in America, excluding important and interesting Indian problems. We shall also outline how the American experience affects the pool of scientists in India.

We begin with a brief description of this group as well as a statement of its quandary. The group is a large, competent body quite uniformly distributed over institutions of higher learning throughout the United States. Although its members have contributed adequately to the general body of scientific knowledge (that is, commensurate with their numbers), they can be credited with a disproportionately small number of fundamental, trendsetting, or strikingly creative contributions to science. The typical scientific career of an Indian in American science may be divided into three phases:

(1) The early educational phase. This consists of graduate studies leading to a Ph.D. degree followed by a few years as a postdoctoral fellow or research associate. This phase lasts anywhere from seven to ten years and, by its end, the scientist is approximately thirty years old (a few exceptional people may reach senior academic ranks by this age). This is the golden period of his or her career. During this time there are examinations to pass, courses and other assignments to complete, sundry well-defined chores to finish, scientific interests to be identified, and working alliances to forge. The average performance is excellent, and most Indian students end up near the top. There is a fair amount of encouragement from the research establishment, represented by the professor and fellow students. This happy state is enhanced by an increase in material comforts, because the life provided by even a graduate assistantship is in many ways superior to a relatively deprived Indian middle class existence, and it is from the middle class that most of our subjects come. We believe, however, that deeper psychological reasons may have much to do with this optimistic and positive attitude. The fact that the young person has competed with his American counterparts, in an American setting and under American rules, and succeeded, gives him a great psychological boost and the expectation of a promising career.

(2) Middle professional life. As a natural consequence of the scientist's coming of age, the godfather role of the professor is withdrawn.

He may even become a competitor. This event ushers in a new era, in which the scientist must succeed on his own. During this time the young person directly faces the scientific establishment, in contradistinction to the earlier phase when he was largely an extension of an established professor. For reasons that we shall discuss later, a strange new phenomenon appears; there is a gradual deterioration in relative performance and productivity. Local people who were behind in graduate school slowly forge ahead in matters that really count: references to their work, invited papers, and award of tenure. The former euphoria is diluted and the days of enthusiasm and optimism vanish.

Two distinct modes of behavior appear at this stage. One group internalizes the "discrimination," accepts the prevailing value system, and settles down to a safe but unexciting and scientifically colorless life, often at levels much lower than they expected. They accept that they will fill the ranks and cannot hope to be in the forefront. The other group resists the tendency to succumb to the injustice of "discrimination," and expects some redress of the unfairness and that something surely will turn up. Usually, it is the more talented and more ambitious who do not give up the struggle. The result of this extended unwillingness to accept the facts is not vindication, but disillusionment and bitterness. Scientific recognition is rare, the awards even more so.

(3) Mature professional life. For the first group, who accept the fait accompli, later life is safe but lacks zest. They become hewers of wood and carriers of water, are well paid, and swell the ranks of scientific manpower. For the second group, life becomes a continual struggle; the disparity between what they expect and what they achieve is a constant drain on their creative energy. There seems little appreciation for past work and less for continuing contribution, except from the local group which directly benefits from the research; even there the credit may be given grudgingly. But one cannot complain or air one's frustrations because no one listens. The consequences are quite grave; nervous tension sets in and heart attacks occur, often at an early age. Lack of professional satisfaction drives many of this group to seek solace and contentment elsewhere. This results in a certain disinterest, not only in scientific institutions but in science itself. Altogether these feelings lead to a definite reduction in scientific productivity, followed by a sense of guilt and further loss of status.

Of course there are notable exceptions, but they are indeed few and far between and may be viewed as statistical quirks. Some others avoid this fate by aggressively adopting as a new value system the ethos and character of the dominant culture.

## Universality of Science?

Anyone attempting to understand the fate of the Indian scientist must begin by digging into Indian history. There is no recent tradition of scientific research in India. There were individuals like Bose, Ray, Saha, and Raman who did enrich the science of their times, but they were singularities, bright stars shining against a background which was largely indifferent to them. They did not create a tradition which could nurture and sustain a modern scientist and give him confidence in his ability independently to produce quality science; they left even less which could inspire him.

There is one strong tradition to which every Indian is heir. This is the tradition which comes of being a colonized people. During India's colonial past, critical and innovative thinking definitely was not encouraged, and often not tolerated. The most talented Indians were trained to value traits which made them excellent sustainers of an already working program. The programs were always those of the British, who also defined the problems and offered the solutions. What was needed was the manpower to put ideas into practice. Excellence, for an Indian, simply meant that he carried out the instructions well, and to the satisfaction of the master. Indians performed at best "at the level of the field captain," and were responsible only for local interim solutions to some operational problems. The success or failure of a pursuit was decided by others. Indians were to understand that they did not belong to the select caste, and hence planning, thinking, and implementing a strategy to deal with important issues were not in their domain. One knew the limits imposed by birth in a subject country and did not try to surpass them. This was the heritage common to all intellectuals: scientists, historians, economists, and others. Could this be damning enough to create the "condition" peculiar to a modern Indian scientist? By itself the answer is "no," but a combination of colonial tradition and absence of a scientific tradition is formidable, and is made lethal by a hearty dose of the much-touted slogan, "Science is Universal."

On the surface, all is well with the concept of the universality of science. Indeed, the language, the methodology, the content, and the results of science are universal, as they must be to be meaningful. Not universal, however, are the institutions of science. What constitutes interesting, important, and even moral scientific problems; how scientific activity should optimally be organized; what the criteria for merit are; how the community rewards good work; and other such questions clearly will be answered in different ways by different societies. It is naive to expect that our sociopolitical and psychological biases will not enter into the institutions of science; after all, these institutions are finally controlled by scientists, who happen to be just as parochial, prejudiced, nationalistic, and political as any other large group of people.

Somehow, the new breed of young scientists, especially in the Third World countries, came to romanticize not only science (often deemed to be a panacea for Third World problems) but the scientist also. The word "scientist" conjures up the kind and benign face of Albert Einstein, and one finds it difficult to associate with him anything mundane or commonplace. This romanticization could have been quite harmless were these scientists never to interact with the real institutions in the West. Clearly, that was not and is not possible. Modern institutions of science are creations of the West, and they hold most of the keys to the doors of modern scientific knowledge. Ambitious scientists from Third World countries had no choice but to come westward and participate in this alien culture. Desiring to jump quickly into this creative activity, they came in droves. The ethos of the university of science, or rather their understanding of this ethos, made scientists disdain ideas of creating institutions and knowledge appropriate to the needs of their own societies. Colonialism in science was accepted with hardly any resistance; in fact, people happily and willingly embraced it.

This acceptance was accelerated by an extremely important postwar development in the United States. The phenomenal prestige gained by American scientists because of the success of the Manhattan project made it possible for them to launch immense scientific projects for which trained manpower was sorely needed. The need became even greater when the ambitious space program was launched. Thus, there was the coincidence of need, and people from the Third World desperate to come. The situation is vaguely reminiscent of the "indentured laborers" who constructed the railways. There are, however, two major differences: this time the laborers came knocking on America's doors (with their master's and doctor's degrees) and the work was physically less hazardous. Thus, this new relationship of submission to the dictates of the American scientific establishment came about smoothly, willingly, with a smile on the face of the Indian scientist and unconditional acceptance in his heart. It was made even sweeter by a significant improvement in his material conditions, and consequent increase in prestige back home. He was able to resist any pangs of conscience that might arise from a feeling of "deserting" the society which educated him by invoking the dogma of the "universality of science" and the "scientist as a citizen of the world." In his naiveté he probably believed in the notion that the scientist belongs to the whole world. We must point out, however, that these notions were taken seriously only by the budding scientists from the Third World; most of the western scientists, even as they entered the profession, were quite cognizant of their nationality.

## The Facts of Life

Let us reexamine the psychodynamics of the Indian scientist's experience in more detail. Their world begins in purity and innocence. Several years later, when there are initial signs of discordance, most refuse to acknowledge them. When reference to their work is not given (unless it is with a well-established American, in which case it is basically taken to be his idea), when scientific societies are found to be a bit slow in inviting them for talks, when funding agencies are not particularly excited to see them as principal investigators, when tenure committees appear to be comparatively more demanding, the era of conflict begins. The scientist's first response is often a resolution to work harder. "If Mr. X made it, there is no reason why I should not be able to." Working harder, however, does not materially alter the situation, and it slowly dawns that the scientific institutions (which control most of their lives and careers) are not totally impartial; their universality is not entirely without exception. The discovery is shattering, all the more so because of the illusion, awe, and respect with which they viewed these institutions. The longer they resist, the deeper is the hurt.

Careful and cool reflection on the state of affairs reveals that there was no institutional resistance to their careers up to a certain level. As long as they were willing to play in an ensemble led by others, there were no problems. The resistance came when they tried to become conductors of the orchestra. They were allowed, even encouraged, to be bright boys, but they were not expected to be powerful and trendsetting men. If ambition were to drive them towards these goals, the task would be uphill and frustrating. They do have a place in the scheme of things but with well–defined limits, considerably lower than the sky.

Unfortunately, this realization comes rather late in the day. By this time the scientists have become accustomed to living in the West, with all its pleasures and comforts, real as well as imagined. Further, their relationship with the land of their birth has grown more and more tenuous over the years. In most cases, the relationship is limited to occasional visits to relatives and complaints about the prevalent inefficiency, dishonesty, and stupidity of all that they left behind. Thus they find themselves in this unenviable position in mid-career. There are three ways by which people learn to cope with the situation:

(1) Adopt the typical immigrant's maxim, "don't rock the boat," and accept one's fate. After all, there is life beyond one's work. This group settles for what we would describe as a safe but scientifically unexciting life. In general, their scientific careers cease to afford them much satisfaction and they seek happiness elsewhere, in the stock market or real estate, in aerobics, in electronic gadgetry, and perhaps even in social and religious practices they would not have touched back home.

(2) Some scientists choose to do unto others what was done to them. They behave like semi-colonial masters in their attitudes to scientists working in India, to hiring practices affecting Indian scientists, and to collaboration with Indian scientists. In this task they are ably assisted by the very people they wish to exploit: an associate professor in a respectable Indian university would happily come to the United States as a post-doctoral fellow at a modest salary.

(3) Some others fight, become very aggressive, and try to get their due by all means available. Such people usually end up spending much time in extrascientific pursuits with minimal results.

Whatever the path, the scientist's productivity usually diminishes as does his interest in science. He strongly resents this decline, is confused and disheartened, and feels at home nowhere. He cannot just pack up and go, certainly not from his scientific work, but he cannot stay and be happily productive. He does not feel a full citizen of the institution which controls his career, yet at the same time he cannot leave whatever the system offers because there is no other secure place to go. Over a lengthy period this situation can become unbearable.

We notice that the entire spectrum of reactions proclaims demoralization and contains very little ongoing and positive thinking. Unfortunately, these are the reactions of a shortsighted and selfish group of people with little social responsibility or concern for the future. We would like to believe that most of them (highly intelligent as they are) do indeed understand or at least sense the basic causes of their dissatisfaction. Therefore, ignorance or lack of awareness could not be the root of their inaction. It is the lack of scientific institutions of their own, built and controlled by themselves, which leads to this unenviable situation.

## Cultural Determinants of Science

It is only natural to ask at this point whether the fate of the expatriate Indian scientist is of more than peripheral interest to the larger question of the fate of the world's third largest pool of scientific manpower, and also whether there is something intrinsically irreconcilable between the culture and tradition of the educated Indian and the modernity represented by contemporary science. We deal with the latter question first, especially because there are concerned social critics who question the wisdom of the country's commitment to a science-based modernization.

Essentially, social critics raise the question of a conflict between modern science and classical Indian culture. It is curious that such a question should arise since classical Indian thinking came very near the common definition of a scientific worldview, a "relentless value-free search for the laws of nature," not only with regard to the external world but to life and any possible afterlife. No predetermined values barred the quest in any field of investigation. The sanctity of the Vedas was questioned by the Jains, the Buddhists, and the Lokayats. God, constraining or condemning man, rarely appears in the classical schools of philosophy. The Jains and the Buddhists, in their relentless search for causality and the apparent inequality in endowments or circumstances, formulated their respective theories of *karma*, in which God is not involved in the causal chain. Among the six canonical "systems" of philosophy, *sankhya*, *nyaya*, and *vaisesika* are equally daring. The philosophic tradition of ancient India is that of valueless and fearless free inquiry. How could that tradition clash with modern science?

Some social scientists point out that these philosophical systems are the expression of the "high, elitist" stream, while the folk culture was fatalistic, animistic, and *karma*-dominated. But this is a double standard. When we judge the scientific worldview we do not equate American science with newspaper advertisement of miracle diets or teenage cosmetics, by advocates of pyramid power, or the Bermuda triangle. Nor does the ever popular astrology column in the newspaper reflect current scientific views on celestial dynamics. Instead, we take the best and the highest as the norm! So if the philosophic traditions of religions originating in the Middle East, studded with their own values and taboos, were no bar to the age of modern science in the West, how could one see Indian philosophic systems as the bar to a full-fledged development of science? We must look elsewhere for the answer.

India is an extremely heterogeneous society. There exist marked differences, not only in food and clothing, but in language and customs, not only from state to state but within a state, and between educated city dwellers and villagers. Yet, in the midst of this great diversity, the common amorphous culture of the urban middle class provides most of the scientific and technical manpower. Before we examine the heritage of the Indian scientist we will briefly say what we believe it is not:

(1) Classical India. The urban, educated Indian youth is not aware of the philosophy of Kapila, Gotama, or Yajnavalkya, nor the science of

Kannada. In most cases, if he has any acquaintance with these names, it would be through children's books like *Amar Chitra Katha*.

(2) Medieval India. Aryabhatta, Bhaskara, Al-Biruni, and Amir Khusro are strange names that he sometimes comes across in a scholarly book, but their discoveries or worldviews have no discernible influence on him. He may pay lip service to J. D. Bernal, Schrachansky, or Joseph Needham but he does not equate their views with his own.

(3) Colonial India. One tries to suppress the memories of the merchants and missionaries (accompanied by the guns and soldiers of an island country) who created the sterile but orderly edifice of colonial India. But, British governance in India made it clear that, scientific or scholarly abilities notwithstanding, men were not born equal. In areas like textile technology, an appropriate Indian technology was replaced by an inappropriate imported technology. India's role in the industrial revolution was not to participate in it but to contribute to its resources.

### The Land of the Free

What then is the heritage and cultural background of the Indian scientist? Our understanding is that it was an amalgam of several half-truths and half-myths, fostered by our system of education and strengthened by the exclusive use of English as the vehicle of communication in the realms of science and technology. Some of these half-myths are listed below.

Western man has built up the entire edifice of the sciences, arts, law, political science, and economics. (We must remember that Greece and the Soviet Union are part of the "West" as far as India is concerned, although we have difficulty considering Japan as "western.") We were colonized and plundered by western man with his military and applied technology, and his science, technology, and culture were held up and accepted as superior and worthy of emulation.

With growing awareness of the West over the last four centuries Indians have come to distinguish the various subspecies of western man: the British, the German, the French, the Russian, and most recently the American. In the postwar era it was very difficult not to be influenced by the generosity, vigor, and the immense resources and resourcefulness of the Americans. We did not want to like the British colonial overlords (though we actually did admire them); the Germans were quite advanced and methodical but we thought them lacking in humanity (we were, in fact, told that they were quite devilish); the Russians had become merciless communists. So the Americans had to be the favorite people for free India to admire, associate with, and emulate.

We knew that they were against colonialism and that they were for justice, democracy, and economic prosperity for all. After all, they rebuilt Europe and dealt generously with a humbled Japan. Their manners were more natural and friendly than those of other westerners. Finally, they were the most innovative people, who not only exported massive quantities of food, but had harnessed the hidden energy of the atom. The postwar ascendancy of American science made believers of the most adamant agnostics.

It is no wonder, then, that the science student in India looked to American institutions and American scientists as the cream of the crop. The most ambitious and promising Indian students went to the United States. While the Statue of Liberty issued an open invitation, the Immigration and Naturalization Service took care that the imported crop was "top of the line." Those that came generally went to the better institutions, were usually euphoric about the academic opportunities, and were often pleased by the ease with which graduate fellowships were made available. The assessment of and acceptance by the scholars at American institutions then became the norm for this better group of young Indian scientists. While the aging academic administrators and civil service officers in India talked about the great British (and sometimes continental) institutions, the young scientists saw that America was the scientific equivalent of the British Museum; the best from many lands was brought there. The result was a subtle but significant transformation; it was not British but American science and technology that became the model.

It was not only the emigration of science students but also the change in the point of view of those who stayed home that contributed to the transformation. Even those who worked only in India looked to American institutions for moral support and sustenance, and it was American recognition that was sought. The physics papers must be published in the *Physical Review* to be "counted." Meaningful reference to one's work must come from scientists at leading American institutions. Personal success in the chosen field must include an appointment offer from a major American university. In this context it is quite clear that to understand the "Indian Scientist" we must study the contrast between the expectations and actualities in the Indian scientist's encounter with the American scientist, not just with American science.

This contrast, and its devastating effect on the productivity of the mature scientists, is seen most clearly in the professional life cycle of the Indian scientist living and working in the United States. To a lesser degree, much of what we have said about the expatriate applies to the homebound scientist, whose success and self-esteem also is thought to depend upon the judgment of and acceptance by the western scientific community.

## Can Science Be "Done" in India?

The analysis that we have presented is not a pleasing one; after all, it seems to tell us that the American scientific establishment is less than "fair" to many of its most outstanding imports. Many will vehemently deny this; others would consider it only marginally relevant. We ourselves are not happy to identify this source of the decline of productivity, but we must protest against attempts to heap such blame on the alleged eternal "fatalism" pervading the body-politic of India and its scientists. Indian classical culture was anything but fatalistic. Teachers and propagandists like Buddha, Mahavira, Ashoka, Nagarjuna, Sankara, and many others actively set out to change the society and its modes of thinking. Medieval India showed remarkable flexibility and adaptation. Its traditional culture survived the onslaught of a dynamic and irrepressible Islam. And most of all, the modern Indian science-technology student (say, at one of the institutes of technology) is a pushy, ambitious, aggressive young man, not essentially different from his counterpart in the prestigious American schools. Even the Indian peasant did not find his concern with *karma* any hindrance to adopting the hybrid strains of wheat, the herbicides, and the chemical fertilizers of the Green Revolution.

Another red herring is that of the poverty of India. In a land of starving masses, where a multitude of pressing problems demand attention, how can science flourish? One might wonder whether only a few societies can afford to sustain and nurture science. These thoughts would be relevant if the Indian government had hesitated in allocating funds for research. This was not the case. The government wisely recognized that the foundation of basic science and research (at the state-of-the-art level in science and technology) is essential if the country is to adopt the "leapfrog" rather than "follow-the-leader" approach to development.

## Epilogue

The principal aim of our essay has been to draw attention to a sad but true fact, and to stimulate thought by and discussion among Indian scientists, technologists, and social scientists. It is a symptom of the malady that there are no proper means by which to air and to clarify this problem. Appropriate organizations are sorely needed. Certainly before we undertake or even recommend an Indian program to erect new scientific institutions, it is pertinent to ask why the existing scientific institutions in India cannot serve the purpose. A detailed examination of this question is beyond the scope of this essay, but what is relevant is how these existing institutions are perceived within the scientific community. We have already pointed out that an average scientist in India is rather eager, even desperate, to come to the United States. Thus the general impression is that, barring a very few highly placed scientists, only powerful scientific bureaucrats and scientists of indeterminate merit stay back. These scientific bureaucrats, whose achievements and activities are modest, pose and behave as scientists and so give credence to the charge that science is not done properly or not done at all in India. Therefore, institutions controlled by this set of people are not likely to excite enthusiasm among scientists living in India or abroad, particularly the latter.

This then is a description of the phenomenology as well as an analysis of the underlying reasons for the state of affairs of the "Indian Scientist." This essay is not meant as an attack on American institutions of science, even though we do point out that these institutions are neither universal nor infinitely benign; no human institutions are. Any large group of people with no organization of their own is likely to feel discriminated against, and unrewarded, and this describes many scientists of Indian origin.

One hopes that this analysis of the past and present will be helpful in pointing some directions for the future. An inevitable conclusion is that Indian scientists must learn clearly to differentiate between science itself and the institutions of science. This realization naturally must force them to create structures suitable to their needs; institutions which safeguard and perpetuate their interests. It is of utmost importance that these institutions be built on solid foundations. They must include a large number of competent and well-trained scientists and they must perform their role honestly and seriously. Only then can the majority of Indian scientists have faith and trust in these institutions and look to them for guidance, encouragement, and intellectual sustenance.

We must not forget that pure scientists are rewarded by the peer appreciation and peer recognition given by scientific societies. Research often is not lucrative, depriving them of financial reward, in contrast to technological ventures where money provides a primary motivation. In addition, scientists place high values on the freedom to decide what research to undertake and on being able to set trends for the guidance of younger scholars. The only way Indian scientists can hope to have scientifically free, exciting, and creative lives is to become their own masters. This is possible if today's scientists begin to build institutions that will secure and guarantee those privileges. They will have to rise above the current confusion and despondency. They must build schools of their own, so that from a large body of dedicated professionals will emerge a significant number of trend setters, extraordinary thinkers, and original creators. And let it be hoped that these will be able to distinguish between the universality of science and the politics of scientific establishments.

Chapter Four

# The Puzzle of
# Religious Modernity[1]

## LAWRENCE A. BABB

If there is any simple formula by which to project Hinduism's future I am unaware of it. Certainly the obvious method, finding the "modern" and extrapolating from it, will not quite do. I think everyone would agree that there is something distinctively modern, and thus probably prefigurative, about the Ramakrishna Mission movement, and the same is surely true of at least the surface features of the film-inspired cult of Santoshi Ma. But if these are two harbingers of a religious world still coming into being, it is far from clear what they have in common, and as the field is enlarged matters become more complex still. If a distinctively Hindu modernism exists, in the literature with which I am familiar it has thus far proven elusive.[2] It is not that plausible examples are lacking, the problem is that there are all too many.

The truth is that we possess no real concept of religious modernity. With regard to technology, economics, and (possibly) social organization, it may still be possible to mobilize something approximating agreement about what is and is not modern. Modern technology, we know, is mostly high-energy technology, and the social and economic systems of the fully industrialized nations give us at least some basis for an idea of the probable directions of socioeconomic change elsewhere. But even these relatively innocuous formulas provoke dissent, and with religion the confusion is fundamental. The problem is not merely the formidable complexity of religious change, but also its inwardness. We may still speak with some clarity of the modernization of an economy, but long gone are those innocent days when serious men and women could speak without embarrassment of "the modernization of the soul."[3] Who would be so presumptuous as to try to characterize the inner landscape of Hindu life now, to say nothing of the year 2000? And even if we shrink from an assay of the present and future Hindu soul, many problems remain.

If we have no clear idea of what religious modernity is, let me nonetheless suggest that we at least have some rough idea of what it is not. To begin with, religious modernity cannot be equated simply with the religiously recent. Modernity is surely recent, but this does not mean that all that is recent is modern. Furthermore, much that we may want to consider modern may turn out to be as old as it is new. This is a highly complex matter. Agehananda Bharati, for example, has suggested that what is recent in Hinduism, at least at the grassroots level, is mostly Sanskritization.[4] Is this religious modernization or not? Sanskritization is not an example of what most people mean by modernization, but if Indian society is becoming more Sanskritized, and especially if the rate at which this is occurring is accelerating (as Bharati seems to suggest), then this portends a potentially fundamental change in the very structure of Indian civilization. Changes of this magnitude may well generate, willy-nilly, their own definitions of modernity. Still, for the present, Sanskritization is not our quarry.

Nor is the religiously modern necessarily the same thing as religiously western. The tendency to equate modernity with westernization is not only a persistent bias in popular thought — eastern and western — but is deeply entrenched in the very concept of modernity as an analytical category. In a variety of academic idioms, modernization is usually characterized as either a borrowing of certain western institutions or an independent reaching of similar cultural-evolutionary "conclusions." In some cultural domains, such as science, this notion may be at least plausible, but in the religious sphere it is misleading and worse. In an Occidental frame of reference it might make good sense to derive a model of "early modern religion" from the Protestant breakdown of this-world/other-world dualism.[5] But even if these ideal types (or their like) have analogues in non-western civilizations, to be held too much in thrall by western-oriented images of religious evolution is to run the risk of being blind to one of the most interesting of all human prospects, namely, that there will be deeply and essentially non-western ways to experience the future spiritually.

There is yet another trap, and this is the temptation to conceive the modern and its future projections in terms of some idea or another of "the best." There are many in India who would really much rather that institutions like the Ramakrishna Mission be taken as auguries of India's religious future than, let us say, the film *Jai Santoshi Ma*. Such feelings should not surprise us, for they exist in other societies too, and have an exact parallel in the deep disinclination of many American Christians to entertain the idea that present-day television evangelism is representative of where Christianity is heading. But the reality of contemporary Christianity is, in fact, whatever contemporary Christians, in their great plurality, take it to be, and the same surely holds for Hinduism. Nobody ever guaranteed that the spiritual future will be in every respect to everyone's taste.

This matter of plurality may, in fact, lead us to the essence of the difficulty in trying to imagine Hinduism's future. This is an immensely variegated tradition. Is there, one may ask, a Hindu tradition as such? Of course there is, but discovering its inner unities remains one of the great problems of Indic studies (and, we must add, a puzzle of Indian national life). What is the common element that unites the meticulous ritualism of the Srivaishnava priest with the deritualized piety of, let us say, the northern *sant* tradition? Something does, but whatever it is, it is subtle and possibly ambiguous in principle. In Hinduism we are dealing with an entire religious world, one far too vast for anyone to be in touch with the whole of it. Even if "present trends" exist, they would be extremely difficult to identify, and this would be so even if sophisticated survey data were available, which they are not. How can Hinduism's future be any less complex than its present? And if its complexity confounds any simple analysis of Hinduism's present, what can we possibly say of its future?

But there may be another way. If a search for Hindu modernism, conceived as a kind of essence, is likely to be futile, then would it not be better to forget about essences and concentrate on what seems to be the only stable fact, that of variety and difference? Such is the anthropologist's inclination in any case. Anthropologists are, as Clifford Geertz once suggested, the miniaturists of the social sciences; by nature wary of grand generalizations, we tend (or at least many of us do) to see the universal (when we are concerned with such grand matters at all) in the parochial and small-scale details of local situations. Surely this sense of things is likely to be the best approach to a future that will certainly be as various as the present.

What is a miniaturist's futurology? I do not know, for as far as I am aware, it has yet to be invented. I suspect, however, that such a futurology would be more illustrative than predictive. By this I mean that it would be less concerned with trying to project trends than with attempting to show how a tradition, in particular instances, has found ways of responding to certain key problems of late twentieth century life; problems that are, as far as we are able to divine such things, likely to be of great human importance in the proximate future. Such a futurology, in other words, is less concerned with predicting what "will be" than with illustrating what "could be," given a tradition's demonstrated creative possibilities.

What follows is offered as an example of a miniaturist futurology in this sense. My focus is a triad of religious movements with which I came into contact while doing field research in Delhi and its environs in 1978-79. They will not strike everyone as felicitous examples, for none of them is without critics in India, and at least one is held in considerable disesteem by many. I believe, however, that each can be interpreted, in part, as a creative response to one of three problems of notable urgency in our era: spiritual parochialism, gender inequality, and cultural rootlessness.


### Saintly Cosmopolitanism

Spiritual parochialism, the first of the problems I address, is the embeddedness of religious experience in the structures of particular groups, castes, communities, and even nations. This tendency is as old as religion itself, and creative responses to it are at least as old as Buddhism. The late twentieth century, however, is an era in which technology has placed vastly different groups and cultures cheek-by-jowl in what has been called a "global village." In this respect our period is one in which human plurality has become a more insistent fact than ever before. A religious challenge to invidious parochialism must take the form of a special type of spiritual cosmopolitanism, by which I mean a religious style that is able to flourish within — and yet transcend — multiple social and cultural worlds, bridging gaps, and defying conventional boundaries. Moreover, this cannot be merely a matter of attracting nominal adherents of varying backgrounds, but of universalizing a spiritual vision that has deep roots in a particular tradition, and that retains something of the authentic wisdom of that tradition even as it becomes socially and culturally mobile. I believe the Radhasoami movement, my first case, to be an example of this sort of cosmopolitanism.

On a relative scale the Radhasoami movement is neither large nor very new.[6] Originating in Agra in the mid-nineteenth century, it represents a recent formulation of *sant mat*, "the creed of the saints," a tradition associated with such celebrated figures as Kabir, Nanak, Dadu, Ravi Das, and others. The movement is divided today between branches associated with Agra and those linked with Punjab, where an offshoot took root at Beas around the turn of the century. In Agra there are three main sub–branches, and the Beas group produced further offshoots of its own, at least two of which are based in Delhi. There are many other smaller groups scattered around northern India, and the movement is well represented abroad. The Radhasoami tradition has been notably prone to schism, and new groups emerge in every generation.

One of the most striking features of this movement is the ease with which it has migrated into the widest variety of socioeconomic and cultural niches. Despite the fact that it is often at odds with itself in schismatic disputes, it has been a bridge between castes, classes, regions, city and countryside, and even East and West. In part this tendency is a product of the movement's older doctrinal heritage. The tradition of *sant mat* has always been impatient with social hierarchy, and this has contributed to the movement's attractiveness to the lowly and excluded. *Sant mat*, moreover, is intrinsically universalizing. Its hostility to image worship and priestly functionaries is, in effect, a rejection of the ceremonial contexts in which hierarchy and social divisions are conventionally dramatized in the Hindu world. And its commitment to the concept of a single, formless divinity — divinity, that is, of a sort that is inherently resistant to the refractions of place or social group — also carries a strong anti-parochial bias.

Alongside this older inheritance are the Radhasoami movement's own sectarian subcultures. Some of these subcultures are particularly attuned to the general outlook of what is today India's least parochial, most mobile, and indeed most "modern" group: middle class, educated men in modern occupations. This, in turn, has provided the movement with an entree into worlds very different from that within which it began. Just why the movement should have developed in this direction is not entirely clear, but it probably reflects its close association with newly emerging bourgeois lifestyles during the critical decades of its early growth. Many of the mostly highly educated and non-mendicant Radhasoami gurus, men who have served as the movement's principal role models, were themselves prototypical of India's modern middle class.

This was not true of Soamiji Maharaj, the movement's putative founder,[7] for he was a holy man of the old style. He was born in 1818 in Agra as the son of a *khatri* moneylender. His education was entirely traditional. Although he married, he was never able to adjust to the demands of an occupation, and he adopted the reclusive existence of a traditional holy man early in life. A personal following soon developed and grew, and in 1861 he finally established a public *satsang*. By the time of his death in 1878, he had initiated several thousand devotees.

He taught a somewhat idiosyncratic version of the existing tradition of *sant mat*. The true self, being distinct from the body and mind, is trapped in this world beneath layers of coarse matter. Salvation is an ascent of the self to the supreme being whose true name is *radhasvami*.[8] Such an ascent is made possible when the self is united with a subtle current of sound-energy, called *shabd*, which originates in the supreme being and reverberates everywhere in the lower creation. This is achieved by means of a spiritual discipline known as *surat-shabd-yoga*. No individual, however, can achieve salvation on his own, for the meshes of the world are far too strong. Thus, a salvation-seeker must submit to a true guru, who is the supreme being in human form.

Soamiji Maharaj's stance toward prevailing social and religious customs was powerfully anti-traditionalist and revisionist, reflecting the heritage of *sant mat* from which his teachings were drawn. He opposed all forms of image worship, and rejected the ceremonial formalism of traditional Hinduism. He took a particularly dim view of priests and other ritual specialists, and of the pilgrimages, fasts, and other rites that support priestly officiants. He rejected caste distinctions as spiritually irrelevant and worse. A wise man, he said, will turn his back on all these worldly traditions, and will see, find, and cling to the feet of a true guru.

There could hardly be a greater human contrast than that between Soamiji Maharaj and his immediate successor in Agra, a man who personally embodied the accommodation ultimately achieved within the Radhasoami tradition between an older religious style and a newly emergent social and cultural world. Soamiji Maharaj was a traditional saint, utterly remote from the world of affairs, and largely isolated from the vast changes occurring in Indian society under British rule. His successor, Huzur Maharaj, was a "new man," an early representative of India's modern educated middle class. He was born in 1829 to a *kayastha* family in Agra. Educated at Agra College, he became a career officer in the postal service. He was at home in English, as Soamiji Maharaj was not, and was familiar with western thought. He was truly skilled in the ways of Anglo-Indian bureaucracy and an immense success in the world of work. His distinguished career as a public servant culminated in his appointment as the first Indian Postmaster General of the North Western Provinces in 1881.

The Agra version of the Radhasoami faith was basically a creation of this man's mind. It is true that the core ideas came from Soamiji Maharaj, but it was Huzur Maharaj who systematized the tradition and gave it institutional form. It was he who provided the faith with a textual tradition (on which both the Agra and the Punjab groups rely) by editing and publishing the master's writings, and it was he who synthesized his master's ideas into a coherent theology in his own writings. It was he, moreover, who in his twenty-year tenure as guru established many of the sectarian usages and customs distinctive of Radhasoami life in the Agra subtradition today.

His career as guru confirmed a pattern of leadership that has been an important factor in shaping the outlook of the movement in recent times. While in no sense a worldly man, Huzur Maharaj was nonetheless a man of affairs, a man of action who knew the world and how to deal with it. From that time to this, most of the gurus of the Radhasoami tradition have had roughly similar backgrounds. They have been men who supported families, who pursued worldly careers, and who did so in modern occupations, as civil servants, lawyers, academicians, and so on.

Such careers have served an exemplary role in defining the kinds of relationships a devotee should maintain with the world. The ideal devotee — an image projected by the personae of the gurus collectively — works for a living, though this does not mean that he allows worldly endeavors to become ends in themselves. In the days of Soamiji Maharaj and Huzur Maharaj *sadhus* (mendicants) played an important institutional role in the movement, but they were stripped of all official status by one of Huzur Maharaj's principal successors. Indeed, in an inversion of the pattern of world-renunciation, the movement has come to regard employment not only as an arena in which to discharge basic obligations of family support, but as a training ground for the inculcation of spiritually valuable character traits. According to Babuji Maharaj, a later guru in the Agra branch, the most fortunate devotee is one who works for a living and whose employment entails submission to authority under "the pressure of gaining a livelihood."[9] Such employment fosters humility and a willingness to accept guidance from superiors, both of which are vital to the successful pursuit of salvation.

There is some indication, moreover, of an affinity between Radhasoami values and the intellectual and emotional demands of certain modern occupational cultures. As active men, devotees must internalize their detachment from the world. A fully internalized — and thus self-policed — disengagement from the world is a religious expression of the same disinterestedness that, when combined with a sense of institutional loyalty, can produce the behavioral consistency, honesty, and fairness so characteristic of the best kind of organization men. And if the workplace can be a school for a religiously valuable outlook on life, as Babuji Maharaj suggests, then the reverse is surely also true. Central to the Radhasoami value system is the ideal of disinterested service (seva) of one's guru. This is an ideal that can potentially be turned to the support of more worldly pursuits.

Because the ideal devotee lives and works in the world, he is enmeshed in a web of social relationships and obligations. He is not, however, at war with them. Just how these matters are dealt with in the Punjab groups I cannot report, but on the Agra side the prevailing attitude is one of detached toleration. I suspect this to be a further reflection of the pragmatic realism of middle class men, but whatever its source, the stance taken toward the extrasectarian world has been to encourage a jealous guarding of vital spiritual interests while allowing a more general accommodation to the demands of an individual's given situation in society.

To the problem of how an individual should react to the ritual obligations of family, caste, and community — obligations often inimical to Radhasoami teachings — the tradition has responded with a strategy of inner compartmentalization. In the interest of civility and social harmony, a devotee may participate, but while doing so he is urged to remain inwardly detached, and to engage in meditation in the Radhasoami manner. What this means, in effect, is that the devotee is allowed to live in local social and cultural worlds, but without being spiritually imprisoned by them.

There is an outer limit to accommodation. The critical issue is that of social claims on an individual's ultimate identity. The tradition allows an individual to behave as a member of a particular caste or other group, but insists that this identity be taken as a matter of mere social convenion and be given up completely when it conflicts with genuine spiritual interests. The principle is illustrated by an incident from Huzur Maharaj's life. We are told that he had to endure severe censure from his fellow *kayasthas* because of his public consumption of Soamiji Maharaj's food leavings *(prasad)*, in their view a flagrant violation of the commensal roles of caste. His intransigence was complete, and the issue was fundamental, for ultimate interests were at stake. In the end a devotee has but one true identity. This identity does not derive from caste, or any other worldly grouping, but is based on his relationship with God. As a taker of a true guru's leavings, the devotee is a *sat-sangi* — one who "associates," through the guru, with the supreme being. As such, the devotee belongs to a universal fraternity, one that supersedes all local social identities, including those of family, caste, and community.

What is it to be a middle class urbanite in a country like India? For many it is, among other things, to be a denizen of a cosmopolitan and socially fluid world that is still emerging from, coexisting with, and being challenged by, an older social order based on what are sometimes called "primordial" allegiances. To live in this world is obviously to confront conflicting claims on one's identity and loyalty, and to be fully at home in such a situation requires that traditional ties be honored at some level, but not in such a way as to leave the individual's deepest feelings of belongingness hostage to them. This applies with special force, perhaps, to those employed in bureaucratic organizations. In its balance of spiritual universalism and pragmatism on issues of parochial ties and obligations, the Radhasoami tradition offers a religious paradigm for precisely this outlook.

The Radhasoami tradition contains a form of Indic piety with an obvious catholicity of appeal. At a purely soteriological level, it can answer to spiritual yearnings of a deeply traditional kind. At the same time, its hostility to social hierarchy gives it a potential following, somewhat differently motivated, among those low on the social scale. Its stress on the value of an active working life, and possibly its historical association — through the principal gurus — with modern occupational cultures, lends to the movement a certain resonance with practical realities of urban, middle class life. And its deparochialization of primary identity seems fundamentally consistent with the attitudinal requirements of urban cosmopolitanism. It is not surprising, therefore, to discover that this religious tradition has found extremely broad constituencies.

Its consolations have been sought by rustic villagers and by members of India's cosmopolitan elites. It has followers among city-dwellers and villagers, and among the poor and well-to-do. It has been all of this not by being all things to all people, but by expressing a spiritual vision that can manifest itself in very different contexts while maintaining its essential integrity.

On a dimension of economic worldliness the flexibility of the tradition is most vividly in evidence in Agra. At one pole is the sectarian community at Soami Bagh, the site of Soamiji Maharaj's *samadh*. Here the purists of the tradition have tried to create a quiet sanctuary in which to pursue what they regard as the original and uncorrupted spiritual practices of the faith. The other pole is represented by the rival community at Dayal Bagh, directly across the street. Here the ideal of service *(seva)* has been transmuted into a work-as-worship ethnic. Founded in 1915, Dayal Bagh was intended to be a utopian community in which spiritual and economic endeavors would blend perfectly. How well Dayal Bagh spirituality passes muster is a matter in dispute (from the Soami Bagh side especially), but in material terms the community has been highly successful. It could be argued, indeed, that during its heyday this community was one of the most striking examples of economic innovation in twentieth century India.

For a full appreciation of the potential social and cultural inclusiveness of the tradition, we must turn from Agra to the Punjab congregations. Although its strongest ties are with the Sikh community, the Beas group has attracted devotees of every religious background. They come from many regions of India and from abroad. It has large followings among villagers and urban poor, as well as the urban middle classes. One of the most striking features of the congregational observances of this group is the immense socioeconomic diversity of the attending crowds.

A particularly impressive achievement of the Beas congregation has been its ability to bridge radical traditional hierarchical divisions. Mark Juergensmeyer reports that this group has had a very strong appeal among untouchables in Punjab, and that its rural constituency is almost exclusively lower-caste.[10] He suggests that this appeal operates on several levels. The utopian city that has been built at Beas projects a vision of a new social order — one of fairness, decency, and modernity in the most general sense — and this exerts a strong pull on the imaginations of the disadvantaged. There is a genuine mixing of high and low castes in *satsang* activities and some of Juergensmeyer's informants spoke of material benefits resulting from their associations with *satsangis* belonging to higher castes. But Juergensmeyer's data indicate that the movement's overall appeal to lower castes is rooted in matters of socioreligious identity. His informants often blamed their lower status on Hinduism and for them the Radhasoami movement represented a non-Hindu (in their view) religious alternative, a spiritual vision that defined them as persons in a way that made no reference to caste.

The Radhasoami movement has had a remarkably strong transcultural appeal. It is hard to see what Punjabi untouchables and New Englanders have in common. Yet, on many occasions I have seen signs advertising offshoots of the Radhasoami movement in public places in the college town of Amherst, Massachusetts. Most of the main branches of the movement have attracted foreign devotees, but the Beas group has been the most successful, with some 20,000 foreign initiates, mostly in Britain, the United States, and South Africa.[11] Juergensmeyer notes, and my own observations confirm, that foreign devotees often have little if any interest in India as such.[12] This is important, because it indicates that the Radhasoami movement has converted a form of Indian religion into a package that can have a spiritual appeal to men and women who have no particular acquaintance with, or predisposition in favor of, things Indian. It is a gateway, that is, to a form of India's religious wisdom that allows adherents to remain, within defined limits, socially and culturally what they were before.

The Radhasoami movement is not the first instance, nor will it be the last, of a powerfully universalizing form of Indian religion. It does represent an excellent example of the type and one that has fared particularly well in the modern world. What may be most important is that it is not a mere religious fragment, but an integral, self-contained tradition. It carries its own rich theology (upon which we have only touched), its own spiritual disciplines, and its own religious sociology centering on the fraternity of *satsangis* as surrenderers to a true guru. This entire complex of elements, a "religious system" if you will, has floated free from its original cultural and social matrix, and is now "in motion," spreading and creating ever newer offshoots. In its country of origin it has transcended every kind of boundary and has shown itself to have the capacity to embark on a worldwide career. It has become a religious global citizen. In this it will surely continue to be at home in the late twentieth century and beyond.

## Otherworldly Feminism

The assertion that gender relations pose one of the most crucial issues on the present-day agenda of humanity will not, I think, provoke much dissent. Traditional female roles are now under determined challenge.

From a worldwide perspective, this is a struggle that is probably only in its initial stages and we cannot clearly foresee its outcome. All that we know for sure is that the issues involved are vastly consequential, for they involve how human beings should be reared and employed, and how they should live together in intimate settings. There are those who believe that this most basic challenge to traditional lifestyles is essentially Euro-American, but there is a growing body of evidence that feminist aspirations are stirring elsewhere. In the second of my cases, the Brahma Kumari movement, we see what I regard as an example of a feminism, religiously expressed, that draws its symbolism and energy directly from the Hindu tradition. As such, it differs considerably in content, but not in modernity of spirit, from its western counterparts.

The Brahma Kumaris are white-hot proselytizers with a visibility all out of proportion to their claimed membership of about 100,000.[13] Working mainly in urban northern India, they are incessant sponsors of "exhibitions" and "conferences" to which they give massive publicity. Their "Raja Yoga Centers" are located at major urban concourses and are very conspicuous owing to the highly distinctive artwork displayed outside. I think it fair to say that the aggressiveness of their self-advertisement is unique in the Hindu world.

The Yoga Centers, also called Spiritual Museums, are the heart of the movement's life. Of these there are some 800, large and small. Inside most centers is a gallery of didactic artwork, the "museum." Visitors are ushered from picture to picture as the doctrinal points they illustrate are explained; they are then urged to attend the meditational sessions and "classes" that are held at each center in the morning and evening hours. To be a lay-member of the movement is to be a regular visitor at such a center and a participant in its various activities. The centers are run by a monastic elite of "fully surrendered" devotees who are the movement's core.

The Brahma Kumaris have faced much hostility and misunderstanding by outsiders. At first glance it is not clear why they should be so mistrusted, for their basic message is little more than a sectarian variant of Hinduism with a millenarian twist. The history of the world, they say, occurs in endlessly repeating 5,000-year cycles of moral and physical decline. The end of the cycle is now imminent, and those who wish to inherit the paradisiacal *satyug* to come must engage in radical self-purification. This purification requires, among other things, celibacy, vegetarianism, abstinence from tobacco and alcohol, and the performance of a form of yoga. In none of this is there anything especially provocative, and yet the Brahma Kumaris have been subjected to derision and disapprobation since the movement's inception.

The source of the difficulty is gender. The Brahma Kumari movement is mainly for women, although men can and do belong. This in itself is not a problem, for women are in fact the principal custodians of popular Hinduism. But the involvement of women in a religious movement that advocates celibacy is quite a different matter. The Brahma Kumaris believe that ours are drastic times requiring drastic measures. If celibacy was once an option only for men, it is now required of all, men and women alike. This advocacy of celibacy for women is an obvious challenge to the traditional role of women in the family and this has touched sensitive cultural nerves.

Although its founder was a man, the Brahma Kumari movement was centered on women from the start, and the social context in which it arose seems, in retrospect, to have been ripe for some kind of female revolt. It began in the late 1930s within an elite class of Sindhi merchants known as "Sindhworkis." This group had prospered greatly after its emergence in the late nineteenth century, and many Sindhworki men were quite cosmopolitan, their businesses having taken them to other areas of India and overseas. Their wives and daughters, however, lived in a far narrower world, for they were subject to the various restrictions of movement and contact with non-kin traditionally imposed on respectable women in many north Indian communities. Moreover, if the accounts of older informants are to be believed, many of the households in which these women were confined were quite troubled ones. Sindhworki men were often abroad on business for years at a time, in effect becoming absentee husbands and fathers. And as if this were not enough, they were widely suspected of keeping mistresses and living dissolute lives while abroad. There was evidently much feminine discontent with this situation. In their own portrayal of the period the Brahma Kumaris stress what they regard as the moral hypocrisy inherent in marriage.[14] Husbands were supposed to be worshipped as "gurus" and "deities" by their wives, but their actual conduct was brutish and ungodlike; certainly they were in no sense worthy of worship.

The movement was born when its founder, a jeweler from Hyderabad named Lekhraj, began to have divinely inspired visions in which he saw the destruction of the present world and the restarting of the historical cycle. A nucleus of followers soon gathered around him, consisting mainly of women from Sindhworki families in Hyderabad. They called him "Om Baba," and the group around him became known as the *om mandli*. In 1937 he established a Managing Committee of several women followers and in early 1938 he turned his entire fortune over to this group. This was the core of what was to become the Brahma Kumari movement.

The immediate result was a savage backlash in Sindhi society. The crux of the matter was celibacy, which was a central Brahma Kumari teaching from the start. We are told that husbands would return from long sojourns abroad only to discover that their wives had made vows of chastity and that their homes were to become "temples" where husband and wife would dwell together in purely "spiritual love." Husbands and their families often responded with beatings and wife-expulsions, and Lekhraj himself came to be regarded as a kind of evil sorcerer whose main motive was sexual misconduct with his female followers. Members were accosted and insulted on the streets, and in 1938 a movement building was set to the torch by an angry mob.

In the end Lekhraj and his followers were driven from Hyderabad to Karachi, where they were left in relative peace to develop their own distinctive style of spiritual and communitarian life. It was during these years that the doctrinal system and subculture of the movement matured into their current forms. In 1950 they moved from Karachi to their present headquarters at Mt. Abu. In the aftermath of this move the outer character of the movement changed fundamentally. What had previously been a reclusive and insular sect became a movement of aggressive proselytizers. Centers were established in major Indian cities and the expansion of the movement began. Lekhraj died in 1969, but the foundations he laid have proven solid and the movement has continued to grow and flourish since then.

At the heart of Brahma Kumari doctrine is what is essentially a sexual theory of historical devolution. The movement teaches that the first half of the 5,000-year universal cycle is a period of plenty, peace, and gender equality. The second half is an earthly hell: a period of strife, suffering, and the subjugation of women. The reason for the transition is sexual intercourse. Prior to the halfway point of history human reproduction takes place by means of yogic powers and intercourse is unknown. At the halfway point these powers are used up; intercourse begins, and with it the subjugation of women. The fall of women is simply a primary symptom of a deeper affliction. Sex lust, the Brahma Kumaris say, is the master-vice that nourishes all forms of "body consciousness," which in turn is the root source of all the miseries of the present world.

Sexuality is therefore at the root of the human predicament. We are all, both men and women, bound by our sexual natures to a corrupt and decaying world. For women, however, the problem is especially acute. According to the Brahma Kumaris, men at least have the option of *sannyas*, but in the world as currently constituted, women have no option save "worldly marriage" (marriage with intercourse). This means that in the present world women are not even seen as moral agents, but only as occasions for choices made by men. Woman is thus regarded as the temptress who pulls men down, as the "door to hell." Women can be free and some women inevitably will be when the historical cycle begins again. But absolute chastity must be both the precondition and essence of women's liberation.

Chastity is probably as susceptible to thematic variation as sexuality itself. It can be post-sexual, the asexuality of the already sexually fulfilled. It can be hypersexual, as in the tantric ideal of erotically energized restraint. Among the Brahma Kumaris, however, the ideal of chastity is conceived mainly in presexual terms, as the sexual innocence of the latency period of childhood. If, for men, the final lifestage of *sannyas* offers the possibility of liberation at life's close, the Brahma Kumaris believe that women (and men too) can become free by recovering life's beginning.

This idea draws its persuasiveness from life-experiences common among northern Indian women. Brahma Kumari doctrine portrays the world as a paradise in its childhood; it is only when the world grows up that the trouble begins. The point is, a similar fall occurs as a woman assumes adult status. When a woman's dominant identity changes from daughter to daughter-in-law, she loses the relative freedom of her father's house. Her position in her conjugal family is often (according to the Brahma Kumaris) one of servitude. This transition is reflected in ritual symbolism. The Brahma Kumaris stress that a *kanya*, an unmarried girl, is considered a goddess, for unmarried girls are worshipped as Durga during the festival of *navratra*. But a woman is not worshipped in this fashion after marriage. Then, say the Brahma Kumaris, it is the husband who is considered "worthy of worship" *(pujya)*, not the wife.

The parallel is clear. Just as the world falls when it matures and sexuality begins, so do women. They were once goddesses, and in order to become goddesses again, they must become children again; they must, that is, be reborn as virgin daughters in the house of their *true* father. Lekhraj, the founder, is known as Brahma Baba within the movement. Therefore, when women enter the movement they become "Brahma Kumaris," meaning virgin daughters of Brahma. They transform themselves from daughters-in-law to virgin daughters and in so doing symbolically recover a preconjugal feminine divinity and liberty.

The Brahma Kumaris believe that they will be reborn as goddesses (and gods in the case of males) in the post-catastrophic world to come, which they characterize as their "inheritance." This too has a wider context. Ursula Sharma has suggested that the hidden agenda of rules of exogamy in northwestern India is to ensure the exclusion of women from the inheritance of land by removing them as far as possible from their natural families.[15] Sharma's analysis fits in well with the Brahma Kumaris' interpretation of women's situation. In present-day society, they say, a woman has "no right" to her father's wealth. The coming paradise, however, is an inheritance from the supreme father and no earthly institution can deny it to them.

It must be emphasized that the Brahma Kumaris are by no means solely concerned with women's problems. Although they have attended to the predicament of women, they conceive this predicament as general; in a sense we are all daughters-in-law, men and women alike. Men have always been an important part of the movement. Men were in fact a majority among the daily attendees at the local center with which I became familiar. Moreover, gender and sexual issues are hardly evident at all in the movement's current public persona, which has been deliberately focused on the culturally more innocuous theme of world peace. Nonetheless, the Brahma Kumari message has a strong feminist emphasis. It is true that this message has not had much appeal. The movement has prospered but is still quite small by comparison with the society in which it has grown. There are many reasons for this, of which the distrust the movement evokes is doubtless one. I suspect that this distrust (which is usually voiced as a suspicion of sexual misconduct) is in part a reflection of the disquiet felt by some when confronted with the spectacle of the movement's dramatic — if mainly symbolic — challenge to patriarchal institutions.

The Brahma Kumari image of women's liberation draws directly on Hindu symbolism and in this sense represents an impressive illustration of how elements of a religious tradition can be turned to uses that are ostensibly quite untraditional. It is also emblematic of a type of modernity. Of the distinctively late-twentieth-century things there are for a person to be, future historians are bound to list such modern occupations as particle physicist, computer engineer, futurologist, and so on. But leaving modern occupational roles aside, surely the most characteristically late-twentieth-century person of all, and the one whose existence is in many ways the most momentous, is woman awake at last to who she is. One need not agree with the Brahma Kumaris' particular vision of the world to see that they show that awakened womankind will inevitably speak in many cultural voices.

## Modernity and Magic

Cultural rootlessness is one of the greatest perils of rapid social change. It arises from a loss of the past, but its result is likely to be a loss of the future as well. Tradition, we must remind ourselves, is not just a source of fixity in human affairs. Not only is tradition itself always changing, but its existence is vital for the coherence of human change in general; to be the agents of our futures we must have some conception, shared with others, of who we are, what the world is like, and what things in it are worth valuing. The religious problem of keeping in touch with the past is that of finding new idioms in which to express older spiritual insights, insights that can continue to impart to a civilization its own particular slant on the world, even in the midst of the most fundamental changes. This is more than finding new bottles for old wine, as exemplified, for example, by televised prayer in the United States or the retelling of mythology by means of film in India. It is a question, rather, of a creative reformulation of tradition of a sort that makes possible a preservation or recovery of the personal relevance of tradition to people whose life-experiences are radically different from those among whom tradition originally grew. I believe the cult of Sathya Sai Baba, the third of my cases, to be an example of such a reformulation.

When I first encountered the cult of Sathya Sai Baba the main issue seemed to be that of authenticity. That the cult was so firmly based among the English-educated and wealthy suggested that there was something spurious about it, that it was a kind of tinsel spirituality having little to do with "real" Hinduism. This impression dissolved as I became better acquainted with the cult's activities and devotees.

Sathya Sai Baba is among the most influential of modern India's religious personalities.[16] As a type he is not new, for figures like him have always been features of the Hindu landscape. No modern Hindu saint, however, has been more successful in gaining adherents from India's educated middle and upper-middle classes, people who better than any other represent the worldwide culture of middle class modernity in its Indian form. The acclaim is not universal; he has many critics and is often accused of fraud and favoring the rich and powerful. But for all the criticism, Sathya Sai Baba remains Hinduism's most significant jet-age holy man.

At one level he is a religious teacher. Although he has no "system" of his own, his teachings embody a coherent (if undistinctive) religious outlook that is consonant with the lifestyle of his active and in some ways rather worldly constituency. He teaches that the pursuit of spiritual goals can be consistent with an active life in the world. He urges his devotees to be familiar with Hindu scripture, to adopt a *sattvik* diet and moderate habits of life, and to engage in periodic meditation. He strongly urges his followers to aid the less fortunate through charity and social service. He is something of a cultural nativist. He regards western cultural influences as highly injurious to the integrity of Indian civilization and believes that too many Indians have sold out their own tradition by emulating western lifestyles. He particularly deplores what he regards as a prevailing ignorance of Hindu scripture among Hindus.

As anyone with the slightest acquaintance with the current religious scene in India knows, Sathya Sai Baba's fame rests not on these teachings but on the miracles with which he is credited. His devotees consider his powers to be limitless. He can travel anywhere instantaneously, appear at more than one location at the same time, cure any illness, raise the dead, and transmute anything into anything else. He can materialize objects and substances from nothing: mostly sacred ash, but also food, books, pictures, watches, and much, much more. He is all knowing, and often tells his devotees what they are about to say before they say it. He is believed to be the author of innumerable uncanny occurrences that take place in his apparent absence. Devotees sometimes smell him in their houses and frequently encounter him in dreams. Because he never appears in a dream unless he wills it, every dream of him is a kind of minor miracle. There are many miraculous households, moreover, in which his powers are continuously manifested from afar. Footprints of sacred ash appear from nowhere, objects change position, edibles are mysteriously eaten, and his pictures exude sacred ash and other substances.

What does it mean to believe that Sathya Sai Baba possesses these powers? This is a question that can be answered on many levels. It is perhaps best to begin to answer not with belief, but with disbelief. In conversations with skeptics, I encountered two views. One was that his miracles were merely sleight of hand. The other, and this was quite common, was that the magic is "real" enough, but is of a non-extraordinary kind; that his powers are really the same as yogically-acquired *siddhis*, or even, as some said, of sorcery. This is important, for it indicates that "belief in" Sathya Sai Baba is not merely a belief in his powers to perform magic; it is a belief that his powers are very special ones, with unique implications.

To his devotees Sathya Sai Baba's miracles are nothing less than the activities of a deity. He is regarded as a "descent" *(avatar)* of God. He himself has made two especially dramatic disclosures of this divine identity. The first occurred in 1940, during his early teens, when, after a brief illness, he declared himself to be a reincarnation of the celebrated Sai Baba of Shirdi in Maharashtra. In 1963, this time a figure of national renown, he again fell ill, and again made a disclosure of identity. This time he revealed that he is Shiva and Shakti in a single body. He further said that his present incarnation is the second of three: Shirdi Sai Baba was Shakti alone, Sathya Sai Baba is Shiva and Shakti together, and still to come is Shiva alone, who will appear as Prem Sai, to be born in Karnataka.

The dominant symbols of Sathya Sai Baba's cult center on this link with Shiva. His iconographic representations often portray him in association with Shiva or with the *linga*, Shiva's conventional emblem. The most important annual occurrence in the cult's sacred calendar is *mahashivratri*, the "great night of Shiva," when he materializes large amounts of sacred ash and produces *lingas* from within his body and ejects them from his mouth. The ash is a vivid link with Shiva. Ash symbolizes Shiva's asceticism and the powers it generates, and is a substance basic to virtually all ceremonies associated with this deity. Therefore, each time Sathya Sai Baba produces ash he dramatically reiterates his identity as Shiva-Shakti.

Because Sathya Sai Baba is a deity, one way to interpret his miracles is as deity-devotee transactions. In the Hindu world, those who worship deities receive *prasad* (divine food leavings) and other items in return. To do so is to express devotional humility while receiving and assimilating the higher virtues and powers of the deity, conceived as divine grace. From this perspective Sathya Sai Baba's magical productions are transactional media, particular forms of his *prasad*. When he materializes something, he almost always gives it to a devotee, and when he does so the item or substance becomes a material vehicle for his personal relationship with the devotee, binding the two together by standing as an emblem of Sathya Sai Baba's personal and benevolent presence in the devotee's life.

The miracles have a deeper meaning yet, for they are projections of Sathya Sai Baba's character as a deity. One of the most obvious features of this deity-saint's persona is his utter unpredictability. He is loving and generous, but also tricksterlike: mercurial, mischievous, full of fun. Where will he be? To whom will he give personal attention? Nobody ever really knows. At this level, his miracles — usually referred to as his "sports" *(lilas)* — are simply one way of expressing this aspect of his character, distillations of his divine capriciousness. Will he perform miracles? Will he produce anything for *me*? One never knows for sure. Devotees' preoccupations with such questions border on the obsessive.

Although this aspect of Sathya Sai Baba's character may puzzle Euro-Americans, it is consistent with certain Hindu concepts of divinity. Hindu deities can indeed be playful, and David Kinsley has shown that divine playfulness has two important dimensions.[17] At one level it expresses the "otherness" of the deities, because its unpredictability confounds all human ethical and theological categories. It also expresses the closeness of the deities to their human worshippers, for the spontaneity of divine play partakes of the spontaneity of love.

Sathya Sai Baba's relationship with his worshippers is precisely an amalgam of otherness and closeness. He is, of course, utterly other, and surrounded by an aura of mystery. He has said repeatedly that no human being can ever fathom him. He does what he does, and the apparent unaccountability of his behavior is thus one of the surfaces of his divine nature. But he is also very close to his playmate-devotees. Indeed, in some ways the most remarkable aspect of his cult is the atmosphere of intense personal intimacy that is maintained, although he is always surrounded by crowds and sustained intimate contact with him is impossible save for a few privileged devotees. True devotees feel that he is a personal and loving presence in their lives.

The apparent paradox is resolved when it is understood that the remoteness implied by his unaccountability is only a delusion arising from human limitations. It is true, for example, that he often fails to reward those whom the world regards as virtuous. It is true, too, that he frequently fails to ameliorate the misfortunes of the apparently innocent, and it cannot be denied that he sometimes lavishes his favor on those who appear too favored already by a corrupted world. But the impression of moral chaos arising from these apparent facts is really only a product of the narrowness of human moral insight. Human beings do not even know their own *karmic* pasts, to say nothing of those of others. Sathya Sai Baba, however, knows everything, "past, present, and future" (as devotees put it). Knowing that he knows everything, devotees know that everything he does is morally informed and consistent with his love and personal concern for them in the end. In this context the very opacity of his behavior becomes reinforcing evidence of his divinity.

The seamlessness of this logic is an important ingredient in the strong sense of reassurance and confidence that devotees gain from their contact with Sathya Sai Baba. They believe that nothing is beyond his powers — thus, they are protected from all harm. Still, nothing is guaranteed. Even the most devoted of his followers experience disappointments and misfortune; they lose loved ones, they have business reverses, they get sick, they die. Nonetheless, a true devotee — one with true faith, that is — knows that everything that "Baba" does or fails to do is for his or her own good in the end. At this level, Sathya Sai Baba's chaotic playfulness is the chaos of human existence itself. What is required of a devotee is total trust in him; and to learn to trust him is therefore to make one's peace with life.

Sathya Sai Baba's sacred persona is a kind of theater and the drama enacted is complex indeed. At one level a mere spectacle, at another his projected character represents a contemporary mobilization of ancient mythical and ritual symbols, especially those clustering around the image of Shiva. It also provides a setting for devotee-deity transactions of a vivid kind. And at the highest level it provides a scaffolding for a religiously-informed outlook that invests experience, even at its most apparently meaningless, with a higher spiritual meeting. Sathya Sai Baba's miracles are not just a conjuring show for the credulous, but represent an expression of distinctive spiritual orientation that utilizes principles that lie deep in the symbolic infrastructure of Hinduism.

There is little in any of this that is truly new, but it is done in a way that is especially in tune with the spiritual needs of cosmopolitan urbanities. Not all such people are Sathya Sai Baba's followers, of course, but a significant number of his followers do belong to this category. One basis of his appeal to this constituency is his soft line on the relationship between spiritual goals and worldly striving, but in this he is hardly unique. The simplicity of his teachings probably appeals to those whose religious sensibilities are, for whatever reason, not very complex. And there are those, no doubt, who are drawn to the cult because of the social chic it has acquired in some circles. Also, the nativistic tone of his teachings has resonance with those whose sense of cultural and perhaps national identity has been challenged by cosmopolitan backgrounds. But as D.A. Swallow suggests, what may be more important than any of these factors is that many of his devotees live in a social world that is, by traditional standards, unnervingly disordered.[18] For them devotion to Sathya Sai Baba apparently helps to restore a sense of the personal relevance and efficacy of a tradition that has come to seem increasingly remote from the landscape of everyday life.

Sathya Sai Baba's real accomplishment is that out of this blend of highly diverse impulses and yearnings he has been able to forge a distinctively focused form of Hinduism, one that uses ancient symbolisms of extraordinary power in a way that is deeply satisfying to followers who are in many ways untraditional. As Swallow puts it, his cult has provided a means for such persons to "think of their many individual and complex problems in terms of traditional dilemmas and conflicts."[19]

Given the up-to-date sophistication of many of his followers, Sathya Sai Baba's emphasis on magic may seem anachronistic. But it is possible that he has found, perhaps inadvertently, a surprising point of contact between a traditional openness to the miraculous and one of modernity's characteristic moods. If his magic is challenged by scientific dogmatism — what some call "the modern superstition" — then this may be eclipsed by the fact that the total symbolic package he presents, of which the magic is only one element, resonates with what in many of his devotees is a deeply entrenched hopefulness. There is something fundamentally confident about the "Sai" outlook on the world. For his devotees the world is suffused with his love, a place in which nothing is impossible, and in which events always serve a benevolent purpose. This view embodies a kind of optimism (though not a Panglossian optimism, as I hope I have shown) that is consonant with the attitudes of those most rewarded by a social and economic order still being born.

## Religious Futures

Each of my examples represents a possible style of religious modernity. Together they show that religious modernity can come in very different packages. Moreover, it must be acknowledged that religious modernities can be antagonistic. Brahma Kumari feminism would not find much sympathy or understanding in Radhasoami circles, and from the Radhasoami and Brahma Kumari viewpoints the emphasis on the miraculous in Sathya Sai Baba's cult is naive and worse. Simply put, these are three quite different religious worlds.

I certainly cannot claim that any of these movements is, in any strong sense, predictive. At most what can be said is that each, in itself, represents a distinctive aspect of the religious present, and in that respect is a weak augury of a fragment of a possible future, a future that is bound to be as complex as the present. In the Radhasoami movement we see a particularly impressive example of a religious tradition that has left the nest and that shows every sign of becoming a religious citizen of the global village. In their critique of one of the most lately-challenged of the ancient status quos, the Brahma Kumaris are a vanguard movement (or, as others would say, a fringe movement). I suspect that this group will be around for quite some time. Although their particular views will probably find no more favor among western feminists than among their own co-nationals, I suggest that if the history of the emergence of women's self-awareness in modern times is written without including them, it will be the poorer for it. The cult of Sathya Sai Baba is more than just another example of fast-food spirituality. It is deeply grounded in tradition and it has made tradition available to modern minds and hearts. Whether his cult survives his departure from the scene remains to be seen. There are, and doubtless will continue to be, many imitators.

At this point foresight fails. I have not pretended that my small examples exhaust the field of contemporary Hinduism, nor have I the temerity to assert that they in any way suggest some grand point of convergence. The only possible generality, I think, is one that involves looking backward as well as ahead. Each of my examples is plainly as Hindu as it is modern. If nothing else, this at least suggests that this is a tradition too rich in possibilities ever to have to retreat from the future. No doubt the grey twilight of secularism will lower over India as elsewhere, but it will certainly not prevail. Nor is there the slightest indication that India will ever have to borrow religious models from other cultures. Let those who fear a planetary future of lifeless cultural monotony take heart. Human variety, by which I especially mean the richly different ways humanity has discovered to construe the world and the human situation spiritually, is among our greatest treasures. It is variety of this kind, after all, that most guarantees an open human future. If the Hindu present is any indication, this precious human heritage will be quite safe in India.

## NOTES

1. This essay is based on research conducted in Delhi and environs between July 1978 and May 1979. The work was supported by an Indo-American Fellowship. I would particularly like to thank colleagues at the Department of Sociology, Delhi School of Economics, for the hospitality, assistance, and intellectual companionship so generously given during my stay in Delhi. I would also like to thank the many members of the religious movements discussed here who assisted me in my inquiries. Responsibility for all errors of fact and interpretation is mine alone.

2. I am leaving aside the equally daunting question of Islamic modernism in India.

3. Robert N. Bellah, "Introduction," *Religion and Progress in Modern Asia,* edited by Robert N. Bellah, New York, the Free Press, 1965, p. ix.

4. Agehananda Bharati, "Hinduism and Modernization," in *Religion and Change in Contemporary Asia,* edited by R. F. Spencer, Minneapolis, University of Minnesota Press, 1971, pp. 73-74.

5. Robert N. Bellah, *Beyond Belief: Essays on Religion in a Post-Industrial World,* New York, Harper and Row, 1970.

6. The development of the Radhasoami movement and its place in the tradition of *sant mat* have been described and analyzed in detail by Daniel Gold, *The Land as Guru in North Indian Sant Tradition and Universals of Religious Perception*, unpublished Ph.D. dissertation, The University of Chicago, 1982; and Mark Juergensmeyer, "The Radhasoami Revival of the Sant Tradition," in *The Sants: Studies in a Devotional Tradition of India*, Berkeley, Graduate Theological Union, forthcoming. For more general accounts see Sant Das Maheshwari, *Radhasoami Faith: History and Tenets*, Soami Bagh (Agra), S. D. Maheshwari, 1954; and Agam Prasad Mathur, *Radhasoami Faith: A Historical Study*, Delhi, Vikas, 1974.

7. There are major disagreements within the movement, especially between the Agra and Punjab wings, concerning the nature of Soamiji Maharaj's contribution, and the role of the Radhasoami tradition in history. I shall not consider these details here. The curious reader is urged to consult Daniel Gold's definitive dissertation (1982), noted above.

8. I am here reporting the Agra version of his teachings. The Punjab groups interpret his teachings differently, and a major point of contention is the significance of the term *radhasvami*.

9. Myron H. Phelps, *Notes of Discourses on Radhasoami Faith Delivered by Babuji Maharaj in 1913-1914* (Phelps' Notes). Soami Bagh (Agra), Radhasoami Satsang, 1947, p. 106.

10. Mark Juergensmeyer, *Religion as a Social Vision: The Movement Against Untouchability in 20th Century Punjab*, Berkeley, University of California Press, 1982, pp. 208-220.

11. Mark Juergensmeyer, "Radhasoami as a Trans-national Movement," in *Understanding the New Religions*, edited by J. Needleman and G. Baker, New York, The Seabury Press, 1978, p. 193.

12. *Ibid.*, p. 195.

13. The Brahma Kumaris have not yet attracted much scholarly attention. I have discussed Brahma Kumari historical cosmology and feminism in greater detail in two publications. See Lawrence A. Babb, "Amnesia and Remembrance in a Hindu Theory of History," *Asian Folklore Studies*, 41, 1982, pp. 49-66; and Lawrence A. Babb, "Indigenous Feminism in a Modern Hindu Sect," *Signs*, 9, 1984, pp. 339-416.

14. Jagdish Chandar, *et adbut jivan kahani*, Mt. Abu, Prajapita Brahma Kumari Ishvariya Vishva-Vidyalaya, n.d.

15. Ursula Sharma, *Women, Work, and Property in North-West India*, London and New York, Tavistock, 1980, pp. 203-204.

16. The best scholarly analyses of the Sathya Sai Baba cult and the Sai Baba tradition that I know are D. A. Swallow, "Ashes and Powers: Myth, Rite, and Miracle in an Indian God-Man's Cult," *Modern Asian*

*Studies*, 16, 1982, pp. 125-158; and Charles S. J. White, "The Sai Baba Movement: Approaches to the Study of Indian Saints," *Journal of Asian Studies*, 31, 1972, pp. 863-878. The cult itself has generated a vast hagiographic literature.

17. David R. Kinsley, *The Divine Player: A Study of Krsna Lila*, Delhi, Motilal Bandarsidass, 1979.

18. Swallow, *op. cit.*, p. 153.

19. *Ibid.*, p. 155.

Chapter Five

# Indian Cinema: Dynamics of Old and New

CHIDANANDA DAS GUPTA

# I

When human beings set foot on the moon, Indian villagers came to hear
of it but many did not believe it. Argument raged for a long time between the old and the young about how it could be possible. In astrolog-
ical reckoning, the moon is one of the planets that influence a human
being's future; what happens when someone simply walks on it? The
question is obviously impossible to answer. Perhaps that is why, when
a reference to moonwalking was made in Ramesh Sippy's popular Hindi
film *Daag*, no direct answer was given. The man who received the news
said, "Maybe, but just now I am more concerned with repairing my
bike."

The problems of modernity and tradition, religion and science, old
and new, East and West—expressions of the same basic conflict—are
central to the Indian cinema today. Cinema is the battleground on which
the old and the new are fighting it out, at least for the masses of people
who have little access to the high culture of the cities and who live insu-
lated within a closed circle on the other side of a great divide.

The relationship of man and woman has always been a preoccupation
of cinema everywhere; it can be seen as the key to the core of a culture,
an index to the inner state of its being, and to the position of woman in
society as a whole. It is, in other words, an essential part of the conflict
between tradition and modernity. In the Islamic countries, the question
of the position of woman has become central to the attitude to
modernization and its apparent concomitant, westernization. In a
similar way in India, different religious groups are in varying degrees
shaken by the basic changes brought about by modern industrialized
society and perceive the position that women threaten to assume in it
as an important symbol of a new social order. This concern is reflected
as sharply in the blockbusters for the mass audience as in the serious
creative cinema of the advanced middle class, but the two cinemas are
ranged on opposite sides of the battleground of ideas. By and large, the
popular cinema stands by the traditional role of a woman; the "new
cinema" of the modern minority advocates her liberation.

In a series of recent films, the mother is the central point around
which the children's fortunes revolve. Indeed, the films of the 1970s are
remarkable for the sharpness of their emphasis on the centrality of the
mother figure. In a number of films starring Amitabh Bachchan, the
biggest star in the Indian firmament, an almost passive mother presides
as the symbol of family unity. Her word is law and her pleasure is her
son's primary concern.

In *Trishul*, a man gives up the girl he loves because his mother extracted a promise from him at her deathbed that he would marry another, a rich industrialist's daughter, who would help him rise in the world. "Remember, before you loved Shanti, you loved me." The rejected girl is, of course, pregnant. When her son grows up she makes him swear vengeance on his father for the maltreatment of his mother. The two protagonists join battle in obedience to their respective mothers. The son finds his father, destroys his position and his wealth, becomes instrumental in his death, and is reunited to him only in his repentance at the moment of death. In *Amar Akbar Anthony*, three brothers are separated from their parents in childhood and are brought up in different religions by surrogate fathers. After they have grown up, the whole family is reunited and all is once more sweetness and joy. In *Deewar*, two brothers, one a policeman and the other a bandit, battle for the love of their mother as though they are rivals for the hand of a girl. The bandit gives his life in order to see his sick mother. It is significant that, in most of these films, the father disappears from the scene at a very early stage but the sons hardly ever lose contact with the mother; in fact, their relationship is strengthened and sanctified by the absence of the father.

This glorification of the mother in the popular cinema expresses many aspects of the crisis of identity that buffets the Indian mind today. I am not going into the psychological theories of the mother complex, or the male fear of the power of the woman, since my concern here is with social transition and the insecurities bred by it. What matters is that this glorification of the mother figure obviously stresses the function of a woman as mother rather than as beloved or wife or independent being. It is interesting to observe that Indian mythology, epics, and Sanskrit drama have few portraits of the Great Mother from which Indian cinema could draw inspiration. Sita in the *Ramayana* is primarily the great wife and so is Draupadi in the *Mahabharata*. Gandhari, aged mother of a hundred slain Kauravas, could have been a candidate but does not shape up to the role. She did mourn their loss on the battlefield, but the dominant impression is of wifely loyalty as she goes about with eyes covered, simulating the sufferings of her blind husband. Damayanti goes through untold suffering for Nala as does Saivya for Harishchandra. Parvati's ascetic feats win her a great husband in Shiva; Savitri's single-minded devotion to her husband defeats death. Kalidas celebrates sexual love in *Kumarasambhavam* and waxes poetic over Parvati's pregnancy, but does not draw a portrait of a long-suffering mother giving up all for her sons. It is the husband who forms life's goal for the great women of Indian mythology. Even the benign and terrible mother images of the puranic pantheon do not provide the true model of the stock figure of the Indian cinema, the widowed mother who gives all for her children. The widow is an archetype manufactured partly by modern literature but mostly by the popular cinema.

In prose literature in modern India, most of which dates from the beginnings of Christian missionary activity, the same centrality of family and sexual love has obtained. This image has necessarily been confined to the educated urban elite, the class most associated with the modernization of the country. The popular cinema has extended these concerns to the masses of the people, eliciting grassroots responses, sometimes radically different from those hopes for change expressed in the Constitution and in the literature of the sophisticated. The fear of the loss of the values of pre-industrial tradition grips the core of Indian popular cinema, behind its garish facade of superficial modernity evidenced by car chases, gang fights, and nightclubs. There also lurks the fear of the unraveling of a social unit bound not only by ties of blood but by the need to work jointly on the land in order to prevent the fragmentation of holdings (an essentially agricultural concept). Geographical delimitation and the lack of transportation and communication reinforced these attachments. Today, self-contained agricultural communities are increasingly being disturbed by industrialization and urbanization. With the expansion of large industry and of urban centers, many rural professions are displaced by mass production. Migrant laborers come together in giant steel plants or power stations, drawn from many regions, language groups, and castes. The workplace becomes more secular and modern, if insecure; the home in the village remains the haven of refuge, the repository of tradition for the members of a family increasingly dispersed geographically and occupationally. There is fear of the disintegration of the family in a period of transition from pre-industrial conditions. Constantly in the popular cinema, the family is broken up early in the film and reunited at the end.

The popular cinema, suspicious of modern western ways, rates traditional modes above them. Some films strain to contrast East and West: *Do Raaste, Evening in Paris*, and *Purab aur Pachhim* declare the East superior and the foreign devil a threat to home and integrity. Others express the same beliefs by implication in an occasional sequence or stretch of dialogue. This often relates to the roles of women. The westernized woman, for instance, is admitted mostly at the margins of society: she is the nightclub singer or bandit, or the golden-hearted prostitute living outside the mainstream of society and therefore well-accustomed to episodes of sex or violence. Sometimes there is a woman doctor or lawyer, a common enough figure, but invariably isolated in a role without family or home. In *Insaaf Ka Tarazu*, the raped woman (whose daughter is also raped) is a consistently underclad photographic model who, it is implied, deserves to be raped. Her lawyer is also a woman of unknown moorings.

In the macho-minded films of Amitabh Bachchan, woman, particularly the more modern woman, is treated as a chattel. As the bandit Don in the film of the same name, Amitabh says, "I dislike two kinds of women; the kind that comes to me too easily, and the other kind that takes too long to come." Girls are depicted going to school or college, but there is an ambivalence as educational institutions are shown as playgrounds for lovers' dalliances, not places to study. The homely girl with old-fashioned rural virtues, good at housework, shy and wary of the other sex, is rated above the better-educated and independent, even though the appearance of the educated girl in the cinema has increased almost in proportion to real life, and women's education as such is not actually denigrated.

Widow remarriage may be hinted at (even advocated, as in *Sholay*), but the girl must die so that the marriage cannot take place. In *Dil Ek Mandir Hai*, a sick husband discovers that his wife and his doctor are in love. Sure that he is going to die, the husband makes the wife promise that she will marry the doctor after his death; but the husband recovers, and it is the doctor who has to die so that widow remarriage does not occur. In *Silsila*, the husband falls in love with another woman but decides, in the moment of truth, that religion and tradition decree that he should remain wedded to his wife even though he will never love her. Thus is the dreaded prospect of divorce, relatively easily granted under present law, kept out of the bounds of reality. Dowry deaths abound in parts of northern India, more especially its Hindi belt. The accounts published in the newspapers are tragic and dramatic, and obvious material for popular cinema; but the subject remains firmly banished from the screen. In the treatment of woman, the popular cinema tolerates some modernity but clearly prefers tradition.

There is hardly any popular film in any Indian language which does not show lovers cavorting outdoors in the lap of nature, like Krishna with the Gopis, to the accompaniment of song and dance. This is the most common form of treatment of love in our cinema. But why nature? Why so seldom within the walls of a home? Why operatically through song and dance rather than realistically through drama? This question can be answered only in the context of separation of fantasy from fact. In real life the free mixing of boys and girls, except in English-speaking upper middle class society, is severely restricted. It is interesting to speculate on the effect that this contradiction has on young people con-stantly exposed to sexual frolic on the screen. Although explicit sexual action, nudity, and even the kiss are not shown, Indian cinema is one of the most sexually charged in the world. Because its openness will not be countenanced by the public and the censors, eroticism goes under-ground. It becomes a persistent leavening to the entire substance of a film.

Take Raj Kapur's *Satyam Sivam Sundaram*. The title enshrines the traditional Indian concept of the unity of the good, the beautiful, and the true. The heroine, Zeenat Aman, is presented relentlessly under-clothed throughout the film. In the same director's *Bobby*, Dimple Kapadia plays the demure adolescent in love; but the moment she breaks into dance, the photography and editing merge to trigger a rapid-fire burst of images of shaking breasts, thrusting thighs, and rip-pling midriff, demolishing the idea of teenage innocence carefully nur-tured by the dramatic sections. In fact, few Indian filmmakers know how to stage, photograph, and cut a dance in any way other than the erotic.

Although the kiss is not shown and direct genital contact is usually avoided, physical proximity is nonetheless considerable. A man puts his arms round a woman, kisses her on the neck, crouches on his knees and embraces her around the waist with his face close to her groin. The sense of sexuality and arousal are, if anything, more than a lip-to-lip kiss would generate. Whenever the kiss becomes unavoidable it is de-flected by an outburst of song and dance. The man and woman separate, singing and dancing, and then come together again renewing the cycle of arousal and dispersal.

Over the last three decades, the romantic view of woman has given way to an assertion of male machismo, tending towards physical domi-nance and rough handling of women. It is possible to relate this to the growing harassment of women in real life, apart from dowry deaths, extending to molestation on the streets and in public conveyances. For young women, particularly the educated and "modern" ones, it has be-come more dangerous to be alone in many areas of the country. The root of this phenomenon may lie in frustration. The sexual fantasies young men and women see on the screen cannot be realized in life. They may work together in government and private offices, but they cannot mix. It would be unacceptable to go to each other's homes. Parents would be present, and as families are large there would be no privacy. If they were found talking to each other, not to speak of holding hands, eyebrows would be raised. If more intimacy was noticed there would be a severe reprimand, particularly for the girl. No wonder the films show hero and heroine playing around in the great outdoors!

Love and marriage, in the context of the dowry system, are two different things for most people. For the bridegroom, it is a matter of direct economic gain; for his family, it is a means of improving its fortunes. It may be a means to luxuries — cars, refrigerators, motorcycles, video sets, and other consumer items normally beyond the reach of the large majority. When a young man and woman are attracted to each other, this, by itself, will play a small part in the business of marriage. Apart from problems of caste and horoscopes, the major question will be, "What will the family acquire in the deal?"

The fantasy of love on the screen and the reality of dowry deaths are in fact the inverse of each other. It is the impracticability of marrying the woman of one's choice after a period of courtship that helps to bring about the element of violence towards women. The more the enactment of love scenes between men and women becomes separated from marriage, the more sexual attraction is made to seem illegitimate, and thus susceptible to violence. It is almost as if the young man feels that since it is his duty to marry to improve his family's fortunes, why should he not have a good time meanwhile as do the heroes on the screen? In order not to miss that dimension in his youth, he has to do something outside of marriage, regardless of the wishes of the woman who may attract him. So the treatment of sex on the screen, and its fantasy and arousal effect on sex-starved youth, often leads to brutality, molestation, and rape in real life, especially among caste Hindus in northwestern India where the incidence of dowry violence is at its highest.

In other words, what some psychologists have rationalized as the "healing effect of collective fantasy" may well be, in India and in matters of love and marriage, the exact opposite. Instead of resolving the inner problem, fantasy aggravates it towards eruption into real life violence.

# II

In two states of south India, Tamil Nadu and Andhra Pradesh, the matinee idol of the regional cinema has become the chief minister. One of many contributing factors to this political impact of the cinema is that it has become the vehicle of expression of a popular will not reflected in the newspapers of the literate or by government-owned radio and television. The privately owned regional cinema expresses, among other things, the fear of national homogenization and the loss of regional ethnic, cultural, and linguistic identity. Such fears have found expression in the violence in the northeast and northwest. In the south also, as the prospect of a stronger national entity is confronted, some of the constituent units are balking. This is certainly not the only cause of regional upsurges, but it is one.

The all-India film has a vested interest in homogenization. It is bred on the superficial factors of commonality brought about by industrialization and urbanization, and stays away from regional reality for fear of destabilizing the precarious unity of its market. Its version of Hindustani has gained more acceptance all over India than the official Hindi. What is called the Hindi film is shown all over the south and in the tribal areas of the northeast where, nonetheless, there is considerable opposition to the official language policy.

One possible factor behind the emphasis on family values, justifying revenge for the redemption of family honor, may well be the mistrust of a larger notion of society developing in a country of shrinking distances and increasingly centralized direction. The motif of revenge, common in the cinema of the last twenty years, is bound up with the concept of family. Together they seem to say that the unwritten but better-known laws framed within smaller units of society, the village and the family, are more to be trusted than those prescribed for the entire population of a vast country. The law is iniquitous and is not honestly administered; therefore the individual must take it into his own hands and dispense summary justice in light of his tradition. In a 1982 film *(Bobbili Puli,* or Tiger of Bobbili), made shortly before he became Chief Minister of Andhra Pradesh, N. T. Rama Rao played an army officer freshly turned bandit. He rounded up the custodians of the law in a cave, and with a battery of guns trained on them by his henchmen, he read them a sermon that ended with Krishna's pronouncement in the Geeta: YADA YADAHI DHARMASYA GLANIRBHAVATI BHARATA/ PARITRANAYA SADHUNAM VINASHAYA CHA DUSHKRATAM/ DHARMASANGSTHAPANARTHAYA SAMBHAVAMI YUGAY YUGAY (From one epoch to another, whenever virtues decline, I manifest myself, to protect the good, punish the guilty, and restore order). When asked about his politics in an interview soon after his election takeover, the Chief Minister said, "You have seen the film *(Bobbili Puli);* there is a man who punishes the bad, there is a man who does justice, there is a man who always sides with the wronged sections of the people. So naturally there is sympathy for the hero. That is the style of the role I perform. So the people expect good things to come of my service to them." Perhaps this could be called a mythological vision of modern India.

This sense of mission is shared by the Hindi cinema in another way. Its concern is not with the deliverance of society at large, but with the protection of its small units. The sights are set increasingly on the family and the group. The suggestion is that society as a whole is too distant and nebulous and therefore a somewhat fearsome concept, compared to the accessible and reassuring values of family and group. Outside the world is a battlground where laws are not respected, if indeed they are worth respecting.

# III

About two years ago, a college-educated girl from a small town near Delhi, with the help of a voluntary organization, came to the capital to seek work, against the wishes of her family. Her brothers followed her and, with the help of the police (according to the newspapers), roughed up the volunteer workers because they would not give them the girl's address. The case went to court and the judge ruled in favor of the girl's constitutional right to determine her future, live alone, take a job — all of which her family considered immoral. In a similar case, the parents roundly abused a judge who ruled in favor of their adult daughter. They stopped only when the threat of contempt of court proceedings was explained to them. Society as a whole is not yet prepared for many of the changes now permitted by law and in evidence among the urban, "westernized," educated groups. There is often a contradiction between what the masses of the people consider proper and what the educated elite has written into the country's laws. In a popular film the conflict between daughter and parents would never be allowed to reach the courtroom; it would be resolved, after some sufferings, on the side of tradition.

Where religion is concerned, within the popular cinema there is a similar unease regarding challenges posed by science. If man struts about on the moon, what happens to God? Products and manifestations of science are increasingly in evidence in the existence of illiterate villagers in remote areas. There is a sense that many of these pose an unspoken challenge to traditional beliefs. Take the popular faith in the purity of the holy river Ganges and the scientists crying themselves hoarse about its dangerous level of pollution. When the subject was last raised in Parliament, the Minister for Tourism said that it was physically impossible for the waters of the Ganges to be polluted.

The insecurity generated by such conflicts has to be neutralized by the cinema in order to set the popular mind at rest. A simple answer is given: separate science from tradition. Hold them in compartments between which osmosis is not permitted. This "ritual neutralization," as Ashis Nandy calls it, is the exact opposite of the dynamic synthesis of old and new that India's cultural and political leadership has sought for one and one-half centuries. To the popular cinema of today, the products of science are for our use but the ideas behind them must not be given prominence. Even in West Bengal, one of the culturally "modern" areas of the country, there was embarrassed silence over Satyajit Ray's *Devi*, which showed a change from superstition to enlightenment through personal tragedy without condemnation. Unlike many other Ray films, this one failed at the box office.

In *Amar Akbar Anthony*, a film mentioned before, the blind mother is taken by her son to see a Muslim saint, Shirdi Sai Baba. In answer to the son's prayers, two masses of light emanate from the saint's eyes, travel across a large courtyard full of devotees, settle in the eyes of the mother, and restore her sight. Thus, in a film full of incidental manifestations of modernity, a miracle — a scientific impossibility — is shown in what might be called a mythologization of the present. The rational thrust of the Gandhi-Nehru era, with its anxiety to lead India towards democracy and modern values, is countered by a rejection of synthesis as a mode of living. Compartmentalization is the cinema's response.

# IV

In the foregoing I have invariably stressed the phrase Indian cinema *today*, because a look back to previous decades gives a rather different picture. The further we go back, the more we find a progressively closer understanding between the attitudes in cinema and the aspirations of the national leadership. The nearer we come to our times, the greater the divergence. Fantasy and fact have increasingly grown apart. The "mythical treatment" of the birth and growth of the hero in relation to his mother and his family gained momentum in the 1970s, and is at its peak today. This is a radical change from the catalytic role often played by pre-independence cinema, with its frequent intervention on behalf of the modern alongside the mythological. Most of the social films of the 1930s were concerned with such problems as caste, dowry, and freedom of choice in marriage.

In Shantatam's *Duniya na Maanay* an old man marries a girl younger than his daughter, but she refuses to consummate the marriage and is aided by the old man's "modern" English-speaking social worker daughter to the extent that the two sing Longfellow's "Psalm of Life" together. The old man is helped by his sister, but has to accept defeat and acknowledge his error. Seen today, the film still retains much of its power. Master Vinayak's *Brahmachari* made fun of obsessive religiosity and defended a modern woman's pursuit of the man of her choice. Such a modern woman would be the object of direct and indirect denigration today. P. C. Barau's *Devdas* became an archetypal film in the romantic advocacy of freedom of choice in marriage. Himangsu Roy and Franz Osten's film, *Achhut Kanya*, deplored untouchability. K. Subramaniyam's *Balyogini* described the plight of child widows. The cinema was in transition in the 1940s, from studio to independent production, from colonial status to independence, from middle class to working class audience, and although innovative it produced fewer big box-office films with social themes. Shantaram's film on Dr. Kotnis' medical mission to China played on India's new-found internationalism. Uday Shankar's *Kalpana* celebrated a new prestige and enthusiasm for the art of dance. Jaigirdar's *Ramshastri* focused on a phase of Indian history and its standards of justice, and a new concern for the downtrodden was shown in K. A. Abbas's *Dharti ke Lal*.

The 1950s evidenced the return to a more vigorous championing of social causes in the films of Raj Kapoor, Bimal Roy, and Mehboob. Kapoor's *Awara* sought to establish the individual's democratic right to an identity of his own, independent of class and privilege, and protested against the glorification of heredity. In Bimal Roy's *Sujata* an outcaste woman is said to have equal rights on the strength of personal qualities, not caste. *Do Bigha Zamin's* hero must struggle against the avarice of the village moneylender and redeem himself. Guru Dutt, the romantic individualist, berated society for undermining the rights of the artist and called for his recognition. The social satire of *Mr. & Mrs. 55* dealt in a forthright manner with divorce, class distinctions, and women's rights. Mehboob's *Aurat*, later remade as *Mother India*, did have a mother, but an active one, not a mythological shadow; the thrust of her actions was positive and forward-looking.

The 1960s saw the dominance of Dharmendra as a kind of muscular-romantic hero. His benign machismo is an independent force projected by his personality, not a reflection of an invisible mother figure providing miraculous impetus. In *Samadhi*, for instance, his fight is for the hand of the woman he loves and for the wellbeing of his son; no mother force lurks behind. The other important hero of the period, Rajesh

Khanna, wields romantic charm and innate kindness on his own, without off-stage promptings from a mother. One of his major films, *Amar Prem*, subsumes the mother aspect of woman into that of the beloved. In its respect for woman, it is remarkably different from the films of the 1970s.

So much for the cultural combustion within the popular cinema's engines, a force that the elite, the engineers of modern India's socioeconomic change, have so far failed to perceive. This is the reason the party in power was twice taken by surprise by the eruption of regional-conservative forces through actors turned politicians. The connection between grassroots democracy and popular cinema in highly illiterate communities is not yet sufficiently understood or appreciated.

# V

The importance of cinema as a medium has not been ignored by India's rulers. In fact, perhaps oddly, India is one of the few non-communist, post-colonial countries to encourage the cinema as a catalyst for social change. The Film Enquiry Committee of 1951 was a high-powered body whose recommendations were approved by Parliament and more-or-less faithfully implemented by the government. The first international film festival in 1952 made a profound impression on the intelligentsia and opened its eyes to the achievements of world cinema from which India had been so isolated. The Film Institute of India and the Film Finance Corporation were founded, as were a Children's Film Society, national awards for excellence in cinema, and a National Film Archive. Of these, the Children's Film Society is the only one still to hover over rather uncertain ground; the others quickly became growth centers for a vigorous new cinema. In 1955, Satyajit Ray's first film, *Pather Panchali*, subsidized by the Government of West Bengal, made history and launched the career of one of the world's celebrated filmmakers. His example, followed by the readiness of first the central and then of some state governments to give aid, led to the making of a new kind of film. The film society movement, launched with missionary zeal by Ray, myself, and others in 1947, had already created pressure towards change in filmmaking norms. Although there had been two film societies before it, both in Bombay, the Calcutta Film Society became the spearhead of a new movement for the spread of a film culture, supported mostly by central and partly by state governments.

With the Film Finance Corporation's readiness to lend money for offbeat films, and the Film Institute's generous facilities for training filmmakers, a new crop of socially conscious, artistically ambitious films were made by creative people of high cultural level in Bengal, Maharashtra, Karnataka, Kerala, and finally even in tiny Manipur in the northeast. These films obtained quick acceptance among the Indian intelligentsia and art film enthusiasts all over the world, winning prizes every year in international film festivals.

The films are firmly aligned on the side of social progress. They are often critical of government, but never of its constitutional goals. They are similarly critical of society, but only in its failure to change. Battlelines with the commercial cinema are clearly drawn over the key issue of the treatment of women. It is the same in many other areas. M. S. Sathyu's *Garm Hawa* (Hot Winds) explored inner conflicts buffeting the large Muslim minority in independent India. This is a subject the popular cinema would not touch with a barge pole; in fact, it is said forces behind the popular cinema attempted to block *Garm Hawa*'s distribution. Ritwik Ghatak's films examined the effects of the partition of Bengal and the advent of the machine in an agricultural society. Mrinal Sen's films concern themselves with the changing aspects of the middle class, and — as in the work of Ray and Ghatak — often look at it through the central position of the woman.

The ordeals of traditional womanhood have been the subject of a wide range of films by Shyam Benegal, Adoor Gopalakrishnan, Girish Kasaravalli, T. Nagabharana, and other articulate and skilled new filmmakers. Benegal's films, in particular, have been revolutionary in their presentation of women in confident self-assertion in *Manthan* and *Bhumika*. The period heroine of *Bhumika* is caught in the very modern dilemma of being unable to live with men or to live without them. The choices she makes are her own, yet this is shown without aggressive emphasis on the modern; the film is based on the life of an actress of old. Direct attacks on hallowed superstitions have been made by a number of filmmakers, one of the earliest of them being Pattabhi Rama Reddy's *Samskara* (Funeral Rites) in Kannada. Political powerplay is ruthlessly exposed in Jabbar Patel's *Simhasana* (The Throne). M. S. Sathyu's *Bara* (Drought) examines the attempts of politicians to foil the attempts of an honest official to relieve the condition of the poor. Younger filmmakers in Bengal have directly concerned themselves with the oppression of the poor and the sentiment for revolution.

Poetic, contemplative films have been made by G. Aravindan, Mani Kaul, and Kumar Sahani. The exquisite textures and sounds of Aravindan's *Pokku Veil* (Twilight) nevertheless present an inverted Dostoyevskian proposition; the rottenness of the society around him forces a sensitive man to take refuge in insanity. The loneliness of an Anglo-Indian school teacher, a member of a tiny minority, is evoked with poignancy in Aparna Sen's *36 Chowringhee Lane*. Minorities again come into their own in Saeed Mirza's *Albert Pinto Ko Gussa Kyon Ata Hai* (Why Does Albert Pinto Get Angry?).

The "new cinema" is thus an avowed social catalyst, firmly supportive of the constitutional goals of the country, its industrialization, and modernization. At the same time it searches for its Indian identity, being isolated from the common man by the western education and the elite status of its filmmakers. This is seen in its highest form of synthesis in the exquisitely paced, contemplative realism of Satyajit Ray's films with their very Indian tranquility and vision. But many younger filmmakers share this need for identification with the characteristics of Indian culture. Ketan Mehta's *Bhavni Bhavai* departs radically from the dominant neo-realistic trend in the new Indian cinema. Using a traditional Gujarati folk song and dance form tinged with a Brechtian alienation, he presents a searing portrait of untouchability. It is a gorgeous, entertaining period piece loaded with trenchant social criticism in a contemporary vein. Mani Kaul's *Dhrupad*, a 70-minute documentary of exquisite artistry, finds a continuous tie between the modern Indian mind and an old and difficult genre of Indian classical music.

# VI

Thus in content as in form, the opposition between the "new cinema" and the traditional popular cinema could not be more apparent. The first is largely sponsored by government; the second firmly in the hands of the private sector, funded often by smuggling and other operations that generate unaccounted money for laundering in the developing tanks of the film industry. The new cinema is unashamedly a proselytizing instrument; the popular cinema is garbed as pure entertainment, yet deriving from old culture and its fundamentalist views. The progressive cinema of pre-independence and the decades immediately following, addressed mainly to the middle class, has now become the realm of the new cinema and its creators.

At the same time, the commercial cinema reaches a vast audience untouched by high art, and its closeness to the grassroots is as undeniable as is the new cinema's lack of such contact. The control of film exhibition is firmly in the hands of distributors of popular films who are not anxious to open the gates to a different kind of cinema. Despite decades of government support for higher forms of filmmaking, alternative channels of communication with the larger public in behalf of the new cinema have not emerged. The result is that purer specimens of the new cinema are unable to get past those who guard the portals of the mass film theaters. The slightly less pure are inevitably diluted in form and content in order to gain entry. The alternatives posed are two: either read pure poetry to fellow poets or create hybrids. No Shakespearean cinema capable of satisfying groundlings and intellectuals alike has yet appeared, although moves continue in that direction.

It seems unlikely that in the remaining years of the century the government impetus will make a strong impression on the form or content of mass cinema. Yet, a large expansion of the number of theaters, increasing to almost three times the present 11,000, has been accepted as a national goal. One effect of this will be a further penetration of the popular cinema's fundamentalism into the urbanizing milieu. In the two southern states which have matinee idols as chief ministers, the density of cinema seats per 1,000 population is twice the national average. It is possible that by 2000 the rest of the country will catch up. In such an event, and without a radical change in the norms of popular film, pressures are likely to grow, especially in the less literate and politically sophisticated areas, to move other film figures into political roles.

Part Three

# Unity
# and Diversity:
# Society and Politics

Chapter Six

# India's Minorities: Who Are They? What Do They Want?

MYRON WEINER

Any attempt to forecast relations between India's minority and majority communities through the year 2000 is bound to be colored by recent turmoil: Sikh terrorism and the army raid on the Golden Temple of Amritsar; the assassination of Prime Minister Indira Gandhi by two Sikh bodyguards; the subsequent Hindu pogroms against Sikhs in New Delhi; and earlier the Assamese-Bengali carnage, Hindu-Muslim rioting in Moradabad, Meerut, Baroda, Bombay, and Hyderabad; and the massacre of scheduled caste agricultural laborers by local landlords in Belchhi, Bihar. To most observers these events are by no means transient, but are indications of increased social conflicts among religious, linguistic, and caste communities. If, as some argue, education is increasing aspirations, economic growth is enlarging economic opportunities, and political democracy is resulting in increased politicization, then one can expect more, not less, competition and conflict among India's many social groups. And, it is further argued, if the competition and conflict continue to result in violence, then the central government is likely to make increasing use of the army, and suspend civil liberties in disturbed areas. Could the fragile Indian democratic political system survive the combined assaults of group violence and state force?

An alternative view is that violence among caste, linguistic, and religious groups is endemic in India's variegated social structure, and that there is no reason to believe that the situation is worse now than in the past or that it is likely to grow significantly worse in the future. One need only recall, it is argued, the communal turmoil at the time of independence and the linguistic agitations of the 1950s to have a sense of perspective and to appreciate the capacity of the social order to generate social conflict in India. All of these recent disturbances have had their precursors. There were Assamese attacks against Marwaris in Gauhati in the late 1960s and against Bengali Hindus in the early 1970s, Hindu-Muslim clashes in Jamshedpur and Ahmedabad, a long history of caste Hindu brutality against ex-untouchables, and the turmoil over the Punjabi Subha movement in the late 1960s. Conditions in the mid-1980s are lamentably bad, but no worse (or better) than those of the 1950s, 1960s, or 1970s, nor are they likely to be worse through the year 2000. Such is the optimistic view!

This essay argues still a third perspective: group conflict is indeed endemic in India and there are forces — some new — that seem likely to worsen minority-majority relations, but what seems most likely to intensify ethnic conflict is the deterioration of political institutions. The capacity of institutions to manage conflict in the 1980s and 1990s is what is at issue. In a period in which majorities are becoming more self-aware, a sense of territorial nationalism is emerging both among majorities and selected minorities, and the international ties of some minorities are growing, political coalitions are in flux, and the problems of conflict management are likely to mount.

## Who Are India's Minorities?

At a conference several years ago a prominent Indian journalist referred to India as a "Hindu island in an Islamic sea." In the same vein, Theodore Wright quotes a Hindu writer as saying that "it is taken for granted that the Hindus are a majority . . . but to say so is totally wrong. The vast mass of people that are called Hindus are a vast congeries of sub-caste minorities . . . whereas the Muslims form the actual majority."[1] These quotes highlight the point that minority and majority status is a matter of self-ascription as well as objective definition. What is a majority from one perspective is a minority from another. Consider the following anomalies:

Until recently most Indians did not regard Sikhs as a minority. Today, they are so regarded and they clearly see themselves as a minority. But in the Punjab it is the Hindus who consider themselves a minority.

The Assamese are among a number of linguistic communities in India with a state of their own, but unlike most of the others they regard themselves as a "national minority." They are surrounded, they point out, by 150 million or so Bengalis. In Assam, however, Bengalis regard themselves as a minority.

Jains are India's oldest religious minority, but the Jains are unobtrusive, politically quietistic, and so intertwined with Hindus that they are often regarded as simply another kind of Hindu rather than a distinctive minority.[2]

Muslims are India's largest religious minority, but in Jammu and Kashmir it is the Hindus who regard themselves as a minority.

Bengalis and Tamils are not generally regarded as minorities, but members of these communities living outside their home state often regard themselves and are regarded by their hosts as members of a linguistic minority.

Scheduled castes are regarded as belonging to a disadvantaged and backward minority, a status also sought by other backward castes often numbering a quarter or more of the population in some states.

Clearly India contains such a medley of religious, caste, and linguistic groups that the sense of belonging to a minority depends upon where one lives, how much power and status one has, and one's sense of community threat. Many Indians narrowly use the term "minority" to refer to those who are not Hindu, a conception which implies that somehow the dominant core of Indian identity is Hinduism, the "mainstream" (to use a favorite Indian word) with which minorities should identify if they want to be regarded as wholly Indian. Thus, some Hindus speak of the need for the "Indianization" of minorities, by which they mean that minorities should adopt "Indian" (i.e., Hindu) names, observe Indian (i.e., Hindu) national holidays, identify with India's historical (i.e., pre-Islamic Hindu and Buddhist) past, its heroes and great events, and be attached to the soil of India (not to Mecca or Rome).[3]

Needless to say, this is not the way India's minorities define the problem. It is not only religious groups who regard themselves as minorities. Caste, tribal, linguistic as well as religious groups can be self-defined minorities for any one of a number of reasons: they have a distinctive group identity that they fear is eroding; they regard themselves as socially and economically subordinate to others; or they believe that they suffer from discrimination, either from others in the society or from the state itself. To regard oneself as part of a minority in India is to suggest that one ought to take group action to remedy one's situation. To declare one's group a minority is, therefore, a political act. In the Indian context, it is a way of calling attention to a situation of self-defined deprivation.

A people who do not share what they regard as the central symbols of the society invariably view themselves as a minority. It is not simply that a community lacks power but rather that the symbols of authority, the values that are propagated from the center, and the culture that emanates from the center are viewed as not theirs. To members of a minority community symbol sharing may be no less important than power sharing. Members of a minority community may refer to those of its members holding high office as having been "coopted" if they share power without the symbols. Moreover, a community may feel threatened because its own members are coming to partake of the symbols, the values, and the culture of the "center" even in the absence of explicit repression.

Once we conceive of a minority as a category defined by the observed rather than by observers, a self-definition by a community itself rather than by others, we are faced with a methodological problem of considerable proportion. If we understand the term "minority" as a socially negotiable concept, then a community that regards itself and is regarded by others as a minority may under some circumstances cease to be a minority, while other communities may become minorities. In the United States, for example, Italian-Americans, Irish-Americans, Polish-Americans and Jews once regarded themselves as minorities, but now are seen by others (and sometimes by themselves) as "ethnics," while the term "minority" has come to be reserved for those who are "disadvantaged." Who belongs to the category "disadvantaged minority," as distinct from "ethnic," is politically and socially negotiable. In India Sikhs and Assamese now loom large as minorities; will other communities join them? In assessing India's future over the next 15 years, we must consider which new minorities will assert claims, what claims will be put forth by the old minorities, and whether some minorities will cease to think of themselves as minorities.

Since we are the observers and not the observed we must fall back upon the communities' self perceptions regarding their minority status. We can then engage in some informed speculation as to which other communities might actively put forth minority claims. It is useful to think of four types of minorities in India: linguistic, religious, caste, and tribal. These can be further divided along three dimensions: whether minorities have a conception of a territorial homeland; the extent of the sense of cohesion within the community; and whether the community regards itself as a disadvantaged or as an achieving minority.

## Linguistic Minorities

Since each of India's states has an official language, those who speak another language as their mother tongue regard themselves as belonging to a linguistic minority. In 1971, in 18 of India's 22 states, plus the union territory of Delhi, 92.8 million people or 17.1 percent of the population did not speak the regional language as their mother tongue [see Table 1].[4] Urdu was spoken by 28.4 million people; 24.7 million spoke a language not recognized as a regional language of any of the states; and approximately 39.7 million people spoke a regional language other than the official language of their state.[5] A projection of these numbers for 1985 shows 174.5 million people belonging to a linguistic minority.

The concerns of each of these linguistic minorities is quite different. Urdu speakers, for example, have called for the establishment of Urdu as an official second language of the states in which they live. There are large Urdu-speaking communities in Uttar Pradesh, Bihar, Maharashtra, Andhra, and Karnataka; in these states an overwhelming majority of Muslims reports Urdu as their mother tongue.

Some minorities speaking "unrecognized" languages have demanded statehood. This demand is often made by those linguistic groups concentrated in a particular region of a state and where the group has a strong sense of its own distinctive identity. The largest "stateless" linguistic minorities (containing more than half a million speakers in 1971) are shown in Table 2.

TABLE 1
## LINGUISTIC MINORITIES BY STATE (1971)
(millions)

| State | Population | Speakers of Official Language | Linguistic Minority | Linguistic Minority (percent) |
|---|---|---|---|---|
| Andhra | 43.5 | 37.1 | 6.4 | 14.7 |
| Assam | 14.6 | 8.9 | 5.7 | 39.0 |
| Bihar | 56.4 | 44.9 | 11.5 | 20.4 |
| Delhi | 4.1 | 3.1 | 1.0 | 33.3 |
| Gujarat | 26.7 | 23.9 | 2.8 | 10.5 |
| Haryana | 10.0 | 9.0 | 1.0 | 10.0 |
| Himachal | 3.5 | 3.0 | 0.5 | 14.3 |
| J&K | 4.6 | 2.4 | 2.2 | 47.8 |
| Karnataka | 29.3 | 19.3 | 10.0 | 34.1 |
| Kerala | 21.4 | 20.5 | 0.9 | 4.0 |
| M.P. | 41.7 | 34.7 | 7.0 | 16.8 |
| Maharashtra | 50.4 | 38.6 | 11.8 | 23.4 |
| Orissa | 21.9 | 18.5 | 3.4 | 15.5 |
| Punjab | 13.6 | 10.8 | 2.8 | 20.5 |
| Rajashthan | 25.8 | 23.5 | 2.3 | 8.9 |
| Tamil Nadu | 41.2 | 34.8 | 6.4 | 15.5 |
| Tripura | 1.6 | 1.1 | 0.5 | 31.2 |
| U.P. | 88.3 | 78.2 | 10.1 | 11.4 |
| West Bengal | 44.3 | 37.8 | 6.5 | 14.7 |
| Total | 542.9 | 450.1 | 92.8 | 17.1 |

TABLE 2
## LINGUISTIC MINORITIES
(millions)

| | | | |
|---|---|---|---|
| Bhili | 3.4 | Konkani | 1.5 |
| Boro | .5 | Kurukh/Oraon | 1.2 |
| Dogri | 1.3 | Mundari | .8 |
| Gondi | 1.7 | Sindhi | 1.7 |
| Nepali | 1.4 | Santali | 3.8 |
| Ho | .8 | Tulu | 1.2 |

Except for Dogri, Sindhi, Nepali, and Konkani, the remaining languages are spoken by tribals. Some tribal peoples, though none speaking the languages listed above, already have states of their own; Meghalaya, Nagaland, Arunachal Pradesh, Dadra and Nagar Haveli, Lakshadweep, and Mizoram are predominantly populated by tribals.

TABLE 3
## LINGUISTIC DIASPORAS (1971)
(millions)

| Language | Speakers | Speakers in "Homeland"[1] | Speakers in Diaspora |
|---|---|---|---|
| Assamese | 8.9 | 8.9 | — |
| Bengali | 44.8 | 38.8 | 6.0 |
| Gujarati | 25.9 | 23.9 | 2.0 |
| Hindi | 208.5 | 197.5 | 11.0 |
| Kannada | 21.7 | 19.3 | — |
| Kashmiri | 2.5 | 2.5 | — |
| Malayalam | 21.9 | 20.5 | 1.4 |
| Marathi | 41.8 | 38.8 | 3.0 |
| Oriya | 19.9 | 18.5 | 1.4 |
| Punjabi | 14.1 | 10.8 | 3.3 |
| Tamil | 37.7 | 35.2 | 2.5 |
| Telugu | 44.8 | 37.1 | 7.7 |
| Subtotal | 492.5 | 451.8 | 40.7 |
| Urdu | 28.6 | — | 28.6 |
| Other languages | 27.1 | 3.4 | 23.7 |
| Total | 548.2 | 455.2 | 93.3[2] |

[1] For the languages listed in Schedule VIII of the Constitution, the homelands include, in addition to the various states, the union territories of Delhi (Hindi), Goa (Marathi) and Pondicherry (Tamil). For "other languages" the homelands include Manipur, Meghalaya, Nagaland, Arunachal Pradesh, and Mizoram.

[2] This number is slightly higher than in Table 1 since all union territories are included.

The third set of linguistic minority groups comprises those who speak an official language other than the language of the state in which they live. These minorities are concentrated in Assam, Karnataka, Maharashtra, Punjab, Tamil Nadu, and West Bengal. There are nearly nine million Bengalis living outside of West Bengal and Tripura, two million Gujaratis outside of Gujarat, 1.4 million Malayalam speakers outside of Kerala, three million speakers of Marathi outside of Maharashtra and Goa, 1.4 million Oriyas not in Orissa, 3.3 million Pun-

jabis not in Punjab, 2.5 million Tamils outside of Tamil Nadu and Pondicherry, 7.7 million Telugus not in Andhra, and 11.0 million Hindi
speakers living outside of the Hindi belt (including 2.7 million people in
Punjab who classify themselves as Hindi speakers) [see Table 3].

Since these minorities, unlike speakers of other "local" languages or
of Urdu, are not regarded as "sons of the soil," they are often the target
of political groups that demand preferences for "local" people in employment and in education. In some instances, most notably in Assam, there
have been demands that the linguistic minorities leave the state and
return to their "homeland."

Special note should be taken of the concern by some linguistic
majorities that they are in danger of becoming a minority within their
own state. The Assamese are particularly fearful for although they account officially for 61 percent of the state's population, it is generally
understood that a substantial portion of the 3.6 million Muslims in the
state who report Assamese as their mother tongue are in fact Bengali
speakers. The influx of illegal migrants from Bangladesh has further
increased the anxieties of the Assamese.

There are a number of cities in which speakers of the state language
are a minority. The Marathi-speaking population constitutes only 42.8
percent of Bombay. Kannada speakers in Bangalore (23.7 percent) are
outnumbered by Tamils (31.7 percent). The Assamese lack a majority
in Gauhati and in several other towns along the Brahmaputra. It is no
surprise, therefore, that these towns have active "sons of the soil"
movements.

## Religious Minorities

According to the 1981 census, Muslims constituted 11.4 percent of the
Indian population (75.5 million), Christians 2.4 percent (16.2 million),
Sikhs 2.0 percent (13.1 million), and Buddhists and Jains 1.2 percent
(7.9 million). Hindus constituted 82.6 percent of the population.

Muslims form a majority in the state of Jammu and Kashmir, but
otherwise they are widely dispersed. They constitute 21.3 percent of
Kerala, 21.5 percent of West Bengal, 15.9 percent of Uttar Pradesh,
14.1 percent of Bihar, 11 percent of Karnataka, and elsewhere they represent less than 10 percent of the state population. No census was conducted in Assam in 1981, but in 1971 Muslims constituted 24 percent of
the population. Two geopolitical features of the Muslims warrant special
attention: they are concentrated in selected districts of these states,
and as compared with Hindus and Sikhs, they are disproportionately
urban.

Muslims are only 8.5 percent of Andhra's population, but they are concentrated in the Telengana region of the state, with their largest concentration in Hyderabad where they form 26.4 percent of the district. (District figures reported here are from the 1971 census since district-wise data for 1981 are not yet available.) Muslims are a majority in Malappuram district in Kerala and they form a substantial portion of the adjacent districts to the north and south. They are numerous in the western portions of Uttar Pradesh, especially in Rampur (45.7 percent), Moradabad and Bijnor districts (one-third of which are Muslims), and there are substantial concentrations in the districts further to the west — Saharanpur, Muzaffarnagar, and Meerut. Similarly, several districts in West Bengal, Maharashtra, and Bihar have well above average concentrations of Muslims.[6] Later we shall explore the political implications of these concentrations.

In 1971, 19.9 percent of the Indian population lived in urban areas, but 28.8 percent of the Muslim population was urban. Muslims constituted one-fifth or more of the population in Hyderabad (38 percent), Kanpur (20 percent), Lucknow (29 percent), Varanasi (26 percent), and Allahabad (24 percent), and they have more than their national average in Calcutta, Bombay, Bangalore, Ahmedabad, Agra, Jaipur, Indore, and Jabalpur. The 1981 census reported that 34 percent of the Muslim population was urban, a significant increase over the 1971 census [see Table 4]. Of special interest is that a number of the urban centers in the north with large numbers of Muslims also have substantial numbers of Hindu refugees who fled from Pakistan at the time of partition; these centers are particularly prone to Hindu-Muslim violence.

India's 13.1 million Sikhs (1981) form a majority of 60.8 percent of the Punjab, but they have been a majority only since 1966. Pre-partition Punjab was 51 percent Muslim, 35 percent Hindu, and 12 percent Sikh. Post-partition Punjab, as of 1961, was 64 percent Hindu, 33 percent Sikh and two percent Muslim; the 1971 figures are 60 percent Sikh, 38 percent Hindu, and only one percent Muslim. These massive changes are the result of the reorganization of the state boundaries in 1947 and again in 1966, and the movement in 1947 of Muslims out of the Indian Punjab, and of Sikhs and Hindus out of the Pakistani Punjab.[7]

From 1961 to 1971 Sikhs increased more rapidly than did both Hindus and Muslims, and from 1971 to 1981 their growth rate continued to be higher than that of the Hindus. Since there is no indication of a higher natural population increase among the Sikhs (Punjab's population growth rates from 1961 to 1971 and from 1971 to 1981 are actually below the national growth rates), this would suggest that there has been a considerable amount of redesignation among Sikhs who previously reported themselves as Hindus. The growth of self-identification and dif-

TABLE 4
## URBAN MUSLIM POPULATION (1971)
(percent)

| Calcutta | 14.2 | Lucknow | 29.5 |
|---|---|---|---|
| Greater Bombay | 14.1 | Howrah | 10.3 |
| Delhi | 7.4 | Agra | 16.3 |
| Madras | 8.5 | Jaipur | 18.7 |
| Hyderabad | 38.0 | Varanasi | 25.9 |
| Bangalore | 14.2 | Indore | 12.4 |
| Ahmedabad | 14.6 | Madurai | 7.6 |
| Kanpur | 20.1 | Jabalpur | 12.5 |
| Nagpur | 9.3 | Allahabad | 23.8 |
| Poona | 9.0 | | |

*Note:* Muslims also have high concentrations in some of the middle-sized cities. They are more than one-third of the population in many of the medium-sized towns in Uttar Pradesh—Bareilly, Meerut, Aligarh, Saharanpur, Firozabad, Shahjahanpur, and they form a majority in Moradabad and Rampur. In addition to the districts of Kashmir, Muslims constitute a majority in the district of Malappuram, Kerala (63.9 percent), Murshidabad, West Bengal (56.3 percent) and in Lakshadweep (94.4 percent). There are 11 other districts in the country, mainly in Assam and in West Bengal, where Muslims constitute 30 percent or more of the population.

ferentiation among the Sikhs and among Hindus in the Punjab has been underway since the turn of the century, but it has accelerated since independence.

One indication of this process is the extent to which Sikhs and Hindus have increasingly distinguished themselves linguistically. After the Sikhs called for the creation of a Punjabi Subha, the Arya Samaj and Jana Sangh urged Punjabi Hindus to repudiate Punjabi as their mother tongue and to declare themselves Hindi speakers. By 1971 only one-half of the five million Hindus in the state declared Punjabi as their mother tongue, and in neighboring Haryana almost no Hindus declared themselves as Punjabi speakers.

The Sikhs now have a homeland, but they also have a diaspora. Of India's 13.1 million Sikhs, 2.8 million — more than one-fifth — live in other parts of India, mostly in Haryana, Rajasthan, Uttar Pradesh, and Delhi. Since the Sikhs in the diaspora are heavily urbanized and are physically distinctive, they are noticeable minorities in cities throughout the country. Moreover, the Sikh diaspora is worldwide. There are substantial numbers of Sikhs in the United States, Canada, the United Kingdom, and West Germany. These diaspora communities are important sources of support for political movements within the Punjab.

India's Christians are more numerous but less politically vocal than the Sikhs. The 1981 census reported 16.2 million Christians, 2.4 percent of the population. The bulk of India's Christians live in Kerala, Tamil Nadu, and Andhra, but the concentration is densest in India's northeast. Christians are a majority in Nagaland (80.2 percent) and in Meghalaya (52.6 percent), but since both states are small and Christians lack the cohesion of the Sikhs neither plays the role that the Punjab does for India's Sikhs. The Christians are dispersed, usually speak the language of the region in which they are located, and in the main are converts from tribes or low castes.

Jains (3.6 million) are so closely associated with Hindus that they are not usually regarded, by themselves or by Hindus, as a religious minority. Also closely associated with Hinduism are the Buddhists (4.7 million); many Buddhists, however, regard themselves as distinct from Hindus.

Two features of India's religious minorities warrant special note. The first is their internal divisions and the second is their relationship with Hindus.

None of the three major religious minorities is cohesive. Sikhs are divided between scheduled caste and non-scheduled caste Sikhs and between Jat Sikhs and other high-caste Sikhs. These divisions have enabled the Congress party to win substantial support from among the Sikhs and have prevented the consolidation of the Sikh vote in the Punjab around the Akali Dal.

Muslims are even less cohesive. The Muslims of the southwest have had long-term ties with Arab countries and they continue to migrate in large numbers to work in the Persian Gulf. They speak Malayalam and in their diet and dress are close to Hindus in the region. The Muslims of Kashmir form a majority of the state, have a strong Kashmiri identity, and overwhelmingly speak Kashmiri rather than Urdu. The Muslims living in the Hindi-speaking region, from the Yamuna north through the Gangetic plains, live in the mainstream of the Turkish, Afghan, Mughal, and Persian invaders, and overwhelmingly (64 percent) speak Urdu. It is here that the two-nation theory had its greatest support and where the Muslim League developed. Still further eastward Bengali Muslims speak Bengali rather than Urdu. Of the nine million Muslims in West Bengal less than one million speak Urdu. These are mostly migrants from Bihar, eastern Uttar Pradesh, and Orissa. The Muslims of Andhra form still another distinctive group. They lived under a Muslim ruler until 1947; their upper classes (some of Persian origin) formed part of the governing elite. Unlike most Muslims living in the south, they are overwhelmingly (91 percent) Urdu-speaking. It is particularly noteworthy that the Muslims in south India, especially in Andhra and Kerala, have formed their own confessional political parties while north Indian Muslims, perhaps "tainted" by their association with the League and the two-nation theory, have frequently participated in mainstream political parties.

Finally, as we have noted earlier, the Christians of the northeast, most of whom are tribal people, are culturally distinctive from the Christians of the south.

The attitude of Hindus toward religious minorities is guided by one central feature of Hinduism: it is an inclusive religion. Unlike Christianity, Judaism, Islam, and Sikhism, which are "exclusive" religions that prescribe rules for membership, insist on adherence to specific dogmas and rules of conduct, and purge the heterodox, Hindus have no clear rules as to what constitutes a Hindu. Hindus view anyone who observes any Hindu rituals, worships any Hindu deities, or philosophically subscribes to any elements of Hinduism as a Hindu. Hindus have no conception of heterodoxy, no notion of apostasy. Islamic fundamentalists in Pakistan have declared the Ahmadiyas, a heterodox sect, to be non-Muslims. Orthodox Jews attack conversions to Judaism by reformed Jews. Orthodox Sikhs have attacked the heterodox Nirankarias. In contrast, Hindu revivalists have sought to incorporate Indians of various faiths into Hinduism.

Hinduism is inclusive in a second sense as well. Hindus regard religions that originated in south Asia, including Buddhism, Jainism, and Sikhism, and variants of Hinduism, such as the Brahmos, Lingayats, and other sects, as Hindu. Article 25 of the Indian Constitution stipulates that Sikhs, Buddhists, and Jains cannot be excluded from Hindu temples, a provision seen by Sikhs as intending to include Sikhs among Hindu communicants. Hindus see no apostasy when members of their religion worship at Sikh Gurdwaras, or at the tombs of saints; it is not unusual for Hindu families to declare one of their male children a Sikh and to give him a Sikh name. Similarly, Hindus incorporate tribal gods into their pantheon as reincarnations of Hindu deities.

Orthodox Hindus do not regard "heterodox" and "reformist" Hindu movements as threatening. India has been rife with religious movements during the past century: the Arya Samaj, theosophists, Vedantists, Brahmos, Lingayats, and numerous "Godheads" or self-proclaimed religious leaders with their own followings. Religious Hindus regard the proliferation of such movements as a sign of religious vitality, not as a threat to any particular orthodoxy. A similar period of religious creativity in sixteenth-century Europe was regarded as a threat to Catholicism.

This tolerance for internal diversity and a readiness to incorporate others is, paradoxically, regarded with distrust by the exclusive religions of Islam, Sikhism, and Christianity. Each has sought, not always successfully, to resist the tendency of their communicants to adopt Hindu customs. Hindus, in turn, regard with equanimity Muslims and Sikhs who succumb to Hindu syncretism. Thus, the Mughal ruler Akbar is highly regarded by Hindus for his efforts to build a composite Indian culture, but by Muslims as an apostate who failed to keep faith. Hindus do, however, regard mass conversion to Islam and Christianity with alarm. The hostility to conversions is largely a reflection of nationalist opposition to religions of foreign origin, but it also reflects the Hindu antipathy towards exclusive religions.

Hindus regard with aversion a philosophical position shared by orthodox Sikhs and Muslims that politics and religion are inseparable.[8] The classical Indian view is that the state preserves order, but it does not impose any particular moral code. Hinduism, unlike Christianity, Islam, Sikhism, and Judaism, has no conception of a universal moral code of conduct and no notion that rulers should act in moral ways according to some religious code. Politics is viewed as an amoral sphere, a notion partly rooted in the conception that Kshatriyas, not Brahmins, are rulers. Men like Maulana Moududi and Sant Jarnail Singh Bhindranwale are regarded by Hindus as "fanatics" for their exclusive attitudes toward their own religion and for their rejection of political secularism.

## Tribal Minorities

India's tribals, numbering 38 million or 6.9 percent of the population in 1971, remain India's largest politically slumbering minority. The tribals largely live in areas they regard as their "homelands," many of which are designated by the government as reserved or "scheduled areas."[9] Some 99,000 square miles are scheduled areas in which legal restrictions are placed on the alienation of land to non-tribals. The six largest tribes are the Gonds of central India; the Bhils of western India; the Santals of Bihar, West Bengal and Orissa; the Oraons of Bihar and West Bengal; the Minas of Rajasthan; and the Mundas of Bihar, West Bengal, and Orissa. These tribes constitute nearly one-half of India's tribal population. Some tribes, though considerably smaller, constitute a majority of the areas in which they live: the Nagas, Khasis and Garos, for example, in India's northeast.[10]

While tribals are a national minority in India, they constitute a majority of the population in several parts of the country. According to the 1971 census, they are a majority in Nagaland (89 percent), Meghalaya (80 percent), and Arunachal Pradesh (79 percent), and one-fifth or more of the population in Manipur (31 percent), Tripura (29 percent), Orissa (23 percent), and Madhya Pradesh (20 percent). Outside of the northeast, tribes constitute a majority of the population in 19 districts: three in Orissa, six in Madhya Pradesh, two in Himachal Pradesh, one in Bihar, two in Rajasthan, two in Assam, two in Gujarat, and one in the Laccadive islands [see Tables 5 and 6].

TABLE 5

## STATES IN WHICH NATIONAL RELIGIOUS AND TRIBAL MINORITIES ARE A MAJORITY OR PLURALITY

| | |
|---|---|
| Jammu and Kashmir | 64.2% Muslim |
| Meghalaya | 52.6% Christian, 80% Tribal |
| Nagaland | 80.2% Christian, 89% Tribal |
| Punjab | 60.8% Sikh |
| Arunachal Pradesh | 79.0% Tribal |
| Mizoram | 83.8% Christian |

TABLE 6

## DISTRICTS WITH A SCHEDULED TRIBE MAJORITY
(percent tribal)

| | |
|---|---|
| Dangs, Gujarat | 92.5 |
| Jhabua, Madhya Pradesh | 84.7 |
| Bastar, Madhya Pradesh | 72.4 |
| Banswara, Rajasthan | 71.5 |
| Lahaul and Spiti, H.P. | 69.1 |
| Kinnaur, H.P. | 62.6 |
| Mandla, M.P. | 61.8 |
| Ranchi, Bihar | 61.6 |
| Koraput, Orissa | 60.9 |
| Mayurbhanj, Orissa | 60.6 |
| Dangarpur, Rajasthan | 60.1 |
| Sundargarh, Orissa | 58.1 |
| Surguja, Madhya Pradesh | 55.6 |
| Shadol, M.P. | 51.4 |
| Dhar, M.P. | 51.1 |
| Surat, Gujarat | 50.0 |

*Note:*   In 19 other districts tribals constitute from 30 to 50 percent of the population.

India's tribes are not wholly isolated, uneducated, and poor, but it would be accurate to say that they have been less affected by the forces of modernization than have other Indians. Their mortality rates are higher, their literacy rates lower; they are less urbanized than other Indians and with the exception of the Santals, few are employed in the modern industrial sector. As a result of the work of Christian missionaries, some of the tribes in the northeast and to a lesser extent among sections of the Santals, Mundas, and Oraons have above-average levels of literacy, but even among these communities only a small number have studied in the universities and entered the professions and senior levels of the bureaucracy.

The tribes are concentrated in three principal regions. One is India's northeast; a second is in middle India and includes Bihar, the hill areas of inland Orissa, southeastern Madhya Pradesh, and a portion of northern Andhra. A third region is in India's west, and includes parts of eastern Gujarat, western Madhya Pradesh, and southern Rajasthan. There is also a small tribal area in the mountain region of Himachal Pradesh and in the Nilgiri hills in Tamil Nadu.

It is particularly noteworthy that the tribals are not only geographically concentrated, but within their respective regions they are overwhelmingly rural while the towns are predominantly non-tribal. In southern Bihar, for example, tribals constitute 58 percent of Ranchi district, 46 percent of Singhbhum district; and 36 percent of Santhal Parganas, but not a single large town in any of these districts has a tribal majority. Control over and access to land and forests is therefore more a concern among the scheduled tribes than among other minorities.[11]

## Caste Minorities

None of India's several thousand castes is in the majority in any region of the country. To speak of a minority caste is to refer not to numbers but to status. Indians generally regard ex-untouchables or scheduled castes as a minority by virtue of their low social status, their economic conditions, and the discrimination to which they have been subjected by caste Hindus. Along with scheduled tribes they are constitutionally guaranteed rights and benefits not provided other minorities. These include reserved constituencies for elections to Parliament and to State Assemblies, reservations for admission into colleges and technical schools, and reserved positions in government employment.[12]

Scheduled castes form 14.6 percent of India's population. The largest single state-wide concentration is in the Punjab where they form nearly one-fourth of the population. There are major concentrations in Uttar Pradesh, West Bengal, Bihar, Tamil Nadu, Andhra, and Madhya Pradesh.

Unlike scheduled tribes, Sikhs, or linguistic groups, scheduled castes do not identify themselves with any homeland or assert territorial demands. Cultural symbols and other measures to enhance group identity have begun to play a role among ex-untouchables as with some other minorities. Efforts to convert ex-untouchables to Buddhism attracted several million in Maharashtra, but the conversion movement has apparently slowed. There have been reports in recent years of conversions to Islam, but while these reports have created anxieties among some Hindus, there is no indication that any large-scale movement is underway.

In recent years a new self-proclaimed caste minority has appeared, the "other backward classes." The "OBCs," as they are called, are referred to in provisions of the Constitution [Article 16(4)] which enables the government to make reservations "of appointments or posts in favour of any backward class of citizens." Dr. Ambedkar, India's Law Minister at the time, who opposed extending benefits from scheduled castes and scheduled tribes to other backward classes, pointed out that the identity of backward classes was so vague that ultimately "a backward community is a community which is backward in the opinion of the government." T. T. Krishnamachari, another member of the Constituent Assembly, described Article 16(4) as "a paradise for lawyers."[13]

While an earlier legislative history settled the identity of scheduled castes and scheduled tribes, Article 16(4) opened up a political debate over the choice of criteria for including particular communities in the category of OBCs. Central government commissions were unable to agree. Some called for the use of objective measures of backwardness such as average education or income levels, while others emphasized position in the social hierarchy: a caste should be classified as backward on the basis of its low status or the inferior treatment of its members by other communities. There was only agreement on the notion that whatever criteria were chosen they should be applied to groups, not individuals. In the absence of a central government consensus, the matter of deciding who was "backward" was left to the state governments.

There thus ensued a political battle in a number of states as castes sought to be included on the list of OBCs and politicians vied for their support. Several states placed a substantial number of castes with large populations on their list. It is not unusual for 20 to 25 percent of the population of a state to appear on the list of backward castes, in addition to those classified as scheduled castes and scheduled tribes. The courts have decreed that the total number of reservations for these three groups for admission to colleges and for positions in the administrative services must be below 50 percent. While that has set a limit as to the size of the OBC it has intensified the struggle to be on the list and over precisely what benefits should be provided. In several states, most notably in Bihar, upper castes have violently opposed the extension of reservations to the backward castes.

In early 1985, decisions by the governments of Madhya Pradesh and Gujarat to extend reservations to the OBCs for engineering, medical, and agricultural colleges — in Madhya Pradesh 80 percent of the seats were in the reserved category and in Gujarat 49 percent — resulted in violent anti-reservation agitation by students. In both states, the reservations were announced on the eve of state government elections and were regarded as measures intended to win electoral support for the governing Congress party from the numerous voters belonging to the backward classes.

### Conclusion: A Statistical Recapitulation and Projection

India's religious minorities, scheduled castes, and tribes constituted 37.2 percent of the country's population in 1971, while the linguistic minorities were 17.5 percent. These two categories overlap substantially since virtually all Urdu speakers are Muslims and a majority of speakers of non-regional languages are members of scheduled tribes. Taking these overlaps into account, approximately 45 percent of the population belongs to linguistic, tribal, religious, or caste groups that regard themselves as minorities [see Table 7]. Since we have categorized "minority" and "majority" from an aggregate national rather than a state point of view, an examination of a few states may better demonstrate how majorities and minorities are distributed.

Consider Bihar, a state with a 1971 population of 56.3 million of whom 7.9 million (14.1 percent) are scheduled castes, 4.9 million (8.6 percent) scheduled tribes, 7.6 million (13.5 percent) Muslims, and 0.6 million (1.2 percent) Christians. The linguistic minorities include 1.9 million Bengalis and 300,000 Oriyas, some of whom are Muslim, Christian, or belong to scheduled castes. If we add one-half of these to our list of minorities, we have 22.1 million minorities (39 percent) and a caste Hindu, Hindi-speaking "majority" of 34.2 million (61 percent).

West Bengal has a population of 44.3 million (1971) with a scheduled tribe population of 2.5 million, 9.1 million Muslims, 250,000 Christians and 8.8 million scheduled castes. These minorities total 20.6 million, or 46.5 percent of the population. There are approximately three million people in West Bengal speaking Hindi, Oriya, Telugu, and other reg-

TABLE 7
## INDIA'S MINORITIES (1971)

|                                        | *Millions* | *Percent* |
|----------------------------------------|------------|-----------|
| Religions, tribes, and castes[1]       |            |           |
| Muslim                                 | 61.4       | 11.2      |
| Scheduled castes                       | 80.0       | 14.6      |
| Scheduled tribes                       | 38.0       | 6.9       |
| Christians                             | 14.2       | 2.6       |
| Sikhs                                  | 10.3       | 1.9       |
|                                        | 203.9      | 37.2      |
|                                        |            |           |
| Linguistic groups                      |            |           |
| Urdu speakers                          | 28.6       | 5.2       |
| Non-regional languages[2]              | 27.1       | 4.9       |
| Minority regional languages[3]         | 40.7       | 7.4       |
|                                        | 96.0[4]    | 17.5      |

[1] These are not mutually exclusive categories since some tribals are Christian and some Sikhs are listed as scheduled castes.

[2] This is a clumsy terminology to refer to local languages not officially listed in the Constitution as regional languages. I have, however, included Sindhi in this category, for though it is recognized as a regional language, it is not the official regional language of any state. I have also excluded Urdu. (The recognized regional languages are in Schedule VIII of the Constitution.)

[3] This refers to those who speak a regional language of a state other than the one in which they live.

[4] The number is slightly higher than given in the text since I have included union territories in these calculations.

ional languages and if one-half of these do not overlap with the other minority categories, then as many as 22.1 million people in the state regard themselves as members of "minorities," a bare majority being Bengali-speaking caste Hindus!

Finally, let us take two states in the south. Kerala's Muslim population is 19.5 percent, its Christian population 21.1 percent, scheduled caste population 8.3 percent, and tribal population 1.3 percent. The caste Hindu population, therefore, is only 49.8 percent, some of whom (3.1 percent) are not Malayalee speakers. In Tamil Nadu, 5.1 percent is Muslim, 5.8 percent Christian, 17.8 percent scheduled caste, 0.8 percent scheduled tribe, these groups together comprising 29.5 percent of the total population. A regional language other than Tamil or Urdu is spoken by 13.5 percent of the population. Assuming some overlap among the categories, minorities form 35 to 40 percent of the state population.

A projection of these figures for the year 2000, extrapolating from current growth rates, gives us 172.0 million Muslims, Christians, and Sikhs, 255 million scheduled castes and tribes, approximately 42.3 million linguistically "stateless" people (without a state of their own), and another 73.7 million people living outside of their "home" state (some of whom, of course, are members of religious minorities or scheduled castes) [see Table 8]. The number of minorities for the year 2000 thus ranges from 472 to 545 million, the difference including many who are "double" minorities. In short, if we think of the dominant majority as those who speak the official regional language as their mother tongue and are caste Hindus, then perhaps only 45 percent to 52 percent of the population can be regarded as part of this "majority" in the year 2000, as compared with a 51 to 58 percent range in 1971. It is likely that the "majority" will fall below 50 percent in several states. Assam, with its Assamese-speaking caste Hindu population already below 50 percent, may foreshadow the anxieties that other "majorities" may feel as their majority status becomes precarious.

### India's Emerging Majorities

To be part of the "majority" is no less a matter of self-identification than to be part of a "minority." The growing articulation of minority claims in India is matched by an assertion of "majority" claims as well. What remains problematic, however, is what constitutes this self-conscious "majority." Two overlapping identities have been competing for majority status: one is Hinduism; the other is determined by various regional languages.

The much noted "revivalism" of Hinduism in recent years is hardly a reassertion of religious piety, for on that score there is no evidence of any decline in the performance of rituals, devotion to deities, participation in religious festivals, religious observance or whatever else one chooses as an indicator of religiosity in a religion that defies easy categorization. Hindu revivalism, or what some Hindus prefer to call a Hindu "renaissance," is a political statement, a reassertion less of religion than of nationalism.

It takes many forms: the militant stance of the RSS toward Christian institutions; the establishment of the Virat Hindu Samaj as an institution both for social reform and for the assertion of Hindu solidarity; the emergence of Bharat Mata as a kind of "national" deity; the call for the establishment of compulsory national Hindu holidays; and Hindu movements for the reconversion of Muslims and Christians and for the Hinduization of tribals.

TABLE 8
## INDIA'S MINORITIES (1971)
### Projections for the Year 2000[1]

|  | *Millions* | *Percent* |
|---|---|---|
| Hindus | 806.8 | 81.2 |
| Muslims | 128.8 | 12.9 |
| Christians | 22.1 | 2.2 |
| Sikhs | 20.8 | 2.1 |
| Other religions | 15.5 | 1.6 |
| Total population | 994.0 | 100.0 |
| Scheduled castes | 170.0 | 17.1 |
| Scheduled tribes | 85.0 | 8.5 |
| Urdu speakers | 51.8 | 5.2 |
| Non-regional languages | 49.0[2] | 4.9 |
| Minority regional languages | 73.7 | 7.4 |

[1] I have used World Bank projections for India's population. The World Bank projects that India's population will grow by 45 percent from 1981 to the year 2000. According to the 1981 census, all tribal, caste, and religious minorities, with the exception of Christians, have increased more rapidly than the population as a whole. In making projections I have assumed that these differences in growth rates continue. Should the population growth rates of the scheduled tribes, scheduled castes, and the various religious minorities decline more rapidly than for the population as a whole over the next 15 years, then these projected increases would, of course, be lower. For the languages I have simply used the projected all-India population growth rates. These projections are to be taken as rough orders of magnitude.

[2] Of whom 6.7 million live in "homelands" in the northeast, leaving 42.3 million "stateless."

*Source:*  The World Bank, *World Development Report 1984*, New York, Oxford University Press, 1984.

The reassertion of Hinduism sometimes takes a defensive form. "How can you expect," asks Karan Singh, Member of Parliament and President of the Virat Hindu Samaj, "millions of people who are called Hindus to continue to accept a second class position in Hindu society?"[14] The sense that India, its secularism notwithstanding, is the heir to Hindu civilization, informs the growing assertiveness of India in its relations with its neighbors and in its commitment to greater military (and nuclear) power. This combined defensiveness and assertiveness of contemporary Hindus is a sentiment that can be tapped by political leaders. It was tapped by Mrs. Gandhi—some say her policies helped create it—

and it has been tapped by Rajiv Gandhi. It was manifest by the support for Congress by the RSS in the December 1984 parliamentary elections, and it was manifest in the fact that for the first time in post-independence elections the Congress party won a clear majority of votes among caste Hindus in northern India.

Among educated Hindus one increasingly hears the view that Hindus should no longer fear Muslims and Sikhs and that the exercise of military force by the government in the Golden Temple complex was not only necessary as an anti-terrorist measure, but was a necessary reassertion of Hindu authority against those who would destroy India. Indeed, the private expression of pride at times seemed to outweigh the official government expressions of regret. So too were the reactions to the pogroms against Sikhs after Mrs. Gandhi's assassination. Rajiv Gandhi captured the mood, coming close to justifying the Hindu mobs, when he said during the election campaign that "when a great tree falls, the ground will quake."

Linguistic regionalism (a form of linguistic "nationalism" as distinct from an all-India nationalism) is the other claimant for majority status. Its perception of the majority-minority distinction is, however, at the regional rather than at the national level. It takes the form of "sons of the soil" sentiments, protection in education and employment against "alien" migrants, the insertion of regional histories, regional symbols, and regional pride into school textbooks and, above all, the demand for greater regional autonomy in relation to the central government. If Hindu revivalism stirs anxieties among Sikhs, Muslims, and Christians, then linguistic regionalism stirs anxieties among linguistic minorities in each of the states and among elites in the center who see regionalism as undermining the creation of an all-Indian nationalism. These latter anxieties are most deeply felt by Hindi-speaking Hindus of the north who see themselves as the center of the center, so to speak.

If the emphasis on group claims and rights for minorities has served to strengthen group assertiveness on the part of various majorities, it is also the case that this new assertiveness has further intensified the anxieties of the minorities. To religious minorities, the embrace of Hindu tolerance, its eagerness to absorb others, is psychologically threatening. To linguistic minorities, the protective, assimilative, and exclusionary stance of linguistic majorities is a cultural threat and a barrier to educational, occupational, and spatial mobility. It is in this context of the new majorities that one must understand the demands of India's minorities.

What Do India's Minorities Want?

In the midst of the black power movement in the United States in the 1960s, a black activist was asked, "What do you people want?" His recorded answer was: "What is it that you have?"

## The Demand for a Homeland

The comparable answer of many members of India's minorities is: "We want a *homeland*." Consider the following:

(1) The demand by India's Muslims before 1947 for a homeland was the driving force among Muslims living in Hindu-majority areas of northern and western India. The demand, fundamentally ethnic, not religious, was for a Muslim-majority state, not an Islamic state. Islamic fundamentalists recognized the Muslim League demand for what it was — a nationalist demand — and therefore rejected it as antithetical to Islamic ideals. The League rejected Indian nationalism, but it was nationalist nonetheless. The demand was also initially rejected by Muslim leaders in Muslim majority states since they had a homeland, but they were ultimately persuaded by the Muslims from the Hindu-majority areas that their homeland would not be secure unless they had a nation-state of their own.

(2) The demand for linguistic homelands or states was the driving force in Indian politics in the 1950s. Minority linguistic groups wanted states of their own where they could become a majority. The movement resulted in the massive reorganization of India's states so as to give almost all of the linguistic groups listed in Schedule VIII of the Constitution (the exceptions were Sindhi and Urdu speakers) linguistic states of their own. The achievement of statehood was thus the means by which some minority groups became a majority.

(3) Prior to independence a demand for a Sikh homeland was made by some Sikh leaders who conceived of India as having three "nations:" the nations of Islam, Hinduism, and Sikhism. The demand became the driving force among virtually all Sikh leaders after 1947 when the possibility of a Sikh-majority state was within their grasp. The achievement of a separate state with a Sikh majority in 1966 left Sikh nationalists unsatisfied largely because divisions within the Sikh community frustrated their efforts to seize power.[15]

(4) The movement in India's northeast among the various tribes was also for a homeland. The initial rejection of these demands by the Indian government led to India's longest insurrectionary movements, which

dissipated (but did not wholly disappear) only after the center agreed to provide the various peoples of the northeast with states of their own.

(5) The unsatisfied demand for a homeland persists in several of India's tribal areas, most notably in the Munda-Oraon-Ho-Santhal region of Bihar, Orissa, Madhya Pradesh, and West Bengal. The movement in part is frustrated by the fact that except in a handful of districts the tribals lack a majority. Nonetheless, the movement for a homeland persists and is unlikely to disappear. There are other areas with sufficiently large concentrations of tribals (though the areas themselves are sometimes small) that have developed homeland movements.

The sense of attachment to "place" in India is as powerful as attachment to group and the two are closely intertwined. Groups often regard the territory in which they live as the site of their exclusive history, a place in which great events occurred and sacred shrines are located. Tribal and linguistic groups often regard a homeland as exclusively their own and would, if they could, exclude others or deny others the right to enjoy the fruits of the land or employment provided within the territory. Hence, India's linguistic majorities define themselves as "sons of the soil" with group rights to employment, land, and political power not granted to those who come from "outside." It is not sufficient that the group occupy the territory that is their homeland; they also seek to exercise political control.

For this reason many minority groups with a territorial base have pressed for statehood. Statehood converts minority status into majority status. It enables minorities to resist assimilation (linguistic or religious) by the majority. And in more practical terms it gives them control over the resources of the government, employment, patronage, and education. In India, where the state exercises so much control over the market, ethnic groups believe that it is essential to hold political power to enable their members to redistribute public goods into their own hands.[16]

It is in this context that we may be able to forecast which groups, now minorities, will seek to turn themselves into majorities by demanding statehood. Any group that has a territorial base that does not now have a state is a likely candidate, particularly if the group has its own political leadership and political organizations to articulate ethnic group interests. Over the next 15 years a number of minority groups will seek majority status by demanding their own states. If I had to predict in which areas, I would focus on districts with tribal concentrations. Resentment over the intrusion of non-tribals into these rural communities is particularly great, while the inability of the tribals to compete for industrial and professional jobs in the urban centers and to gain access to senior administrative positions is a source of considerable anger on the part of educated tribals. The government's policy of fostering the industrial development of districts without industries, many of which are tribal-populated districts, could serve to increase migration into these localities and further widen the gap between the tribal and non-tribal populations.

The achievement of statehood by the tribals of the northeast stands as a model for others. There have already been demands that a Bodo-state be carved out of Assam and for a Jharkhand state to be carved out of Bihar. One could imagine these demands becoming more articulate. Tribals in other parts of the country will seek statehood or greater autonomy within their states not only to gain control over state resources, but to place restrictions on the entry of non-tribals into the local labor market.

In addition to the tribal areas there are indications that a distinctive identity exists among some linguistic groups not listed as official languages in the eighth schedule of the Constitution, and there are indications of a territorial-cum-cultural identity in the hill regions of Uttar Pradesh and in subregions of Andhra and Maharashtra. Among any of these peoples there could be a demand for statehood.

Some ethnic groups do not have a sufficiently large population in any single district or region to seek statehood, but many of these same groups would substantially increase their political power were they in smaller states. Indeed, a Jharkhand state would not have a tribal majority, but tribal power would be substantially greater than it is now in Bihar. Similarly, were West Bengal, Maharashtra, Uttar Pradesh, and Bihar reorganized into smaller units as some have proposed, the proportion of Muslims in several of the resulting smaller states would be substantially higher than in the present states. A decision to reorganize these states would result in the mobilization of Muslims (along with tribals and the Nepalis) to seek gerrymandered borders that would concentrate and maximize their numbers in the newly formed states.

The close association between group identity and political power has been put forth by every group in India seeking statehood. One scholar quotes a Sikh leader as saying, "No nation can maintain itself without political power."[17] He quotes another Sikh politician as saying, "Akalis seek some sort of cultural and religious freedom by which they could keep the cultural identity of the Sikhs intact. Furthermore, they also feel that without political power in the hands of the Sikhs, this may not be possible."[18] The same statement could easily have been made by Mizo, Naga, Munda, Oraon, Ho, Assamese, Nepali, Telugu, and other tribal and linguistic leaders.

## Linguistic Recognition

A major demand of a number of linguistic groups is that their language be included in the eighth schedule of the Constitution. Inclusion in the list enables a linguistic group to take all-India examinations in their own language. Similarly, recognition as an official language of a state enables a people to compete for positions in the state services without having to take examinations in another language. Official recognition, linguistic minorities argue, reduces the pressures for linguistic assimilation and enables the group to strengthen its identity and solidarity.

It should be noted that linguistic minorities are allowed to have primary and secondary school classes in their mother tongue when there is a sufficient number of children to form a class. But the question of whether linguistic minorities have classes in their own language at the university level and whether examinations for state employment can be taken in their own language have been bitter political issues in several states. The issue has been pressed, among others, by Nepalis living in Darjeeling and Dehra Dun, by Marathi speakers in Karnataka, by Bengalis in Assam and by Urdu speakers in almost any state in which they are numerous.

## Reservations

The alternative to statehood for dispersed minorities is to have reserved seats in legislative bodies and in the administrative services. The Indian Constitution, as we have already noted, legitimizes claims for groups' rights. The Constitution provides for group benefits for scheduled castes, scheduled tribes, and other backward classes. In addition to group representation through reserved constituencies in elected bodies, the government can provide for quotas for appointments in the administrative services, and admissions into colleges, universities, and medical and technical schools.

The system of reservations has a long history in India. Under the Morley-Minto reforms of 1909 separate electorates were established for Muslims. The British subsequently provided separate electorates for Sikhs, scheduled castes, Anglo-Indians, and other minority groups. With partition and a new constitution all separate electorates were abolished except those for scheduled castes and tribes.

While the Government of India has steadfastly held to the position that only these groups are entitled to reserved constituencies, reservations have been extended to others in education and employment.[19] They were first extended, as we have discussed earlier, to "other backward classes." In recent years legislation has extended group rights to "sons of the soil," that is, people who speak the recognized regional language of the state or, in at least one case (Telengana), to the "native" people of a subregion of the state. The principle of reservations has thereby been extended to a majority that wants to be protected against competition from a successful minority.

State and central governments in India have moved toward the principle that membership in educational institutions, in state and central administrative services, in the military and in public sector employment should ultimately reflect the demographic division of the country. While that policy is welcomed by some minorities (and some majorities!), it leaves two groups unhappy: those who are left out and those who lose.

Muslims, once the primary beneficiaries of reservations, are now excluded from reservations, although Muslim leaders have called for reservations on the grounds that they too are backward in employment and education. The Government of India has, however, consistently refused to extend reservations to religious groups on the grounds that it would be divisive. The government's opposition to reservations along religious lines strikes many Muslims as discriminatory, given the government's willingness to grant benefits to caste, tribal, and linguistic groups.

Sikhs have reacted against the government's reservation policies, not only because they are excluded from the system of reservations, but because they view the government's policy to achieve a greater ethnic balance in the military by proportional recruitment in the states as having the effect of reducing the number of Sikhs in the armed forces. It has been estimated that Sikhs have comprised as much as 15 percent of the military, though they constitute less than two percent of the population; proportional recruitment would thus very substantially undermine the opportunities of young Sikhs to seek military careers.

Among higher caste Hindus there has developed resistance to reservations, most recently in Madhya Pradesh, Gujarat, and Bihar. The backlash is not only against the demand of the other backward classes but in some instances even against reservations for scheduled castes and tribes. The more successful reservations become at improving the capacity of scheduled castes and tribes to compete for jobs in the administrative services, the less willing are others to support a system of employment based on group membership. Reservations in India, as elsewhere, has left all communities dissatisfied — beneficiaries because they believe that the reservations are not satisfactorily administered and those who are excluded because they view the system as discriminatory.

## Security

Minorities in India, as elsewhere, are particularly concerned over their security. Poor and dispersed minorities, most especially members of the scheduled castes, are particularly vulnerable to attacks from the majority. In recent years, there have been repeated charges from minorities that they can no longer rely upon the police to assure them of protection and that the police themselves have attacked minorities or provided support for attackers. There is considerable evidence from media reports that the police in India have become increasingly politicized and that factions of the governing party and their supporters within local communities have used the police to their own advantage. The collusion of sections of the police with sections of the Congress party against minorities was particularly evident in the attacks against Sikhs in the capital city following Mrs. Gandhi's assassination. Not until the army was called in did the attacks subside.

In other recent ethnic conflicts in Maharashtra, Assam, and Punjab the police have been ineffective. Their weakness acknowledged, the central government has turned to the military. In the Punjab, for example, the central government charged the state government (though run by its own party) of failing to deal with Sikh terrorism, failing to provide adequate intelligence to its own police and to the army, and having its administrative services and police taking a partisan position toward the various groups.

The use of the military to deal with ethnic conflict entails very substantial risks for the military itself, as the mutiny of Sikhs within the army after the assault on the Golden Temple demonstrated. Moreover, as the government contemplates the use of the army to deal with ethnic conflicts and consults with army personnel, the army itself may become politicized.

The inability of the government to provide the military with adequate intelligence as to the numbers of terrorists in the Golden Temple and the quantity and type of military equipment led to a prolonged battle and heavy loss of life and casualties for the military. The resulting anger and humiliation has embittered sections of the military. The consequence is likely to be pressure for growing involvement of the military in subsequent political decisions to use military force.

Even if the military remains non-political, the frequent use of armed forces (including the Central Reserve Police and the Border Security Forces), usually accompanied by the suspension of the state government and the imposition of restrictions upon the press and upon the opposition, involves a suspension of democratic procedures and represents a significant erosion of the democratic process and democratic institutions.

While opposition leaders have not disagreed with the government's decision to deploy the army in Punjab, Assam, and other regions of ethnic conflict and violence, critics have argued that Mrs. Gandhi often failed to take political measures prior to the outburst of violence. Indeed, many went further in arguing that actions by the government often precipitated the violence which was then used by the government to justify the use of force and thereby win popular credit for restoring law and order. Thus, say the critics, the decision to hold elections in Assam prior to an agreement over disputed electoral rolls made violence more likely; and in the Punjab, the exclusion of the Akali Dal from political power in the state, and steps taken by Congress leaders to encourage Bhindranwale's attacks against the moderates in the Akali Dal, served to strengthen the radical terrorist elements. It has been noted that Hindu-Muslim clashes grew in Hyderabad at the very moment when Mrs. Gandhi's supporters were seeking to bring down the state government, charging it with weakness in the handling of communal disturbances. These are persuasive criticisms, highlighting the inability of a weakened governing party to share power with minorities, and the temptation on the part of some government supporters to encourage ethnic strife so as to justify central government intervention, and to win support from majority communities. There is in India a deep and justifiable fear of uncontrollable violence among religious, caste, and linguistic groups. This fear serves to legitimate armed intervention by the state and can easily be played upon by a government. A government whose leaders and supporters deliberately or through inaction enable such conflicts to grow, however, is in danger of unleashing uncontrollable forces that could ultimately lead to its own undermining.

## Politics: The Problem or the Solution?

Indians have two views of the impact of politics on ethnic group conflict: that it worsens group relations and that politics is the way to reduce group conflict. Both views are correct.

The distribution of education, employment, and wealth in India is largely determined by the political process. This central feature of political life means that each ethnic group can best improve its share of education and employment by increasing its political power. The twin objectives of all ethnic groups in India — to strengthen their group identity and to improve both the social status and economic well-being of the group — can best be achieved through the route of politics. It is this central fact that induces politicians to appeal to their ethnic group for votes.

In this sense, politics can intensify and sometimes even create group consciousness, but it is by no means the only determinant. How group consciousness develops has been a subject of considerable scholarly inquiry.[20] A review of that literature is not called for here, except to say that most scholars give considerable importance to such matters as the impact of external threats, the influence of cultural and intellectual elites, the effects of government policies and programs, and the growth in mass communications, education, and urbanization. Often of critical importance are an increase in social mobility, a rise in education, and gains in employment that exceed the traditional status held by a social group. This tension between aspirations (and sometimes material achievement) and status often arouses group consciousness. The reverse, a decline in income which threatens to lower social status, can also arouse group consciousness. In India it is the former rather than the latter that has more often been the stimulus to political action.

It is not necessary that we know which of these factors will strengthen group consciousness in India over the next fifteen years. It is sufficient to know that group consciousness has been growing and that it shows no signs of withering under the forces of modernization.[21] It is important to note that it is in the perceived interests of caste, tribal, religious, and ethnic groups to seek political power to improve their status and economic well-being.[22] Ethnic groups have interests no less than do classes. In India, as in other multi-ethnic societies, individuals are members both of a class and an ethnic group. In a society without ethnic divisions class consciousness develops more easily, but in a society divided along ethnic lines historical and comparative evidence overwhelmingly suggests that ethnic group consciousness is likely to prevail. The fictive ties of kinship that characterize ethnic groups provide a more affective sense of attachment than do the appeals to interests made on the behalf of classes. Class has its affective appeals, but the sense of class comradeship is often of a lesser pull than the attractions of blood ties, real or imagined.

Class appeals are of growing importance in India. Punjabi farmers have sought to influence government policies on agricultural prices and access to irrigation and to electric power. The middle classes in Assam have called for more job-producing central government public sector investments. And Maharashtrian factory workers have demanded higher wages. But these same individuals organized to make class demands have assumed quite a different garb with other claims when they act as Sikhs, Assamese, and Muslims.

Heightened group consciousness does not necessarily result in intergroup conflict. Group consciousness may lead to a sense of pride, may result in a more strict observance of cultural and religious practices, may lead members of a group to help one another. Conflicts arise when a group asserts its identity by attacking the identity of other groups and, above all, when a claim for group rights and group power is perceived by others as threatening.

Conflicts among ethnic groups and between ethnic groups and the government are unlikely to abate over the next fifteen years. In India it is particularly important to note that governmental instability and perceived governmental weakness exacerbate social conflict. At one level Hindu-Muslim conflicts in Maharashtra and Andhra, Sikh-Hindu conflicts in Punjab, and Bengali-Assamese conflicts in Assam can be understood in terms of particular social changes at work in each of these states and among each of these communities; but at another level they can be explained by the weakening of the governing Congress party. The loosening of the bonds between the Congress party and ex-untouchables and Muslims has created new conditions for caste and communal conflict. The failure of state Congress parties and their governments to be responsive to local religious, linguistic, caste, and regional concerns has sometimes led to the channelization of protests into regional and ethnic parties and movements. Weak political institutions are more often a cause than a consequence of growing social conflict.

## Conflict Management in the 1980s and 1990s

The organizational decline of the Congress party at the state and local level, and the politicization of the police and the lower levels of administration, do not augur well for conflict management by government. Moreover, a number of public policies which had mitigated group conflict in the past have now themselves become sources of conflict. Reservations ameliorated the plight of scheduled castes and scheduled tribes but the pressure for their extension to other groups has now made reservations a divisive issue. Federalism and the rearrangements of state boundaries to provide statehood for linguistic, tribal, and (in the case of Punjab) religious minorities worked well for reducing conflict in the 1950s and 1960s, but it is not working well in the 1980s, as many of the states now seek a rearrangement of center-state powers and resources. The earlier government policy of seeking to reduce foreign influence (particularly with respect to foreign missionaries) works less well when India's Muslims employed in the Gulf are sending remittances home, Sikhs are living in western Europe and North America, Bangladeshis are moving into Assam, and Tamil-Sinhalese conflicts in Sri Lanka arouse south Indian Tamil sentiments.[23] Even the language formulas of the 1960s are questioned as Urdu-speaking Muslims, Nepalis, and other linguistic minorities press for official recognition. Nor do strategies of sitting it out, waiting for ethnic feelings to dissipate, or of incorporating leaders of ethnic groups seem to work as well in the 1980s as those strategies did earlier.

In the next 15 years the demands of ethnic groups, majorities or minorities, are bound to force a rethinking of many of India's hitherto successful policies to manage conflict.

One major policy thrust over the next 15 years is likely to be a growing concern for what can loosely be defined as "majority" interests. Government officials are already concerned that some minorities could coerce the national government through their control over critical resources or critical institutions. The threat by Sikh militants to block the sale of grains to the central government has made officials eager to reduce the nation's dependence upon Punjabi grain and, more generally, to prevent any region from, as one official privately put it, "placing a ransom" on the government. Attempts by Assamese to prevent the movement of oil from Assam to refineries is another case in point.

Military officials are similarly concerned that military units be ethnically diversified and that Muslims, Sikhs, and other self-conscious ethnic groups not be in a position to undermine the use of military power in domestic crises. The government's policy of diversifying military recruitment geographically has been vindicated by recent developments. So too has been the government's policy of recruiting for national administrative service with some regard for geographical distribution, even at the cost of purely "merit" considerations. Similarly, some regard for geographical distribution, since geography is a surrogate for linguistic and religious affiliation, is an important consideration in the selection of students by the central universities and the national institutes of engineering, management, and medicine. Wide geographic representation assures that the next generation of the country's scientific, engineering, management, and medical personnel is ethnically diversified.

The state governments are no less likely to protect their interests than is the central government. Even as the states make claims upon the center for more resources and greater autonomy, so too will tribal and linguistic minorities make claims upon the states. And just as the central government will resist demands made by the states, so too will state governments resist demands made by the minorities. Under such circumstances local minorities turn to the center for political support; indeed by generating violence and creating disturbances that the state government cannot handle, local groups (notably opponents of the government) hope to force central government intervention.

The less able are state governments to manage majority-minority relations the more likely it is that the central government will intervene. Of critical importance, therefore, in the future of majority-minority relations in India is the viability of the state governments. Rajiv Gandhi's overwhelming victory in the national parliamentary elections will be of little avail in the peaceful management of ethnic conflict if state governments are weak. Should minorities become more assertive and conflict prove to be unmanageable by state government authorities, then the powers of the central government will increase.

A pessimistic scenario is one in which majority-minority conflicts increase, state governments do not demonstrably increase their capacity to deal with these conflicts, the center by its actions provokes opposition to central authority, and the growth of violent conflict leads to greater coercion and the use of the armed forces.

An optimistic scenario is one in which leaders at both the national and state levels demonstrate their skill at accommodating the demands for substantial administrative decentralization and prove skillful at reassuring minorities without threatening the cultural identity and interests of majorities. We can make no predictions about which scenario is most likely.

# NOTES

1. Theodore P. Wright, Jr., "The Ethnic Numbers Game in India: Hindu-Muslim Conflicts over Conversion, Family Planning, Migration, and the Census," in *Culture, Ethnicity and Identity*, edited by William McCrady, New York, Academic Press, 1983, p. 412.

2. R. A. Schermerhorn, *Ethnic Plurality in India*, Tucson, Arizona, University of Arizona Press, 1978, pp. 101-127. Schermerhorn's book on minorities is one of the few comprehensive treatments.

3. Balraj Madhok, *Indianization? What, Why and How*, New Delhi, S. Chand and Co., 1970.

4. Throughout this analysis I have used 1971 census figures on language and caste since state-wide figures for 1981 have only been released for religion. While the absolute numbers have, of course, substantially changed, the percentages are not likely to have changed a great deal.

5. For the construction of the tables included here I have drawn the data from K. P. Ittaman, "Social Composition of the Population" in *Population in India*, New York, Economic and Social Commission for Asia and the Pacific, United Nations, 1982, pp. 233-254.

6. Nafis Ahmad Siddique, *Population Geography of Muslims in India*, New Delhi, S. Chand and Co., 1976. According to Siddique, Mus-

lims constitute a majority in nine districts (mainly in Kashmir), 35 to 50 percent of the population in ten more districts, and in 20 more districts they comprise 20 to 35 percent of the population.

7. The demand for a Punjabi Subha was a way of pressing for a Sikh majority state within the framework of a policy that accepted *linguistic* states but rejected statehood on the basis of religion. This view was articulated by Master Tara Singh, leader of the movement for a Punjabi Subha, who was asked by the then Chief Minister of the state in 1955, "So you want a land wherein the Sikhs should dominate?" to which Tara Singh replied, "This is exactly what I have in mind," and continued: "This cover of a Punjabi-speaking State slogan serves my purpose well since it does not offend against nationalism. The government should accept our demand under the slogan of a Punjabi-speaking State without a probe. What we want is Azadi (independence). The Sikhs have no Azadi. We will fight for our Azadi with full power even if we have to revolt." Baldev Raj Nayar, *Minority Politics in the Punjab*, Princeton, Princeton University Press, 1966, p. 37.

8. Master Tara Singh, a dominant figure among Sikhs for over a generation, said that "the Khalsa Panth will either be a ruler or a rebel. It has no third role to play." (Schermerhorn, *op. cit.*, p. 140). Sikhs share the Muslim view of the inseparability of religion and politics, a position considered anathema by most Hindus.

9. Schedule V of the Constitution provides that selected tribal areas should be administered by the state governments, with the Governor of each state given the power to modify central and state laws for the scheduled areas and to frame regulations protecting tribal land rights. Special funds are provided by the central government for the development of scheduled areas. Central government responsibility for the areas is in the hands of the Home Ministry.

10. For this discussion of the demography of India's tribes I have drawn from Myron Weiner and John Osgood Field, "How Tribal Constituencies in India Vote," in *Electoral Politics in the Indian States*, vol. II, edited by Myron Weiner and John Osgood Field, New Delhi, Manohar Book Service, pp. 78-85.

11. Land Alienation and Restoration in Tribal Communities in India, edited by S. N. Dubey and Ratna Naidu, Bombay, Himalaya Publishing House, 1977. This is a useful collection of papers on the growing problem of land alienation among tribals in Andhra, Maharashtra, Gujarat, Rajasthan, Madhya Pradesh, West Bengal, Orissa, and Bihar.

12. See Barbara R. Joshi, *Democracy in Search of Equality: Untouchable Politics and Indian Social Change*, Delhi, Hindustan Publishing Corporation, 1982.

13. On the backward classes: who they are, how they are statutorily

defined, and how they seek preferential status, see Marc Galanter, "Who Are the Other Backward Classes? An Introduction to a Constitutional Puzzle," *Economic and Political Weekly*, October 28, 1978, p. 1812.

14. Karan Singh, "Hindu Renaissance," *Seminar*, April 1983, p. 17.

15. After the Punjab was reorganized on a linguistic basis in November 1966, the Akalis were able to form a government for the first time, but their hold on political power was tenuous. It was not simply because the Sikhs constituted only 60 percent of the population, but because a substantial portion of the Sikh community, the scheduled caste Sikhs, in their antagonism to Sikh Jats, voted for the Congress party. For a time the Akalis were in coalition with Congress, then with the Jana Sangh, then with the Janata party. Thrust out of power in Mrs. Gandhi's Congress victory of 1980, the Akalis adopted a more radical posture, articulating an earlier demand for more autonomy for the Punjab, but also explicitly articulating Sikh religious concerns as well.

For an informative analysis of the Sikh issue, see *Seminar*, February 1984, devoted to "the Punjab Tangle." The issue contains articles by I. K. Gujral ("The Sequence"), Rajendra Sareen ("Source of Trouble"), Attar Singh ("What Went Wrong"), T. V. Sathyamurthy ("Crisis Within the Crisis"), Prakash Tandon ("Another Angle"), Sajjan Singh Murgin Puri ("Sanctuary"), and K. R. Bombwall ("Ethnonationism"). The issue also contains an excellent bibliography.

16. The American liberal view, to quote Arthur M. Schlesinger, that "politics, after all, is in the art of solving problems" and that "political tendencies rise or fall depending on the results they produce" ("The Elections and After," *New York Review of Books*, August 16, 1984, p. 35), hardly fits the Indian view of politics. For Indians politics means acquiring power over others, maintaining or elevating one's status, and using power to provide patronage to one's supporters. Policies and issues have little to do with politics. While dozens of governments have fallen, I can think of none where a split in the government party on an issue of public policy led to a legislative defeat in the assembly.

17. M. S. Dhami, *Minority Leaders Image of the Indian Political System: An Exploratory Study of the Attitudes of Akali Leaders*, New Delhi, Sterling Publishers, 1975, p. 34.

18. *Ibid.*, p. 35.

19. For an analysis of the ways in which preferential policies, once restricted to scheduled castes and scheduled tribes, have been extended to other groups, including the majority communities, see Myron Weiner, "The Political Consequences of Preferential Policies: A Comparative Perspective," in *Comparative Politics*, October 1983, pp. 35-52.

20. For an analysis of the impact of politics on shaping linguistic and religious group consciousness in India, see Paul Brass, *Language, Religion and Politics in North India*, Berkeley, University of California Press, 1974.

21. An elderly Indian socialist, Achyut Patwardhan, reflecting on the ways in which Marxism affected his own capacity to understand the determinants and durability of religious and ethnic group consciousness in India, had this to say: "There is another error which is now equally apparent in retrospect which must be confessed frankly. Pt. Jawaharlal Nehru and the younger section of Congressmen (among these must be counted the present writer and his other socialist colleagues) sincerely believed that regional and parochial loyalties would be defeated logically and inevitably by more basic 'class' loyalties. Our generation was under the spell of Marx and Lenin and economic factors seemed to us far more decisive in determining the direction of world history. We felt, therefore, that Indian Muslim masses would be weaned away from the reactionary sectarian domination of the Mullahs." Achyut Patwardhan, foreword to M. A. Karandikar, *Islam in India's Transition to Modernity*, Westport, Connecticut, Greenwood Publishers Corporatin, 1969, pp. vii-viii.

22. Since Marxists see "interests" only in class terms they are unable to see religion, tribe, language, and caste as rational bases for social action or political conflict, and when they analyze such behavior it is either seen as derivative of economic differences or as a false consciousness. For a statement of the Marxist view of interests, see André Beteille, *Six Essays in Comparative Sociology*, Delhi, Oxford University Press, 1974. Beteille, a leading Indian sociologist, writes that "the task of sociology, as I see it, is to study the dialectical relationship between ideas and interests" (p. 98). "The study of class and class conflict is rooted in a sociology of interests of which Marx, more than anybody else, laid the foundation. Marx himself saw not only the conflict of classes but the division of labour itself as being rooted in the structure of interests" (p. 103). "The important step," continues Beteille, "in the study of interests is to go beyond the individual and to see how interests are socially structured . . . Interests have a dual role: they unite people into a class and they divide one class from another although this division may be masked by an ideology . . . Those who work on the land have similar interests whether they speak Bengali or Santali, or practice Hinduism or Animism" (pp. 104-105). This notion that people in the same occupation "have similar interests" precludes an understanding of how individuals and groups define their "interests," and it fails to recognize that people in the same class but in different ethnic groups (Bengali and

Santali peasants, for example, or Hindu and tribal middle class) may in fact have competing interests in land or employment.

23. The movement of Bangladeshis, Tamils from Sri Lanka and Nepalis into India and of Indians into Nepal, the Gulf states, West Europe, and the United States has created new internal and international relations issues for India (some of which led Mrs. Gandhi to speak of a "foreign hand") that cry out for a full-scale analysis.

Chapter Seven

# The Language
# Issue Revisited

ROBERT D. KING

Is it possible to imagine an India in the twenty-first century without a
language problem? Certainly not. That much at least is clear. If long-es-
tablished nations with as few as two languages continue to have fester-
ing disagreements about language policy (Canada and Belgium come to
mind), then one would be a hopeless optimist to imagine an India in
which language had ceased to be a problem altogether. Dozens of different languages are spoken in India, each by millions of people, each having extraordinarily powerful claims on ethnic, regional, religious, and
ancestral loyalties, and each loaded with sublime symbolism for its
speakers. And India, unlike China, does not have the advantage of a
single script and a single way of writing its diverse languages.[1]

The twentieth century has come to regard a one-to-one relationship
between nations and languages as virtually the only natural one. Countries with a single language—Germany, France, the United States,
Japan—have clear advantages in regard to ease of communication and
even political stability. When even two languages are spoken by large
segments of the population, as in Belgium, Canada, Sri Lanka, or any
number of newly formed African states, it becomes hard to create a
stable society. Actually, it is something of a miracle that India became
and has remained a single nation, much less a democratic one, and I say
this strictly as a linguist. Political scientists and sociologists will have
their own reasons for astonishment that India became and remains, in
some palpable sense, a single nation.[2] This is a part of the "paradox" of
which Salman Rushdie wrote in the wake of Mrs. Gandhi's tragic assassination.[3]

India will always have language problems, so it is the question of degree that become important. Since independence in 1947, several manifestations of the language issue have pushed India to the brink of serious disorder. A large amount of political energy was expended on
ameliorating the language controversy during the 1950s and 1960s, but
there are cycles in this, as in most areas of sociocultural development,
and language in India today is not the burning issue that it was in 1955
or 1965.

I am optimistic that the most serious language problems are behind.
I think (and I hope) that it is possible to envision an India in the not-too-
distant future in which language will have become about the same kind
of political problem that it has become, say, in eastern Canada. It is
certainly a problem there, but not on a scale that threatens the unity
of the country or even appreciably diverts energies from more substantial concerns. This improvement in the Indian linguistic scene will take
place quite independently of what the government chooses to do or not
to do. It is, in short, no longer really a matter of government policy,

and the less the government says, and especially the less the government does, almost surely the better.

To anyone who has followed linguistic controversies in India, such optimism can seem little more than a mindless expression of faith. In July 1960, headlines in the international press read: LANGUAGE RIOTS IN ASSAM! SCORES KILLED! 40,000 FLEE! Madras had ugly scenes over language in 1965. In August 1967, in Ranchi, supporters of Hindi clashed with Muslims seeking acceptance of Urdu as the second official language of Bihar and the violence cost at least 70 lives.[4] Even today it is a rare week when an Indian newspaper does not report some language confrontation such as the problems of Urdu in Hyderabad or Uttar Pradesh, the status of Punjabi, an anti-English incident, or linguistic minorities claiming bias.

In fact, there is almost no sociolinguistic problem that India has not experienced, is still experiencing, or threatens to experience. Obviously, the problem is rooted in the presumably desirable attempt to agree upon a national language in a country in which many regional languages are spoken, a problem in nation-building since the end of World War II. There has never been a time in Indian history when the different vernaculars did not carry the main burden of oral communication in the villages and the major regions. But there have always been "link languages" facilitating relations and communications beyond the vernacular boundaries.

Sanskrit was the earliest such language that we know about, and in some ways its pan-Indian importance in Hindu society continues today. The importance of a language is not measured only by the number of its speakers. Persian came with Muslim rule, was made the court language of the Moghul Empire, and achieved a cachet that endured in some places — though not very deeply on the whole, I think — to the middle period of the British raj.[5] In those parts of the country under strong Moghul hegemony, north India and pockets in the Deccan, Persian assumed some of the linking function of Sanskrit. English was for the British what Persian had been for the Moghuls and Sanskrit for the pundits, so that by 1947 English was the only language with substantial currency among the elite throughout all of India.

I say "among the elite." It is perfectly clear that no language has ever had pan-Indian currency in any very profound sense except among the elite, and I doubt that any ever will. I have never seen an estimate of English speakers in India greater than two or three percent, and that is probably on the high side (though one must remember that small percentages in India still indicate millions). These are the "elite" of public life and commerce as well as those who, like hotel clerks and airline personnel, depend on some knowledge of English for their livelihood.

Before I make my predictions about the language situation in India, let me briefly describe the major linguistic issues the country has confronted since independence. On the whole, regional languages have done very well for themselves. They have modernized, taken on new technical terms and new uses, and secured for themselves a proper place at the state level. The reorganization of states according to linguistic boundaries — the creation of Andhra Pradesh (Telugu), Kerala (Malayalam), and the division of single predecessor states into Maharashtra (Marathi) and Gujarat (Gujarati), and into the Punjab (Punjabi) and Haryana (Hindi) — was inevitable, however much geographers, economists, political scientists, and other rationalists might have wished that other factors (like trade relationships) had played a larger role in determining state boundaries. Commonsense considerations often go against the grain of what now seems recognized as an imperative of nationhood in the twentieth century: one state, one language; one language, one state.

Language disputes have often served as surrogates for more fundamental disagreements among Indians. The argument over Hindi versus Urdu, a debate prominent before partition but only occasionally since — and then, for obvious reasons, only at the state level — is seen in retrospect as not much more than the continuation of the Hindu-Muslim struggle by other means.[6] Gandhi's advocacy of a slightly factitious official "Hindustani," neutral between Hindi and Urdu, was less an advocacy of something linguistically real than a well-meant effort to preserve communal peace. It is a sadly ironic symbol of its linguistic ephemerality that Hindustani, as an official language, died for lack of one vote in the Constituent Assembly in 1946 when the reality of partition was apparent.[7] A real language cannot be *voted* out of existence.

More recent arguments about the status of the Punjabi language and the Gurumukhi script, arguments all too sadly current today, are reminiscent of the Hindustani question, in that the fundamental issue is not so much a linguistic one as it is a question of the rights and claims of a minority (Sikhs). The problems are real and require resolution, but the language conflict is a symptom of a deeper quest for recognition and power in a multi-ethnic nation. Having said that, however, let me emphasize that the linguistic issue *is* real, if secondary: never underestimate the power of a language as symbol, least of all in Asia.

The thorniest linguistic issue until the mid-1960s was the question of "national" language versus "official" language; more specifically, the question of the choice between Hindi and English.[8] The framers of the Constitution of India accorded constitutional standing to most of the major regional languages of India and to Sanskrit, but they chose Hindi,

the regional language with the most speakers and the heaviest political
clout, as the official language of the union. English was to coexist
alongside Hindi for official national purposes, but was to be phased out
by 1965; this has not happened, of course, and never will unless India
moves in an unforeseeable direction.[9]

Our knowledge of languages, and of how they develop within a country, makes it clear that the movement to replace English by Hindi for
national purposes was bound to fail. India's elites have conversed with
each other in English, no matter what their native languages, since the
beginning of the twentieth century; by 1900, English was the only
genuine link language on the subcontinent. Not much can be done in a
free society to force unwilling people to accept one regional language
as the national language, even when that regional language has more
native speakers and a better political power base than the others. It is
one thing to enforce a national standard language in China, in Tanzania,
or in Kemal Ataturk's Turkey; it is quite another to try to do so in a
society as diverse and democratic as that of India. It takes fines, prison
sentences, and firing squads to force people to use a language or a script
they do not want to use.[10]

Which is perhaps the major point to be made in this essay: there is
very little the government of a free country can do to change significantly language usage and practice, to force its citizens to use certain
languages in preference to others, and to prevent people speaking a
language they wish to continue to speak. Language is conservative, the
most conservative form of cultural behavior, even more so than religion.
In a free society it is almost immune to government intervention. It
resists legislative and bureaucratic injunctions.

This point, accepted and well understood by linguists, is insufficiently
appreciated by everyone else, politicians and social engineers in particular.[11] It is a fact that government actions can induce major changes in
many kinds of group behavior and attitudes; insistent policies of the
federal government of the United States have led to a welcome revolution in race relations in the American south since 1954. But it is not a
fact that governments other than harsh dictatorships can do much to
change linguistic behavior.[12]

The government of Ireland has, since independence in 1921, done everything it can to promote the Gaelic language — financial induce-
ments, preferments, massive educational initiatives — to no avail. English wins and Gaelic loses speakers every day. The Welsh language is
alive and well in Wales today, and what the government has chosen to
do or not to do is almost totally beside the point.[13] The Yiddish language, a language which never even had a territory to call its own, prevailed against gross discrimination in Eastern Europe for centuries. It

took the massacre of most of its speakers to put Yiddish on the list of endangered languages. Romani, the language of the Gypsies, yields a similar story of survival against powerful governmental efforts to suppress it. Even dictators have trouble mandating linguistic choices that are unpopular. People simply do not like government meddling in a personal matter like language and a wise government will steer clear of official language policies.

What do I predict for language in India in the year 2000? My view is that nature will take its course and what the government does will be largely beside the point. The linguistic "marketplace" — by which I mean a good deal more than the economic marketplace — efficiently dictates the large and small decisions alike. If I am right where India is concerned, this means several different things:

(1) English will continue to be the language of national discourse and national politics, as well as the language with the greatest pan-Indian intellectual appeal. Anyone with a moderately important role in running the central government will use English most of the time.

(2) English will grow in importance as the language of commerce and business as India continues to develop economically. Most conversations on topics that cross state lines will be in English, as they are now, and as they have been since the earliest days of the Congress movement.

(3) "Indian English" will continue to diverge from standard British or American English. Indians whose English is used only with other Indians will speak a very different kind of English from that spoken by, let us say, Indian diplomats abroad. (Linguists call this "diglossia.")

(4) The movement to make Hindi the national language has lost its vitality and will continue to weaken. The "three-language formula," in any of its variants, is dead.[14] Hindi will continue to gain moderately in speakers because there are advantages for the Indian who speaks Hindi well, especially in the civil service. Hindi's gains will be greater and more secure the less the central government says and does, since any overt campaign, ushered in by the usual extravagant rhetoric, will always breed fatal opposition, in Dravidian India and West Bengal if nowhere else.

(5) The regional languages will expand virtually to the limits of the state boundaries. Within the states, the regional language will be the language of instruction at all levels, including, probably, all but a few universities.[15]

Language is far from being the major problem that India faces; overpopulation, the cost of oil, Balkanization — any one of these is a greater threat to the union than anything linguistic. Language is not "of no intrinsic importance," as the Report of the Official Language Commission of 1956 put it (how quaint that sentiment sounds in 1985), but one should not overstate its importance.[16] Nor should one ever forget that language in India is as often a symbol of protest as it is a cause: what the Sikhs want is certainly a good deal more than respect for the Gurumukhi script.

The best language policy the government of India can adopt is no language policy. If that is asking too much, which it is as a matter of realpolitik, then a policy of linguistic benign neglect will do nearly as well.[17] The potency of government initiatives in the field of language policy is simply not very great, not in India, not in any relatively free society. Here, finally, is an area of policy in which the government need not do anything in order to accomplish good: less is better.

The unique genius of India, probably its greatest legacy from Hinduism, is the ability to absorb conflicting ideas and create harmony out of opposing views. India is a tolerant land in spite of communal conflicts. It lives every day with a degree of diversity unknown in the countries of the West. The language conflicts of post-independence India go against the grain of this tradition of tolerance. They are, as it were, the spiritual legacy of Aurangzeb rather than of Akbar.

I believe, though often in the face of sad evidence to the contrary, that the Indian genius for reconciling dualities will prevail in language as well as in other matters. If this is true, then I do not think we will need to spend too much time worrying about language conflicts in the India of the twenty-first century. The linguistic "marketplace," together with a little luck and a great measure of traditional Indian tolerance, will solve most of the problems.

## NOTES

1. The literature on language in India is by now so voluminous that it would require a lengthy bibliography to list only the major items. A few of the more balanced and sophisticated treatments dealing with different aspects of the problem are: J. Das Gupta, *Language Conflict and National Development*, Berkeley, University of California Press, 1970; Baldev Raj Nayar, *National Communication and Language Policy in India*, New York, Praeger, 1969; E. Annamalai, editor, *Language Movements in India*, Mysore, Cultural Institute of Indian Languages, 1979. For a more general treatment of language problems in developing countries see Joshua Fishman, Charles A. Ferguson, and J. Das Gupta,

editors, *Language Problems of Developing Nations*, New York, Wiley and Sons, 1968.

2. See the comments by Einar Haugen on language and nation alignment in his essay, "Dialect, Language, Nation," *American Anthropologist*, LXVIII, 1966, pp. 922-935.

3. *The New Republic*, November 26, 1984, p. 17.

4. Das Gupta, *op. cit.*, p. 149.

5. *Ibid.*, p. 40.

6. Cf. Kerrin Dittmer, *Die indischen Muslims und die Hindi-Urdu Kontroverse in den United Provinces*, Wiesbaden, Harrassowitz, 1972.

7. Das Gupta, *op. cit.*, p. 123. My colleague Herman van Olphen has pointed out that, in a real sense, it is the "official" versions of Hindi and Urdu rather than Hindustani that are fictitious, "since they were brought into being by government and religious organizations over a long period of time. It was not Hindustani that died by a one-vote margin in the Constituent Assembly in 1946, but the use of Hindustani by the Indian government. It (Hindustani) is still the *lingua franca* of a large part of South Asia." I agree with this perceptive comment; the argument has to do with the difference between a language (i.e., a code of communication using spoken words) and an officially recognized language (with a script, codified rules, and so on).

8. Das Gupta, *op. cit.*, p. 36.

9. See S. Dwivedi, *Hindi on Trial*, New Delhi, Vikas, 1981, for a lengthy treatment of the status of Hindi before and after independence.

10. This point, the conservatism of linguistic behavior, is virtually axiomatic in linguistics. It is a basic part of almost any introductory course in linguistics. For a very brief exposure to the subject one might consult Victoria Fromkin and Robert Rodman, *An Introduction to Language*, New York, Holt, Rinehart and Winston, 1978, chapter 10 *et passim*, and Jacob Ornstein and William W. Gage, *The ABC's of Languages and Linguistics*, Philadelphia, Chilton Books, 1964, chapter 10.

11. Well, by almost all linguists, and certainly by every linguist *qua* linguist. The fact is that most of us, linguists included, want to believe that most things can be changed by government for the better; and we often find it hard to accept the repeated failures of government efforts to accomplish our favorite goals (there always seem to be extenuating circumstances). The plain fact is that government action can effect little changes at the margins in linguistic behavior, but it cannot succeed in changing the big things — not in a free country. One need only study bilingual education in almost any country where it has become public policy. Not to put too fine a point on it, bilingual education has, quite simply, failed virtually every time it has been tried. While it is a noble

experiment and a few people do end up managing two languages reasonably well, not very many do.

12. Except at the margins, see 11.

13. In fact, in not-so-distant times the Welsh language was actively suppressed by the English government. Suppression did not work; the people would not have it.

14. The "three-language formula" came down to the compulsory study of three languages, e.g., Hindi, English, and the regional vernacular; but the formula had all sorts of varied nuances. The idea was to make all Indians fluent in the three languages that they would need to function well in modern India. See Nayar, *op. cit.*, pp. 152-163.

15. This may occur although any university that abandons English in favor of the vernacular will lose its all-India student body and its prestige, ultimately becoming a provincial institution.

16. Quoted in Das Gupta, *op. cit.*, p. 160.

17. India would do well to look to its large northern neighbor as a useful model. The Soviet Union, with all its myriad languages, has for the most part followed a policy of linguistic benign neglect since Lenin's day. The Soviet Union has had relatively little overt linguistic trouble since the October Revolution; however, the Soviet Union has never had the slightest hesitation in crushing languages of minorities who have come into official disfavor — Ukrainians, Jews, White Russians, and others: but it is after all a totalitarian country, a fact which makes its linguistic liberality all the more surprising.

Chapter Eight

# Center-State Relations In India: The Federal Dilemma

PAUL WALLACE

Two factors provide the ordering framework for center-state relations in India: first, the political status and style of the dominant party; second, and not to be underestimated, the regional forces and groupings operating in and between the states. These regional groups are highly adaptable protean elements that may be submerged by a passing electoral wave, but inevitably rebound because they are the very stuff of society. Two other considerations provide a larger environment for this perspective. India's constitutional structure is federal, if somewhat qualifiedly, and federalism is becoming increasingly important as economic changes — in the form of commercializing agriculture and burgeoning industrialism — enhance social, political, and economic interdependence.

India's federal dilemma for the year 2000 is highlighted by the need for more effective central political and governmental institutions that can respond more positively to the acute need for decentralization. A wild card complicating the always hazardous task of prediction exists in the person of the new Prime Minister, 41 year old Rajiv Gandhi. It is not that he lacks a record since his mother induced him into the political arena in 1980; stated simply, he has yet to chart a clear course. His all-things-to-most-people image has yet to be clarified. Nonetheless, discernible patterns and trends will continue until the end of the century unless they are deliberately altered.

## Personalism and Centralization

Centralization was so clearly the pattern of the Congress Party under Indira Gandhi as to occasion, in the words of W. H. Morris-Jones, "the decay of center-state relations." He argues that her political "style transformed these relations from ones of political bargaining to ones akin to feudal tutelage."[1] Prime Minister Rajiv Gandhi inherited a party which had undergone twin processes of personalism and de-institutionalization in its political apparatus and style. India's eighth general elections in December 1984 can be interpreted as a massive mandate for Rajiv Gandhi and as a sympathy vote for his mother who was assassinated on October 31, 1984.[2] Congress (I) won four-fifths (401 out of 508) of the Lok Sabha seats decided in December. His initial appointments confirmed that Rajiv was in command with a personal authority that did not differ markedly from the pattern established by Indira Gandhi.

Feudalism is an apt term for the personal relations that relate Congress (I) lieutenants to a dominant leader; an infrastructure of leadership does not exist. The form political leadership in the party has assumed is more like the structure of the pre-independence Muslim League led by Muhammad Ali Jinnah than the shape of the Congress of Mahatma Gandhi and Jawaharlal Nehru. Feudalism, however, is an inappropriate word for the centralizing consequences of the altered political relationships. Mrs. Gandhi's predecessors formulated, whether consciously or not, a pattern of center-state relations that can be described as federalist — regardless of the difficulty of using the term. In both the ruling party and at various levels of government, power was decentralized to the degree that a bargaining process was necessary.[3] Political leaders at each level had bases of support that resulted in the minimal degrees of autonomy essential to a federalist political pattern.

Factionalism within the dominant Congress and the vitality of regional, ethnic-based parties provided the political context for federalism in India. The political dynamic of that context underwent a massive change as Mrs. Gandhi reacted to what she perceived as challenges to her political power. Beginning with the party split in 1969, the Congress system itself changed radically with the forced departure or "domestication" of formerly autonomous leaders. National figures such as Kamaraj Nadar from Tamil Nadu, Sanjiva Reddy from Andhra Pradesh, Atulya Ghosh from West Bengal, and Morarji Desai from Gujarat, collectively known as the "Syndicate," challenged a seemingly insecure Indira Gandhi over the issue of the Union Presidency.[4] They lost.

The Syndicate's party became known as Congress (O). The "O" stood for "organization," representing these leaders' central importance to the party machinery and their collective voice in decision-making. Each maintained a base of autonomous support in his home state, and with their defeat an intricate system of bargaining between powerful leaders gave way to a new pattern. In this changed power configuration, Mrs. Gandhi not only centralized power horizontally at the center in both the government and her party, but she centralized power vertically through appointees at the state level directly dependent upon her.

Centralization of the government, party, and center-state levels after 1969 was only partially complete. Some political leaders with independent or autonomous support bases remained with Mrs. Gandhi. Y. B. Chavan from Maharashtra, Swaran Singh from Punjab, and *harijan* leader Jagjivan Ram were three of the most important examples. Devraj Urs achieved a similar stature in Karnataka.

Regional political parties have provided another state level dimension inhibiting a thorough-going centralization. Most notable have been the National Conference in Kashmir, the Akali Dal in Punjab, the CPI-M in West Bengal, and the AIADMK and the DMK in Tamil Nadu. The Jana Sangh and the Charan Singh-led Bharatiya Kranti Dal (subsequently the Lok Dal and, in 1984, the Dalit Mazdoor Kisan Party or

DMKP) also resisted the centralizing efforts. By 1974, Jaya Prakash Narayan became the most significant force outside of regular party channels as he attempted to mobilize opposition to Mrs. Gandhi, particularly in Bihar, through his movement against corruption and for "total revolution." Mrs. Gandhi felt politically threatened by these forces as well as by a petition that challenged her election, thereby raising the possibility of her losing the Prime Ministership.

The Emergency, which began on June 26, 1975, allowed the Prime Minister to accelerate the process begun in 1969. Major elements of India's democratic political system were subjected to centralization, under the aegis of Mrs. Gandhi and her younger son Sanjay, and with much repression. Centralization affected political parties, even the ruling Congress Party, the press, associational rights, trade unions, the judiciary, and center-state relationship.[5]

The precarious balance between the center and the states swung sharply toward centralized and authoritarian modes of political operation. Yet, in a sense Mrs. Gandhi had only accelerated tendencies inherent in India's constitutional structure. Since 1950, scholars have debated the extent to which the Indian system is truly federal. Kenneth Wheare emphasized centralizing features of the Constitution such as the emergency powers, presidential rule, the center's power to alter state boundaries, the incorporation of state constitutions within the Union constitution, and the dominant role of the center in financial matters as qualifying Indian federalism.[6]

K. Iyengar Santhanam stressed the centralizing role of the Planning Commission in enhancing the national government's dominance over the states.[7] Taxation, always weighted toward the center, flows in ever larger proportions to New Delhi "because the states . . . are deprived of productive and elastic sources of revenues." Commercial developments have led to "an increasing tendency towards centralization of these taxes."[8]

Constitutional features, and the development of central government institutions, such as the Planning Commission, worked in favor of the center long before the Emergency, but in practice accommodative federal politics sustained a federal and pluralist system. Thus, the federal political process eroded from at least 1969, and was directly attacked beginning with the Emergency in 1975, although Constitutional limits were not violated.

Since the Emergency did not provide a permanent legal framework for escalated centralization, constitutional changes were thought necessary. Various types of restructuring were considered, including a changeover to a presidential system; but instead of the writing of a new Constitution, an overhauling of the existing framework occurred. A new legal structure designed for the post-Emergency period emerged in November 1976 in the 42nd Amendment to the Constitution. Increased powers of the Prime Minister included the authority further to amend the Constitution by executive order for a period of two years. Fundamental rights were substantially replaced by a new section on fundamental duties. The judiciary was subordinated to Parliament. In sum, the amendment appeared to give "a new permanence to a state of affairs that had originally been presented as temporary."[9]

India's electorate reacted strongly to what it perceived as Emergency excesses and the March 1977 elections brought the Janata Party coalition to power with a large majority. Dismantling of the Emergency apparatus followed, including abrogating the 42nd Amendment. A more open system and broader sharing of power enabled the resumption of federalism. The Janata Party stressed decentralization, particularly in regard to rural development. Mostly dormant *panchayati raj* institutions were once again emphasized for local, rural self-government, and a revised model was recommended to the states for adoption and implementation.[10] An entire new scheme, *antodaya*, was designed to reach the very poorest at the village level.

This thrust toward decentralizing public policy shattered on the shoals of the party's internal differences. Despite their personal relationships developed in prison, and the drama of reaching the heights of political power, Janata leaders could not hold their alliance together. Broad consensus on decentralization, civil liberties, and rural development could not withstand intergroup and intraparty conflict. The coalition collapsed in July 1979; six months of an ineffective Charan Singh-led Lok Dal caretaker government completed the disintegration of the Janata alliance and undermined its popular support. The constituent groups staggered separately and unsuccessfully towards the elections of January 1980.

The "Indira wave" and the rejection of the Janata and Lok Dal returned Mrs. Gandhi to power with a large majority. It is important to note, however, that neither Janata's decentralization attempts nor its policies were the focus of Congress (I)'s and the public's criticisms during the election campaign. Mrs. Gandhi's call for a strong, stable government underlined the management failure of the Janata and Lok Dal, particularly as contrasted with the image of economic progress and social discipline that she projected as characteristic of her earlier rule. Effective management — "the party that governs," as the Congress (I) promised — rather than ideology or center-state relationships became a powerful and electorally advantageous theme, notwithstanding questions about her own record of "delivering the goods."

In fact, before the Emergency, Mrs. Gandhi's management of India's problems had been severely criticized. One of her critics pinned the difficulty on overcentralization: "Basically, it is a crisis of non-performance — of a system that has become so centralized and so disoriented and cut off from the people that it is unable to produce results."[11]

It had become clear by 1980 that the recentralization of party and government under the Congress (I) grew more from Mrs. Gandhi's personal political style than from center-state considerations or from a particular ideology. Her split with the Syndicate in 1969 eliminated most of the brokers with whom she shared power. Her leftist policies at the time resulted in symbolic acts such as the abolition of privy purses and bank nationalization. Her opposition to "monopoly houses" in the publications industry was aimed more at her critics than at monopolies themselves. Prior to and during the Emergency she did not hesitate to suppress trade unions and to provide more liberal opportunities for big business.

Similarly, in her relations with state governments, she had a pragmatic and mixed record. As early as 1959, while President of the Congress, Mrs. Gandhi reputedly had a significant role in toppling the Communist government of Kerala. Similarly, she engineered the imposition of President's rule to replace a Communist government in West Bengal in 1971. At other times, including the Emergency, she coexisted with communist regimes in West Bengal and Kerala, and even entered into a successful alliance with the CPI in Kerala. Moreover, she alternately allied with the DMK in Tamil Nadu in 1971, the AIADMK in 1977, and again the DMK in January 1980. In Punjab, she consistently opposed the Akali Dal at the state level, but accepted the support of Akali members of Parliament from 1969 through 1971 when she lacked a clear majority.

Rajiv Gandhi became a junior partner, however reluctant, in perpetuating this pattern of personalism and centralization following his brother's death in 1980. By this time the remaining Congress (I) leaders with autonomous power had followed those earlier challengers of Mrs. Gandhi and had to find political homes elsewhere. Individuals who returned to the Congress (I) were "domesticated;" their autonomy was curtailed. These included Y. B. Chavan, Swaran Singh, Jagjivan Ram, Devraj Urs, and H. N. Bahaguna.

## Center Hegemony versus State Autonomy

Indira Gandhi's 1980 electoral wave left intact a few bastions of opposition party control at the state level, most notably in Kashmir, West Bengal, and Tamil Nadu. These were joined by two former Congress core states in the south, Andhra Pradesh and Karnataka. On January 6, 1983, they fell to the Telugu Desam and a Janata-led alliance respectively.[12] More basic political problems existed in Assam, centering on the volatile issue of the status and rights of indigenous people versus Bengalis who are perceived as outsiders. Above all, India's most prosperous state, Punjab, became a center of violence, terrorism, and massive central government intervention.[13]

The manner in which Congress (I) behaved in each of these situations did not deviate from the pattern of personalism and centralization established earlier. Toppling the government of a state ruled by an opposition party by questionable means succeeded in Kashmir. In what was described as "a campaign of political violence," the party began a movement in January 1984 to oust its opponents in Srinagar.[14] It weaned away enough of the ruling National Conference MLAs so that a rump section of that party, supported by the Congress (I), could be installed without benefit of an Assembly vote. The action took place in July despite the opposition of the state's governor, B. K. Nehru, who was replaced by the Gandhi loyalist Jagmohan.[15]

Similar attempts in Karnataka and Andhra Pradesh failed. Karnataka's Janata Party Chief Minister tape-recorded efforts in late 1983 to buy off members of his Assembly party, resulting in what became known as "India's Watergate."[16] Andhra's case almost turned into a political Waterloo for the Congress (I) when the 20-month old Telugu Desam ministry of N. T. Rama Rao was dismissed on August 15, 1984. Like a hero in one of his approximately 300 films, Rao rebounded from increasing political criticism and a triple coronary bypass operation. He gathered his supporters in a massive campaign which he took to New Delhi. Even the pro-Gandhi *Hindustan Times* headlined its editorial "Shameful," while the neutral *Times of India* ran a front page editorial calling for the removal of the state's governor. *India Today* headlined its cover story "Democracy Betrayed." On September 16, one month after being deposed, N. T. Rama Rao returned to his *gaddi* as Chief Minister of Andhra Pradesh.[17]

National government intervention through the instrumentality of the ruling party and its control over the constitutional machinery, in these cases the centrally appointed state governors, seriously weakened genuine federalism. Punjab's situation raises the same fundamental questions concerning the nature of center-state relations. In this case, the problems are more complex and the stakes even higher than in Kashmir, Karnataka, Andhra, and in Sikkim where a popular Congress (I) Chief Minister was dismissed by New Delhi in May 1984.

The methods used by the Congress (I) to weaken its opponents provide a common strand linking Punjab to the other states. Ayesha Kagal attributes the rise of Sant Jarnail Singh Bhindranwale, the leader of the terrorist movement in Punjab, to the Congress: "The irony, of course, is that the Sant was originally a product, nurtured and marketed

by the Center to cut into the Akali Dal's spheres of influence." About
Amrik Singh, President of the All India Sikh Student Federation and
one of Bhindranwale's major lieutenants, Kagal writes that he "was
fielded against the Akali Dal's candidate Umranangal in the 1979 SGPC
[committee which controls the Sikh temples in Punjab] election."[18]
Joseph Lelyveld reports the widely held belief that Bhindranwale "had
been initially recruited into politics by Sanjay Gandhi after his mother's
fall from power in 1977."[19]

Further corroboration of the relationship between Bhindranwale and
the Congress (I) is provided by the highly respected Punjab national
columnist, Kuldip Nayar. Giani Zail Singh, Darbara Singh, and Sanjay
Gandhi are all linked to the building up of Bhindranwale as a counter
to the Akali Dal. Giani Zail Singh, Chief Minister of Punjab until the
Congress debacle of 1977, became the Home Minister of India in 1980
and, subsequently, President of India. Darbara Singh served as the
Congress (I) Chief Minister of Punjab from 1980 until the advent of
President's rule in 1983. Nayar concludes that "little did they realise at
that time that they were creating a Frankenstein."[20]

Bhindranwale's campaign of assassination and terror escalated sys-
tematically from at least September 1981 when Lala Jagat Narain, a
prominent Punjab Hindu newspaper publisher, died from a hit squad's
bullets. Bhindranwale, however, has to be distinguished from his Sikh
co-religionists in the Akali Dal. Relations between the Akali Dal and
the national Congress government were central to the climate which
enabled Bhindranwale and his followers to prosper. From the government perspective, numerous attempts at negotiation, detailed in its
*White Paper* of July 10, 1984 were not productive because of Akali Dal
intransigence and terrorist pressure. Most Sikhs and many Hindus concluded that the Congress government did not bargain in good faith, undermined possible agreements, and maintained the Punjab problem so
as to exacerbate the differences within the Akali Dal and further to
divide the Sikh community. Furthermore, an undercurrent of speculation questioned the communal aspects of the Punjab problem. As early
as 1983, serious questions were raised in India as to whether a Sikh
versus Hindu tactic was being pursued by Mrs. Gandhi in Punjab as
part of a larger strategy to gain Hindu votes in the forthcoming general
elections.[21] The fact that these questions were taken seriously indicates
the strain on India's federal institutions.

Following the June 1984 military assault on the Golden Temple in
Amritsar (Operation Bluestar), even moderate Sikhs such as
Khushwant Singh charged the Congress (I) with exploiting com-
munalism, pitting Hindus against Sikhs. "I said for once that I was not
living in a secular India but in a Hindu India," he stated in an interview.
And he concluded that he opposed "this kind of army action" as what

he feared had occurred, "a total polarisation of views between the Sikh and the Hindu."[22] Mrs. Gandhi's assassination by two of her Sikh bodyguards in October unleashed a Hindu backlash in which over 2,700 Sikhs were killed.[23] In Delhi, the hardest hit area, independent investigating teams published evidence of organized efforts involving "important politicians of the Congress (I) at the top and by authorities in the administration."[24]

Punjab provided the catalyst for the continuation of new ordinances and legislation restricting due process — in the tradition of preventive detention acts, and further limiting the federalist dimension of center-state relations. Most notable are the National Security (Second Amendment) Ordinance, promulgated on June 21, 1984, and the Terrorist Affected Area (Special Courts) Ordinance, promulgated on July 14, 1984 under which all of Punjab was declared a terrorist affected area. Both ordinances were passed by Parliament in August 1984. These acts, maintains the People's Union for Civil Liberties in Delhi, can be used "against dissenters and for narrow political ends by the ruling party."[25]

In criticizing the Terrorist Affected Area Ordinance, eminent jurist V. M. Tarkunde points to the broad definition of "terrorist." He concludes that workers who go on strike in the railways or postal service could come under the definition. Special courts under the Ordinance can hold trials *in camera* and the names of witnesses do not have to be disclosed.[26] In August 1984, the *Indian Express* reported that four special courts were to be set up in Punjab, in addition to an initial three, and noted that there were "about 5,000 cases under 'Specified Charges' registered since January 28" when the Ordinance first came into force "retrospectively."[27] A subsequent *Indian Express* editorial describes the terrorist measure as "one piece of legislation which fits in with the scenario of authoritarian rule and which must ring an alarm bell."[28]

Restrictive legislation, a centralizing national government, and the machinations of the ruling Congress Party have been at least partly checked in the past, with the exception of the Emergency, by a credible if fragmented opposition at national and state levels. This buffer has been markedly diminished. Elections in December 1984 greatly reduced opposition numbers in Parliament. Cartoonist Abu Abraham pictured the opposition as a museum piece labelled "Homo Oppositinus Indicus," while a catalog entry states, "Presumed Extinct."[29]

Only one of the so-called national parties, the CPI-M, won more than ten seats; 18 of its total of 22 came from West Bengal. Janata's total of ten is the second highest among national parties. The regional Andhra Pradesh party, Telugu Desam, emerged with 28 — the largest bloc among the opposition. Another regional party, the AIADMK from Tamil Nadu, with 12 seats ranked third. Of the national leaders only Charan Singh survived the onslaught, but in the process he lost his DMKP parliamentary party as it shrivelled to three seats. A fractious leadership made it unlikely that the truncated opposition would rapidly recover, even with the Indira sympathy wave a matter of history.

Nonetheless, regional political parties and groups continued to maintain effective if diminished areas of political power. N. T. Rama Rao's Telugu Desam rode the reaction to the abortive toppling attempt —and his own sympathy wave — to a major victory in Andhra Pradesh. His Karnataka neighbor, Ramakrishna Hegde, lost the parliamentary electoral battle but his state Janata Party remained intact, and his post-election political acumen salvaged future prospects. As a consequence of the parliamentary defeat he submitted his state government's resignation, even though his Janata Party-led coalition maintained its majority in the state assembly. This display of integrity led to a surprising response from New Delhi. Prime Minister Rajiv Gandhi requested that Hegde serve as a caretaker Chief Minister until state elections were held in March.

Tamil Nadu maintained its distinctive political character although the Congress (I) made inroads. M. G. Ramachandran's AIADMK had its turn to ally with the Congress (I) which, coupled with a sympathy vote for the ailing film star, assured continuation of the AIADMK regime. The CPI-M suffered unanticipated parliamentary defeats in urban West Bengal, but retained its rural strongholds and control of the state government. Farooq Abdullah countered the Congress (I) wave in the parliamentary elections in Kashmir, and will continue with renewed force his efforts to return his National Conference to power. Sharad Pawar similarly resisted the Congress (I) wave in Maharashtra, becoming one of the few younger opposition leaders who may be capable of building an effective party — if he does not join the Congress. Open politics in Punjab surely will see the reemergence of the Akali Dal.

In early March 1985, non-Congress (I) elements received a strong boost as a consequence of the results of assembly elections held in 11 of India's 22 states. Delinking of state and national voting, the waning of the Indira sympathy wave, local factors and issues, and perhaps even a reaction to the December 1984 landslide combined partly to restore the federal political balance.

N. T. Rama Rao's Telugu Desam and Hegde's Janata Party retained control of the southern states of Andhra Pradesh and Karnataka with increased margins. A rout of Congress (I) in the tiny Himalayan state of Sikkim, where it won only one of 32 seats, is attributable to the earlier dismissal of Chief Minister Nar Bahadur Bhandari by the Congress (I).[30] The credible showing of opposition parties in seven of eight states retained by the Congress (I) is significant. Only in Gujarat did the party increase its percentage of popular votes over the parliamentary elections. A radical change in neighboring Maharashtra reduced Congress

(I) seats from 186 to 162. Moreover, the party is now confronted by Sharad Pawar's Congress (S) with 58 seats, as part of the Progressive Democratic Front (which he leads) with 106 seats.

Perhaps the most important contrast with the parliamentary elections is the return of the opposition to the Hindi heartland, India's electoral core. Congress (I) recorded a drop of almost 25 percent from its parliamentary landslide in Uttar Pradesh, Bihar, Madhya Pradesh, and Rajasthan. Charan Singh's earlier version of the DMKP won 59 seats in the Uttar Pradesh assembly in 1980. This time it won 85, and increased its strength in Bihar from 37 to 44. By contrast, it won only three seats nationwide in the parliamentary elections.

One Indian commentator summarized the significance of the March 1985 assembly elections by stating that "the Opposition pulled itself up by the bootstraps from the pit to which it had been relegated in December."[31] Electoral waves may swamp, but they do not drown opposition parties and groups. Leadership and party name changes certainly will occur by the year 2000 and new splits and amalgamations will occur, but the social and issue support bases will remain.

## Two Scenarios

The nature of center-state relations to the end of the century will depend on the course charted and pursued by Prime Minister Rajiv Gandhi in his first term. Two different scenarios may follow the initial period of rule by the third member of the Nehru dynasty. One possible outcome is continuation of the personalism and centralizing pattern established by Indira Gandhi. The other is a return to accommodation politics, with a conscious effort to reverse centralizing tendencies which have reduced inexorably the federal elements of center-state relations as well as the delegation of power within the central government itself.

Holding onto power and enhancing it almost regardless of means is the modus operandi of the continuation of the personalism and centralizing scenario. Rajiv certainly made known his displeasure with some of his brother's political cronies. Some were forced out of office; others were denied Congress tickets to contest the parliamentary and assembly elections. Whether these actions reflect political style and social backgrounds, or signify conscious efforts to reestablish more democratic norms remains to be seen. It is clear that Rajiv increasingly became the center of power, quickly developing his own coterie — including the Doon School group.

Sharing that power may be as difficult for Rajiv as it was for his mother. His first post-election appointments resulted in the dismissal

of Finance Minister Pranab Mukherjee, Special Assistant to the Prime
Minister R. K. Dhawan, and the downgrading of Khan Chowdhury from
Railways Minister to one of the general secretaries of the Congress
Party. One of his inner Doon School group, Arun Nehru, did not receive
an expected Cabinet appointment. Instead, the quip in Delhi was that
he was shunted from the center of power to a second-level ministerial
position in the Ministry of Power. One interpretation of these changes
is that Rajiv simply is selecting his own team rather than warding off
potential rivals. Nonetheless, he stood virtually alone as his administration began. Nor did he alter the powerful role of the Prime Minister's
secretariat.

Another aspect of Rajiv's ability to enhance personal power was manifest during the immediate post-assassination period, the ensuing election campaign, and the opening weeks of the new term. Rajiv Gandhi
is enormously effective on television and radio. A new adjective may
be added to his existing characterizations as Mr. Clean and Mr. Efficient; he is also Mr. Cool. His composure during the turmoil following
the assassination, and the soft, reassuring manner in subsequent tele-
casts and broadcasts to the nation, greatly impressed almost all who
saw or heard him.

More ominous, considering the heightened sense of communalism
stemming from the Punjab developments, is the nature of the Congress
(I)'s election campaign. The new leader relentlessly hammered on the
theme of the unity and integrity of India. To many, these were code
words for a secessionist threat seemingly posed by Sikhs in Punjab. At
the same time, Gandhi appeared to spread this blanket indictment over
the opposition by criticizing it for being sympathetic to Akali Dal demands. The strength of his message, reinforced by powerful party election posters stressing this theme, gained the support of even some
Rashtriya Sevak Sangh (RSS) elements which normally support only
the Hindu-oriented Bharatiya Janata Party (erstwhile Jana Sangh).
Certainly, the Hindu backlash or Hindu factor was channeled toward
support of the Congress (I).[32]

In sum, the personalist, centralizing scenario presents a new individual employing his own style, but a continuation of the old pattern.
Although public policy may be more coherent, more efficient methods
of administration may develop, and Rajiv may be less abrasive even to
his opponents than was his mother, it is nevertheless possible that he
is driven by the same compulsion to centralize power under his personal
control as was his mother. Consciously or subconsciously, he may con-
clude that centralizing and consolidating power is the only way to maintain the unity of India. Problems confronting him during the first
months of his regime included not only those in Punjab and Assam, but

anti-reservationist riots in Gujarat, communal problems in Maharashtra, the aftermath of the Union Carbide tragedy in Bhopal, Sikh terrorist activity in Delhi and adjoining states, and further Tamil-Sinhalese violence in Sri Lanka with its south India spillover. As Pran Chopra said of Rajiv's mother in 1983, he may lose interest in the art of the politics of accommodation.[33]

Another scenario, also possible for the year 2000, could return India to accommodation politics and revitalize center-state relations. It can be argued that the intensity of Mrs. Gandhi's thrust toward personalism and centralization was in fact contrary to other basic forces in modern India, that it was an aberration abetted by a series of extraordinary events and her own personality.

Susanne and Lloyd Rudolph boldly stated in 1980 that "the most striking feature of Indian politics is its persistent centrism" with its dominant party relying on "a pluralist basis of support."[34] In brief, their seven major points stressed a weak class consciousness, the fragmentation of the "confessional" or religious majority, the electoral strength of religious and social minorities, the political strength of "bullock capitalists" and "backward classes," the imperative of capturing power in Delhi, the constraints imposed by cultural diversity and social pluralism in the federal system, and the advantages conferred on a centrist national party by the electoral system.[35]

An even more striking and surprising case, emphasizing centrism rather than extremism with concomitant decentralizing union-state consequences, is made by Paul Brass. He examines various data that connect pluralism, regionalism, and decentralizing tendencies in center-state relations.[36] These include newspaper circulation by language, the transfer of resources from the center to the states by the Finance and Planning commissions, election statistics, and the incidence of imposition of President's rule. Certainly Brass is no apologist for Prime Minister Indira Gandhi; to the contrary, he persuasively points up her efforts toward centralization. Nonetheless, he stresses that she neither became free from the need for support from "regionally powerful rural landowning castes" nor from dependence on the states — whose instability resulted at least partly from her centralizing efforts. Except for an authoritarian option, he concludes "that centralization and consolidation of power in India's federal parliamentary system are bound to be ephemeral. . . ." Authoritarianism and centralization are not viable options as they "promise ultimately a violent breakdown."[37]

Rajiv Gandhi's style, particularly following the elections, can be seen as reinforcing a more accommodating, centrist approach to society and politics. Bhabani Sen Gupta emphasizes the positive traits displayed by a young Prime Minister representing a new generation and benefitting from a massive mandate: "As the medium is the message, so is political style the political leader. Rajiv Gandhi has suddenly changed the political climate of India from one of confrontation to conciliation."[38] He contrasts Rajiv's signficant freedom of action with Indira Gandhi's dependence on the Syndicate as she became Prime Minister in 1966. Rajiv has been able to make significant changes of personnel who "in the public eye [were] symbols of political amorality and arbitrary use of power."[39] Even Charan Singh, normally a vitriolic critic of the ruling party, gave the new government high marks: "They have begun well and with humility."[40] A new leadership presents the opportunity for new initiatives, or even processing old initiatives more effectively. The term, "a healing touch," is now a cliche in India; nevertheless, given the continuing regional and social problems, it is precisely such a touch that is needed.

Significant first steps toward reconciliation and accommodation with the Sikhs were taken by Gandhi early in 1985. Eight major imprisoned Akali Dal leaders were released on March 11 and Arjun Singh, a confidante of the Prime Minister and a respected political leader, became the new Governor of Punjab even as it continued under central rule. Recognizing the interrelationship between Sikh and broader Punjab concerns, the Prime Minister visited Punjab and announced an economic package for the troubled state which includes an integral railway coach factory, the first major heavy industrial plant for the state.[41]

Three specific Akali Dal demands were at least partially redressed on April 11. Justice Ranganath Mishra was appointed to head a Commission of Inquiry into the allegations of organized violence against Sikhs following Mrs. Gandhi's assassination. The government lifted the year-old ban on the All India Sikh Student Federation and stated it would release more jailed Sikhs. In early 1985, at least 1,200 were under detention.[42] Somewhat euphorically, *India Today* concluded that "in one stroke the most relevant demands of the Sikhs had been conceded."[43] In fact, there are a number of issues that remain to be negotiated and, equally important, implemented. Moreover, renewed terrorism, first in Chandigarh, and then in Delhi and the nearby states of Haryana, Rajasthan and Uttar Pradesh, will test the patience, skill, and accommodative abilities of all parties.[44,45]


**Continuing State Pressure**

Regardless of which scenario dominates the next fifteen years, center-state relations will continue to be first order concerns for the Indian polity. These are old, persistent issues regardless of the age and inclinations of the political leadership. The appointment of the Sarkaria Commission in March 1983 — Mr. R. S. Sarkaria being a retired Supreme Court Justice in the Indian tradition — is merely the latest in a series of individuals or groups charged with examining center-state relations, beginning with the drafters of the Indian Constitution.

In the 1960s, the Administrative Reforms Commission concluded that existing constitutional provisions "are adequate" for the functioning of harmonious relations between the center and the states. Nonetheless, the Commission did recommend measures, including an interstate council, to enhance the management of center-state relations. The proposed council would have included the Prime Minister as chair, the Ministers for Home and Finance, the Leader of the Opposition in the Lok Sabha — or another individual elected by the opposition — and one representative each from the five zonal councils. Invitations to a cabinet minister or a Chief Minister concerned with a subject under consideration were envisioned. Neither the Congress nor Janata regimes was, however, inclined to implement the recommendation.[46]

A detailed reexamination and extensive recommendations were provided by the Rajamannar committee appointed by the Tamil Nadu government in 1969. Dr. P. V. Rajamannar headed an inquiry committee charged to "examine the entire question regarding the relationship that should subsist between the Center and the States in a federal setup." Its 1971 report contains an extensive listing of recommended changes, with proposed constitutional amendments designed to give more autonomy to the states within a continuing federal system.[47]

Chief Minister Jyoti Basu of West Bengal was unsuccessful in a 1977 attempt to persuade the Janata Party government of Prime Minister Morarji Desai to reconsider center-state relations. In a covering letter to a detailed submission by the state government, Basu wrote:

> The unity of our country has been subjected to considerable strain during the last few years. This, in our view, has been caused mostly by an overbearing and, if I may add, obsessive preoccupation on the part of those who were in authority at the Centre to concentrate all power and responsibilities in their hands.[48]

Another attempt to review and recommend changes in center-state relations took place during the period of Janata rule, when all five southern Chief Ministers met in Bangalore on July 16, 1978. The six resolutions forwarded to the center by Tamil Nadu's Chief Minister, M. G. Ramachandran, included non-imposition of Hindi on non-Hindi speaking people, protection of the interests of linguistic and cultural minorities, an increase in fiscal allocations to the states with a review of this subject by a committee of the National Development Council, parity in the subsidy for wheat and rice, and a regional wage policy. The Congress (I) Chief Ministers from Karnataka and Andhra Pradesh joined in this collective but again unsuccessful effort.[49]

In addition to the various governmental bodies to have examined and recommended changes in center-state relations, innumerable academic meetings have dwelt on this subject. One example will suffice, selected because it illustrates the intensity of feeling as well as a focus on the Planning Commission. At a five-day seminar on center-state relations organized by the Tamil Nadu Academy of Political Science in Madras in January 1984, the eminent jurist Nani Palkhivala criticized the Planning Commission in his keynote address. He asserted that it "had arrogated to itself the right to allocate almost 70% of the central resources to the States, which was wholly unconstitutional and the States must have the courage to stand up to this body."[50]

As one looks back at the mid-1980s from the perspective of the year 2000, the continual pressure to readjust center-state relations to changing times will be seen as the impetus for significant adaptations. Undoubtedly, the Sarkaria Commission will be utilized by Rajiv Gandhi's government in an attempt to cope with its most immediate crisis in Punjab. A revised list of demands, as presented in the various Akali Dal Anandpur Sahib resolutions, probably will be its first order of business. Certainly, no national government will accept all of the initial demands — restricting central authority to defense, foreign affairs, communications, railways, and currency — as set forth in October 1973.

Simple rejection or acceptance of the Anandpur Sahib resolutions is not the issue; in fact, there is no one document embodying all the demands.[51] What Anandpur Sahib signifies is that the Akali Dal, like many groups through time and throughout the country, wants a reconsideration of center-state relationships, as well as of specific matters relating to Sikhs. Many of the demands were conceded in principle by the government, either in negotiations or in statements by authoritative officials. Thus, they would appear to be negotiable if the political climate is minimally conducive to rational discourse. The Sarkaria Commission can be inordinately valuable in this process, as well as in regard to comparable concerns found in most states.

A regularized process for continual reconsideration of center-state concerns may be in place by the year 2000, in addition to such already established machinery as the Planning Commission, Finance Commission, and other government bodies which are viewed by the states as operating from an overly-centralized perspective. At the same time, the unwillingness or political inability of the states to make more effective use of their own taxing powers, e.g., with regard to agricultural production, will increase their dependence on central resources.

Punjab's situation in the 1980s underlines the need for effective institutions. All authoritative institutions virtually collapsed in the state in the period from the summer of 1981 to the army action in June 1984. Political parties, including both the Akali Dal and the Congress, the state government, the police, and the bureaucracy lost their authority, enabling Sant Jarnail Singh Bhindranwale increasingly to fill the growing void. India cannot afford to continue to use the military as often or as intensively as in the last few years if a civilian regime is to continue. Between 1980 and 1983, "the Army went to the aid of civil power on as many as 747 occasions — of which 350 account for internal security and law and order." Another 137 were for disaster relief, 39 for maintenance of essential services, and the others fall in the miscellaneous category.[52]

Revitalizing the institutions and performance of the dominant party is one alternative to increased reliance on the military. During Indira Gandhi's personalist and centralist reign, Congress party institutions atrophied. Party elections were not held after 1972. Prime Minister Rajiv Gandhi has taken the first steps toward rebuilding; in May 1985, at a meeting of the All India Congress Committee in New Delhi, he announced that a list of Congress members would be published by December and elections would take place in 1986.[53]

Effective governance is essential if India is to continue its proud tradition of civilian and democratic rule. The federal dilemma is that increasing complexities in the political, economic, and social spheres reinforce the pressures for centralization. At the same time, mobilization and politicization of formerly dormant groups such as the backward castes, the *harijans*, and the tribals, as well as the various "sons of the soil" movements, result in still more demands for resources and political access.[54] In such circumstances, an adequate and acceptable response by government and political institutions is increasingly difficult.

India will not have found a solution by the year 2000 to what is in reality an old problem for this heterogeneous society. One may be cautiously optimistic, however, that an opportunity now exists to move significantly to cope with the dilemma by enhancing the role of the states in a manner that enhances the effectiveness of the national government. Engaging in adjustment and adaptation within a federal structure is not necessarily a zero sum game.

## NOTES

1. W. H. Morris-Jones, "India — More Questions Than Answers," *Asian Survey*, August 1984, p. 811.

2. This analysis benefits from my opportunity to conduct post-election research in India in December 1984 and January 1985. I gratefully acknowledge financial support from the Smithsonian Institution, although all opinions and conclusions are my own.

3. For the most detailed statement of the system, see Rajni Kothari, *Politics in India*, Boston, Little, Brown and Co., 1970. Restated with some changes in "The Congress System Revisited: A Decennial Review," *Asian Survey*, December 1974, pp. 1035-54. For an earlier, and somewhat similar model, see O. P. Goyal and Paul Wallace, "The Congress Party — A Conceptual Study," *India Quarterly*, April–June 1964, pp. 180-201.

4. Joseph Lelyveld contrasts "the self-perpetuating dynastic figure she became and the painfully insecure woman she usually seemed when she was just getting used to her job as Prime Minister." *The New York Times Magazine*, December 2, 1984.

5. For descriptions and analysis of the Emergency period, see the following: Henry C. Hart, editor, *Indira Gandhi's India: A Political System Reappraised*, Boulder, Colorado, Westview Press, 1976; W. H. Morris-Jones, "Creeping But Uneasy Authoritarianism: India, 1975-76," *Government and Opposition*, Winter 1977, pp. 20-41; J. Anthony Lukas, "India Is As Indira Does," *The New York Times Magazine*, April 4, 1976; Paul Wallace, "Centralisation and Depoliticisation in South Asia," *The Journal of Commonwealth and Comparative Politics*, March 1978, pp. 3-21.

6. Kenneth C. Wheare, *Federal Government*, 3rd edition, London, Oxford University Press, 1953.

7. K. Iyengar Santhanam, *Union-State Relations in India*, New York, Asia Publishing House, 1961.

8. P. K. Bhargava, "Transfers From the Center to the States in India," *Asian Survey*, June 1984, pp. 666-668.

9. *The New York Times*, November 3, 1976.

10. Former Minister of Community Development, S. K. Dey, concluded in 1977 that *panchayati raj* institutions remained, but "as skeletons devoid of soul or substance with not even an election in ten years and more in most states." S. K. Dey, "Rural India — A Reminder," *The Tribune* (Chandigarh), May 14, 1977.

11. Rajni Kothari, *Democratic Polity and Social Change in India: Crisis and Opportunities*, Bombay, Allied Publishers, 1976, p. 25.

12. *The New York Times*, January 7, 1983.

13. For the government version, see Government of India, *White Paper on the Punjab Agitation*, New Delhi, July 10, 1984. An unqualified indictment of government policy and actions is presented by Sachchidanand Sinha, Jasvir Singh, Sunil, and G. K. C. Reddy in *Army Action in Punjab: Prelude & Aftermath*, New Delhi, Samata Era Publications, 1984. Two of the better journalistic efforts are by Kuldip Nayar and Khushwant Singh, *Tragedy of Punjab: Operations Bluestar & After*, New Delhi, Vision Books Pvt. Ltd., 1984; and Amarjit Kaur, et al., *The Punjab Story*, New Delhi, Roli Books International, 1984. Also see Paul Wallace, "The Dilemma of Sikh Revivalism: Identity vs. Political Power," forthcoming in *Fundamentalism, Revivalists, and Violence in South Asia*, edited by James W. Björkman, Riverdale, Maryland, The Riverdale Company, 1987.

14. Mary Ann Weaver, *The Christian Science Monitor*, February 7, 1984.

15. Detailed coverage is provided by the cover story in *India Today*, July 31, 1984, pp. 8-14.

16. *The Christian Science Monitor*, February 7, 1984.

17. *India Today*, September 15, 1984, pp. 6-17, and October 15, 1984, pp. 12-14.

18. Ayesha Kagal, *The Times of India*, September 12, 1982.

19. *The New York Times Magazine*, December 2, 1984.

20. Kuldip Nayar and Khushwant Singh, *op. cit.*, p. 31.

21. National columnist Pran Chopra wrote in 1983 that "there is bound to be a Hindu backlash." Hindus, he writes, "have herded under the Congress (I) umbrella, since Mrs. Gandhi has so well cast herself now in the image of a Hindu goddess. Herding them [Hindus] in is one part of Mrs. Gandhi's motives, as it was in Jammu too; another part is to use 'insecurity' on the border for beating her drum of 'India in danger'." *Illustrated Weekly of India*, December 11, 1983, p. 11.

22. Interview with Khushwant Singh in *Choice* (New Delhi), September 1984, p. 8.

23. *The New York Times*, March 16, 1985.

24. *Who Are The Guilty? Report of a Joint Inquiry into the Causes and Impact of the Riots in Delhi from 31 October to 10 November*, New Delhi, People's Union for Democratic Rights and People's Union for Civil Liberties, 1984, p. 1.

25. *Black Laws 1984: The Terrorist Affected Areas (Special Courts) Ordinance, Ordinances Amending the National Security Act*, New Delhi, People's Union for Civil Liberties, August 1984.

26. *Ibid.*, p. 9.

27. *The Indian Express*, August 26, 1984.

28. P. A. Sebastian, *The Indian Express*, October 8, 1984.

29. *India Today*, January 31, 1985, p. 18.

30. *The New York Times*, March 7, 1985; *India Today*, March 31, 1985, pp. 8-21.

31. Sumit Mitra, *India Today*, *ibid.*, p. 19.

32. For a clear analysis written shortly before the elections, see D. L. Sheth, "Wooing the Hindu Voter," *Indian Express Magazine*, December 9, 1984, p. 1. A contrary view is expressed in *Sunday*, January 6-19, 1985, pp. 26-27.

33. Pran Chopra, *op. cit.*, p. 8.

34. Susanne Hoeber Rudolph and Lloyd I. Rudolph, "The Centrist Future of Indian Politics," *Asian Survey*, June 1980, p. 575.

35. *Ibid.*, pp. 575-594.

36. Paul R. Brass, "Pluralism, Regionalism, and Decentralizing Tendencies in Contemporary Indian Politics," in *The States of South Asia: Problems of National Integration*, edited by A. Jeyaratnam Wilson and Dennis Dalton, Honolulu, The University Press of Hawaii, 1982, pp. 223-264.

37. *Ibid.*, pp. 238-239.

38. Bhabani Sen Gupta, "The New Politics," *India Today*, January 31, 1985, p. 59.

39. *Ibid.*

40. In his interview, he did add the fear that Rajiv "may follow in the footsteps of his mother who followed a megalomaniacal policy based on elitist philosophies." *India Today*, January 31, 1985, p. 21.

41. *The New York Times*, March 17, 1985; *The Christian Science Monitor*, April 1, 1985.

42. *The New York Times*, April 12, 1985; *India News*, May 6, 1985.

43. *India Today*, April 30, 1985, p. 8.

44. Krishan Lal Marchanda, a Hindu leader, and a Sikh student leader were gunned down in Chandigarh. *The Christian Science Monitor*, April 1, 1985.

45. Bombs within booby-trapped transistor radio cases were placed primarily in bus and train stations. Delhi served as the major target with at least 19 bomb blasts. Explosions with a heavy toll of death and injury took place on May 10 and 11. "The Return of Terrorism," *India Today*, May 31, 1985, pp. 8-19.

46. K. K. Katyal, "Centre-State Relations," *The Hindu* (Madras), March 28, 1983.

47. Anirudh Prasad, *Centre and State Powers Under Indian Federalism*, New Delhi, Deep and Deep Publications, 2nd edition, 1984, pp. 274-284. All of its recommendations are reproduced in this section.

48. K. K. Katyal, *op. cit.;* S. K. Sahay, "The Sarkaria Commission," *The Statesman*, March 31, 1983. The full text of "West Bengal's Memorandum on Centre-State Powers" is contained in Prasad, *op. cit.*, pp. 287-292. It was adopted by the West Bengal Government on December 1, 1977 and circulated to other state governments and leaders with the intent to initiate a national debate on center-state relations.

49. K. K. Katyal, *op. cit.*

50. *The Statesman*, January 7, 1984.

51. For the various versions of what generally is referred to as the Anandpur Sahib Resolution see: Government of India, *White Paper on the Punjab Agitation, op. cit.*, pp. 88-97; Prasad, *op. cit.*, p. 286.

52. G. C. Katoch, "Soldiers as Policemen: Peril in Riding the Military Tiger," *The Statesman*, January 18, 1985, p. 4. See also the perceptive article by Giri Deshingkar, "Growing Insurgency," *Seminar*, January 1985, pp. 37-41.

53. James Traub, "The Sorry State of India," *The New Republic*, June 4, 1984, p. 21; *India Today*, May 31, 1985, p. 22.

54. See Myron Weiner, *Sons of the Soil: Migration and Ethnic Conflict in India*, Princeton, N.J., Princeton University Press and Delhi, Oxford University Press, 1978.

Part Four

# The Economy:
# The Pursuit of
# Growth With Equity

Chapter Nine

# The Economic Outlook For India

RAJ KRISHNA

*Editor's Note: Professor Raj Krishna died suddenly of a heart
attack in Rome on May 20, 1985. He was still working on a final
draft of this paper. The essay printed here is based largely on a
transcript of his original presentation in Austin on February 9,
1985. There has been some rearrangement of material and a few
connecting sentences have been inserted, but his arguments and
conclusions stand as delivered. Professor Susan Hadden was of
invaluable assistance in helping to prepare the transcript for
publication.*

I have been asked to write about the economic outlook for India in the
year 2000, but that topic is much too large for one essay. Therefore, I
propose to narrow it by focusing on three dimensions of economic development: growth, investment, and poverty. This means that I will
not discuss many other important aspects of development, including unemployment, self-reliance, structural change, regional shifts, and
technological progress. Growth, investment, and poverty are most critical and in many ways form the context for discussing any of the other
factors.

## Growth

The economic outlook for India is strongly dependent on economic
growth. We economists make projections into the future to see how
different factors will affect growth. Projections can be made from
trends or by use of a full-scale model. Four or five groups have already
constructed models that attempt to project critical numbers for the Indian economy for the year 2000: these include the Operations Research
Group at Baroda; the Second India Group; the National Committee of
Science and Technology; the Planning Commission in the Sixth Plan
document; and the Centre for Policy Research. I will be using some of
their numbers, although most of them have already become obsolete.
The actual performance of the economy has shown that all of these models have underestimated growth in population, growth in investment,
and the capital-output ratio. In any case, the growth rate was never
determined by the models; it was exogenously assumed and the models
only worked out the implications of alternative growth rates.

Simpler ways of projecting trends are often useful, particularly because India, addicted as it is to stability, has shown very stable trends.
I have elsewhere listed some 10 or 12 critical growth rates and ratios
which have been unusually stable in India over the last 20 to 30 years.
The economic growth rate has been stuck at 3.55 percent; the growth

rate of agricultural output at 2.6 percent; the Gini coefficient (which measures inequality, in this case of rural land distribution) at 0.65 percent; the rural poverty ratio (according to one estimate) at 58 percent; the urban poverty ratio at 50 percent; and the unemployment rate at 8.2 percent. The allocation of investment between sectors has been very stable. The foreign trade to GNP ratio has also been stable. What is most telling, the proportion of the labor force in agriculture has not diminished significantly. All around us in Asia it has declined noticeably from around 70 percent to 40 percent, but in India it remained at 69 percent in the census of 1981. In fact it has been stuck at around 70 to 72 percent, not only in recent decades but since the census of 1911. We are indeed a very stable society and, as the agricultural labor force numbers suggest, this record of stability in crucial parameters is unusual in the history of development.

One can easily project these stable growth rates and come up with some numbers for the year 2000. The only thing to do then is to assess whether there is reason to believe that there will be significant departures from the trends. The examples above do not include three parameters that have been unstable. Unlike the agricultural growth rate, the growth rate of industry has not been stable; it declined from seven percent in the 1950s to six percent in the 1960s to 4.5 percent in the 1970s. The capital-output ratio has not been stable. It has risen from 3.4 to nearly six. This means that it now takes six rupees to generate one rupee of national income. The investment rate has gone up dramatically, from 11 percent in the First Plan to 24 percent in the Sixth Plan.

Thus, three crucial parameters — the investment rate, the capital-output ratio, and the industrial growth rate — have shown remarkable trends. It is important to notice, however, that two of these cancel one another. The rise in the investment rate meant that more capital was available for development, but the rise in the capital-output ratio meant that inefficiency in the use of capital rose correspondingly, leaving the overall rate of growth unchanged at 3.55 percent.

What do these numbers mean for the growth outlook? The short-run rate of growth in the Sixth Plan period (1980-1985) has been about 4.1 percent, a little higher than the long-run trend. Although officially it was frequently claimed that the short-run rate was more than five percent, the Seventh Plan quantitative frame accepted the 4.1 percent figure. Does this improved performance of the last five years suggest a structural change in the growth rate? The short answer is no. Although there was a high rate of growth in 1983-84, the long run rate from 1951 to 1985 has not really changed from about 3.5 percent. The rate probably will not change, even with the four percent short-term growth rate achieved in the last five years and in 1984-85 because of bumper crops.

There have been six previous occasions since independence when the yearly rate of growth has exceeded four percent, but invariably above-average years have been followed by below-average ones and the long-run average remains the same. From this previous experience, we know that if we can maintain a four percent rate of growth over two entire plan periods, or obtain an explosively high rate of about seven percent during a single period, then there will be a statistically significant jump in the long-run growth rate.

The stable, low rate of long-run growth that has prevailed has allowed only a 1.3 percent rate of growth in per capita income. This statistic is very low if we compare it with the growth in per capita income in other countries: India ranks 56th out of 80 developing countries, or 80th out of 106 countries if we include the advanced nations. If this trend continues, our present $260 per capita will be only $328 by the year 2000. In contrast, China, which started after the revolution at roughly the same per capita income as India at independence, at $310 already exceeds our per capita income. From 1968 to 1982, a period of 22 years, growth in China's per capita income averaged five percent annually, despite the excesses of the pre-Deng period. By 2000, China's per capita income will be $746. Middle income countries have been increasing income at 3.6 percent and will have per capita incomes around $3,000 in the year 2000.

More important than a comparison with other countries, however, is the fact that the low growth in per capita income is unacceptable if we ever hope to reduce poverty. China is especially striking, because there per capita income has increased at four times the Indian rate. Even if we raise our overall growth rate to four percent and our per capita growth rate to two percent, income would be only $371; it would take an overall growth rate of about 4.5 percent before poverty would begin to diminish, and even then per capita income would be only $574 at the end of the century.

What role has agriculture played in India's growth? At least it has not hindered, and many commentators believe that it has aided. Agriculture is one of the sectors with a stable growth rate: a steady 2.6 percent per year, both before and after the Green Revolution. Before, growth in agriculture arose from increases in the amount of land under cultivation; afterwards, it came from increases in the productivity of land already in use. This rate is sufficient to enable India to meet its food requirements to the year 2000, whether measured in minimum amounts for subsistence — 385 grams per day per capita — or the 500 grams per day maximum which has been proposed. We are already producing in excess of the maximum requirements. If the present rate of growth is maintained over the next 15 years, India will have a food supply adequate to meet the maximum caloric needs of 1.05 billion people.

Not only is a 2.6 percent rate of growth sufficient for agriculture, it would be very difficult to achieve a higher rate than that. The post-Green Revolution growth has come from very high rates of increase in three critical inputs: 10 percent annual growth in the area planted with high yielding varieties, 10 percent growth in the availability of nitrogen/potassium/phosphorus fertilizer, and about 2.3 million hectares added to irrigated areas every year. This irrigation increase is one of the highest recorded anywhere and India has reached it each year for five years. The other rates are also high, but the increase in irrigation alone is almost enough to ensure that Indian agriculture can continue to grow at 2.6 percent per year.

The agricultural picture is bright in another way. Based on achievements in demonstration plots, yields of most crops can be increased by two to 11 times. Not only is this substantial increase possible, but there are some 60 million acres of irrigable land still to be brought under cultivation. Professor C. S. Shah's projection shows that even if all irrigation potential is utilized in the next 15 years, the rate of growth of agricultural output will still be 2.5 percent. In contrast with overall growth, India's ability to maintain an annual agricultural growth rate of 2.6 percent is an exceptional achievement; even Japan's output grew at only 2.2 percent. In developed nations long-term agricultural growth is much less than two percent, although some have experienced short periods of increase of three or even four percent.

Continuing success in agriculture will be increasingly costly. In the last 13 years the cost of each unit of output in agriculture has risen by 32 percent. Normally technological change brings down the cost, but this has not occurred in India; the excellent growth rate has taken place despite increased costs. In fact, recent studies demonstrate — contrary to common belief — that the capital-output ratio has always been higher in agriculture than in industry despite the apparent capital intensity of industry.

To sum up, growth in India has been slow, and has not reached levels which will allow it to overcome both poverty and increases in population. Agriculture has been a bright spot in the overall picture, but the industrial sector has not contributed as it might have, despite a high rate of investment. Let us consider why this is the case.

## Investment

In contrast to the rather dismal growth picture is the fact, already noted, that the investment rate proportional to GNP has risen remarkably, from 11 percent to 24 percent. This extraordinary jump is the result of very heavy taxation, nationalization of banking, and other institutional devices. Although reaching a 24 percent rate is a great achievement for a poor country, it is obvious that this growth cannot continue. The best we can expect in the next five years, the Seventh Plan period, is that it may average 25 percent, which is what the Planning Commission is projecting. In later plan periods the rate may rise to 27 or 28 percent at most, where it will level off for a long time. In the development literature there are only a few countries (and among the low income countries only China) which have achieved a saving rate over 23 percent and a concomitant investment rate of 26 percent. Therefore, it is not surprising that the model builders underestimated the investment rate in India.

Similarly, no one expected the capital-output ratio to rise to six. As noted, that rise cancels growth in investment, because more units of capital are required to obtain the same amount of growth. Again, planners were reluctant to admit this rate, but in the Seventh Plan quantitative frame a 5.6 capital-output ratio is accepted. Unfortunately, it is difficult to change the whole pathology that underlies the inefficient use of capital in India. Therefore, it is unlikely that the ratio will fall much below five and it is possible that it will stay at six.

The pathology of inefficient capital use is complex, but two basic components are the lag in project completion and the low capacity utilization. Most observers of the Indian economy note that very few projects are finished on time; it seems to take seven to 25 years to finish a project which takes fewer years elsewhere. Out of 192 major irrigation projects started between 1951 and 1980, only 42 have been completed. This is also true for coal, power, and other critical industries. Delay raises the capital costs of producing the desired output, both because the goods cannot be produced until the project is completed and because the cost of capital rises with inflation over the life of the project.

Even after capacity is installed, the Indian economy utilizes it at a very low level. In the power sector, it is a world-wide scandal that India's power capacity utilization ratio varies between 45 and 47 percent; that is, capital has been invested to generate 100 units but it is generating only 45 to 47 units. As in other matters, Bihar holds the lowest utilization record at 37 percent. The capital-output ratio will of course be very high if capital is locked up unproductively in unfinished projects or is not fully utilized when projects are finally completed.

Because growth, the capital-output ratio, and investment are all interrelated, we can use them to make predictions. If the capital-output ratio remains between five and six, the growth rate cannot go much higher than 5.4 percent; it will range downward from that figure to 4.3 percent. Therefore, the critical question is whether the capital-output ratio in India can be reduced. This requires a major policy and managerial revolution because, contrary to common belief, the ratio has not been rising as a result of capital being switched to more capital-intensive sectors. In fact, three-fourths of the rise is due to the increase in inefficiency of capital use rather than to switching of capital.

Considering especially the industrial sector, the revolution that will lower the capital-output ratio has two features. First, government must rationalize and reduce its controls over investment. There are 86 different enactments and control agencies to be satisfied by an investor before he can set up a plant; about 28 agencies have control over daily operations. In light of this, it is more surprising that the rate of industrial growth is so high than that it is so low. Many committees have recommended reduction in controls, but they have not been reduced and the reason is obvious. Originally set up in accord with Fabian socialism, which dominated economic planning in India even before independence, the controls now create the livelihood of a class of 16.4 million people, mostly government employees, many of whom will lose income if controls are reduced. Rather than ideology, controls are maintained as the class interest of a "third class," identified by Marx as part of the transition to mature capitalism. Elsewhere, I have quoted extensively from Marx's texts to show that the mid-nineteenth century examples he and Engels examined conformed to this description of Indian bureaucracy.

Second, the state must abandon its monopolies in critical sectors except in the case of weapons. Many public enterprises are generating losses. They are not generating surpluses and their services are of poor quality. One justification for state monopoly is to provide services that the private sector would not otherwise provide, or to ensure that these services are priced so as to be widely accessible. Yet, public sector pricing in India has become consumer-exploiting, monopolistic pricing of the worst kind. Pricing of public utilities is now a mode of taxation. A tool for promoting economic equality has become the captive of a class-based state.

In general, denationalization of industry is not necessary; more important is to revolutionize management in the public sector. We must rid ourselves of the idea that officers of the Indian Administrative Service can do anything from diplomacy to development to electronics to fertilizer. At present, by the time an officer understands something about fertilizer he is shifted to power and then to shipbuilding. At any given moment the absence of relevant knowledge by managers is guaranteed.

A management revolution can be achieved in several ways. One is to allow officers to develop and use their expertise. If for some reason this is not feasible, agencies can contract with professional managers to run their operations. Another means of achieving more efficiency is to build into the public sector incentives for performance and punishment for non-performance. Now, inefficient managers can only be promoted or transferred, and they carry inefficiency or corruption with them to the new post. But such change runs counter to the interest of a large class, and it will take strong government action to impose it. Statements by some in the new government indicate that there is understanding of this problem.


## Poverty

Discussions about growth and investment depend strongly on data. Almost unique in the developing world, India has a long time series record of the number of people below the poverty line. The Chinese, in contrast, have never conducted annual consumer surveys or sought to measure poverty, or if they did the results were never published. India conducts consumer surveys every year and measures poverty regularly, so that at this point we have 13 separate observations from the 1961-1970 period. This means that it has been relatively easy to show that little progress has been made in the struggle against poverty. Perhaps this is the reason surveys are now conducted only at five year intervals and the results are published after about six years. The 1983 results will be available, I hope, in 1990!

As in the United States, there are different standards by which to measure poverty. One measure uses Rs. 15 of expenditure per capita per month for rural people and Rs. 20 for urban dwellers, based on 1961 prices. In 1980, these levels were Rs. 76 for rural people and Rs. 88 for urban. This means that, in 1980 prices, we are talking about a poverty line drawn at a maximum expenditure of two and one-half to three rupees per day.

Because of the discrepancies in obtaining and interpreting data different observers discern different poverty ratios; lower figures show 48.5 percent of people below the poverty line while higher figures show 57 percent below. Percentages must always be considered along with absolute numbers. Using the lower set of figures, we get an annual increase of 3.7 million people below the poverty line; using the higher, 5.8 million people are added every year to the poverty category.

In 1978, official estimates of poverty ranged between 309 and 371 million; the Sixth Plan document mentions 320 million. If we assume that increases will continue at the same rate, we reach the frightening conclusion that there will be 390 million Indians below the poverty line in the year 2000. It is frightening because such a poverty population will be more than the total population of India when she became free at mid-century.

The poverty ratio is another statistic that remains stable, but stable ratios combined with population growth mean that the absolute numbers below the poverty line are always increasing. Actually, the lower series does show a reduction in the urban poverty ratio; in those areas there is some response to growth in per capita income, but there is absolutely no effect on the rural poverty ratio. This is therefore invariant, and we can expect it to remain so because the agricultural growth rate is not likely to increase. If, however, the industrial growth rate increases, and urban per capita income grows faster, we can expect some reduction in urban poverty. That is why it is so important that the industrial growth rate be increased to at least seven percent.

This conclusion represents a change in my thinking. I have usually argued that high industrial growth does not influence poverty, but two exercises I conducted recently at the World Bank showed that if India's rate of growth can be increased from 3.5 to 6.5 percent, and held there for the next 15 years, the stock of capital can be increased by seven instead of five percent a year. I also found, at least theoretically, that this growth would almost eliminate our eight percent unemployment rate by the end of the century. This happens, not by increasing employment in the modern sector, but by increasing employment in the more informal small-scale sector. The ratio between the growth rate of informal small-scale employment and formal modern sector employment is almost one; in other words, the elasticity of small-scale employment with respect to modern sector employment is almost one. If the modern sector grows one percent, the informal sector grows 0.9 or nearly one percent. Informal sector employment is already enormous, therefore the multiplier effects are considerable in the urban areas. This linkage between the two sectors exists because the modern sector buys quantities of goods from the small-scale sector, which constitutes 80 percent of the labor force in the cities and towns. The modern sector also spends a large proportion of its income on goods and services produced in the informal sector. This multiplier effect of high industrial growth in the modern sectors is the reason that high industrial growth will so dramatically reduce unemployment.

The overlap between unemployment and poverty is very high; indeed, 80 percent of both unemployment and of poverty are accounted for by only two groups: the landless and the small farmers. Overall, however, there are six times as many poor in India as unemployed, so that reducing unemployment will have an effect on poverty but it will not be so great as one might hope.

The administrative revolution and the policy revolution are preconditions for a seven percent growth rate, which is what it was in the 1950s and which is the absolute minimum for reduction of poverty. Such a rate is perfectly possible so far as access to resources is concerned: we have skilled and unskilled manpower, a large national market, and natural resources. Despite the fact that there are no economic impediments to industrial growth, the Indian rate is much lower than that in east and northeast Asia. The fateful question is whether India can achieve the efficiency necessary to reduce the capital-output ratio from six to five, and thereby raise productivity and per capita income and reduce poverty. No one knows whether this will occur. The new regime recognizes the problem, but it will come up against strong and perhaps irresistible class interest. Predictions cannot be very cheerful. India's situation is well described in the words of T. S. Eliot: "Between the intention and the act falls the shadow."

Chapter Ten

# Paradoxes of Planned Development: The Indian Experience

## C. T. KURIEN

# I

In 1985 India completes the Sixth and starts on the Seventh Five Year Plan. There is a note of optimism as the transition takes place. The Sixth Plan set a target of an annual rate of growth of 5.2 percent and indications are that actual performance will be fairly close to it. What is even more significant is that foodgrain production in 1983-84 reached a record of over 150 million tons and the expectation was that 1984-85 would be even better. In a vast country at low levels of consumption, it is not surprising that food production becomes a crucial index of economic performance. From that perspective India's record of planned development has been quite impressive. In the early 1950s, when the government turned to planned development within the framework of parliamentary democracy and a mixed economy of private and public sectors, foodgrain production was in the neighborhood of 50 million tons. In a little over three decades food production has tripled. This period was also one of very rapid population growth of around 2.2 percent per annum, with total numbers increasing from 360 million in 1951 to over 700 million today. Thus while population almost doubled, food production nearly tripled. Moreover, in terms of industrial output India today ranks tenth in the world.

The performance of the period of planned development stands in striking contrast to the period immediately preceding. The Sixth Five Year Plan document gives an account of this contrast. Between 1950-51 and 1978-79 national income grew at an annual rate of 3.5 percent, agricultural production 2.7 percent, industrial production 6.1 percent, and per capita income 1.3 percent. In the first half of the century (between 1900-01 and 1945-46, to be precise) the annual growth rates were 1.2 percent in national income, 0.3 percent in agricultural production, and 2.0 percent in industrial output. Although the pre-1947 period had a very negligible rate of increase in population there was hardly any change in per capita income. Hence the Sixth Plan's assessment that "one of the most significant achievements of our development policy after independence has been the fact that the handicap of stagnation was overcome and the process of growth initiated" is quite correct.

To this list of achievements of planned development at least one more must be added. The rate of savings in the economy has registered a very substantial increase. Development theorists in the 1950s considered the biggest handicap of the so-called underdeveloped countries to be their inability to save more than about six percent of their national income because of the vicious circle of low productivity, low incomes, and low capacity to save and invest, which perpetuated low productivity. It was argued that if the level of savings could be raised to something like 12 percent, development would then become largely self-sustaining. But this necessary doubling of the rate of saving was considered to be an uphill task which the poor countries would not be able to accomplish by their own efforts. The early Indian plans reflected this view. In the long-term profile produced by the Second Five Year Plan, one of the major objectives was to raise investment as a percentage of national income from a little over seven percent at the end of the First Plan to 17 percent at the end of the Fifth Plan. The document noted that a steep stepping up of investment in the Second and Third Plan periods was called for in order to cross the 12 percent barrier, and noted that "the crossing of this 'threshold' at a time when living standards and saving potential are low calls for a measure of external assistance to supplement domestic resources," thus conceding that domestic savings would not rise as rapidly as the postulated increase in investment. But what was thought to be difficult, if not impossible, was achieved almost effortlessly. The rate of savings crossed 12 percent by the mid-1960s and moved up to 17 percent in the early 1970s, crossed the 20 percent level by the mid-1970s and reached almost 25 percent in 1978-79. Preparatory papers of the Seventh Plan postulate a rate of savings of 26 percent during the plan period. This unexpected performance has raised many questions, but what needs to be noted is that the Indian economy has not only grown but is demonstrating its continued capacity to do so.

India's development planning was not meant only to give a boost to the economy's growth. From the very beginning the objectives of planned development were much wider, "to open to our people opportunities for a richer and more varied life," as the First Plan document put it. The paradox of planned development in India has been that in spite of a not insignificant achievement in terms of growth, the broader objectives to which growth was to contribute have not been realized. After a careful evaluation of the first three decades of planned economic development, in which the progress achieved on many fronts was fully acknowledged, the *Draft Five Year Plan 1978-83* document stated: "We must face the fact that the most important objectives of planning have not been achieved, the most cherished goals seem to be almost as distant today as when we set out on the road to planned development." More specifically, the document indicated: "It is a cause of legitimate national pride that over this period a stagnant and dependent economy has been modernized and made more self-reliant . . . . On the other hand, the numbers of unemployed and underemployed are still very high and more than 40 percent of the population lives below the poverty line." (The poverty level was officially defined in the early 1960s as Rs. 20 per

capita per month. This norm still continues to be used. In current prices
it is about Rs. 80, or less than eight U.S. dollars.)

It is now well known that this is not a peculiarly Indian paradox. Making a review of the experience of a large number of underdeveloped
countries, a study for the World Bank came to a similar conclusion in
the mid-1970s. "It is now clear," said the authors, "that more than a
decade of rapid growth in underdeveloped countries has been of little
or no benefit to perhaps a third of their population. Although the average per capita income of the Third World has increased by 50 percent
since 1960, this growth has been unequally distributed among countries,
and socio-economic groups."[1]

What the present essay proposes to do is to examine this paradox in
some depth, to seek some explanations for the Indian experience, and
to indicate what seem to be the prospects in the immediate future.

# II

Discussions about the economic policies of an independent India had
started and were actively pursued well before the country actually became free. These discussions spoke largely in terms of changing the
structural aspects of the economy. To give just one example, the Indian
National Congress's National Planning Committee (chaired by
Jawaharlal Nehru) stated in 1938:

> Under planned economy no rights of property or inheritance in any form
> of national wealth, e.g., land, mines, forests, etc. should be allowed. The
> ultimate property in these forms of wealth must vest in the people
> collectively . . . . All cultivation should, ordinarily be in common, and
> according to the plan applying to each unit . . . . Industries which are
> under private ownership, but which are or become of national
> importance, owing to the scale of their operations, the labour employed,
> the nature of the commodities or services supplied, or for any other
> reason connected with the local or foreign trade of the country, its credit
> or finance, must be put under rigid control by the state . . . . New
> industries, suitable only for large-scale work by power-driven machinery
> and for standardized mass production . . . must be established and
> conducted as public enterprises. All key industries must be state-owned
> and state-managed.

When the Constitution of the new Republic was written, it outlined
the kind of socioeconomic order the country should aim to establish:

> The State shall strive to promote the welfare of the people by securing
> and protecting as effectively as it may a social order in which justice,
> social, economic and political, shall inform all institutions of national life

. . . . The State shall, in particular, direct its policy towards securing:
(a) that the citizens, men and women equally, have the right to an
adequate means of livelihood;
(b) that the ownership and control of the material resources of the
community are so distributed as best to subserve the common good;
(c) that the operation of the economic system does not result in the
concentration of wealth and means of production to the common
detriment.

In the early years of the formulation of economic policy it was recognized that major economic and social changes, as well as increases in production, were required to tackle the problems facing the country, and especially that of mass poverty. But it was stated that as a matter of pragmatic necessity the initial emphasis had to be on increasing production and ensuring sustained growth. A long period of economic stagnation, against the background of increasing population pressure, followed by the burdens of World War II, had weakened the economy. Partition uprooted millions of people and dislocated economic life. Productivity in agriculture and industry was at low levels. Rebuilding the rural economy and laying the foundation of industrial progress on a scientific basis were essential. Thus planned development came to concentrate on production, productivity, mobilization of savings, and allocation of investment. It was reasoned that increases in production, especially of basic goods like food, were not only necessary to cope with problems of mass poverty, but possibly even a sufficient accomplishment if it could be assumed that an increased output would be matched by a more adequate pattern of distribution. Thus in the early 1960s, when it was documented that over 50 percent of the population was below the officially accepted poverty line, the Planning Commission produced a model to show how accelerated production growth alone could eradicate mass poverty.

Such reasoning began to change, nationally and internationally, in the late 1960s and early 1970s. Both economic and political factors were involved in a shift in strategy toward a redistributive pattern favoring the weaker sections. The economic rationale of the new strategy was officially propounded in a preparatory document of the Fifth Five Year Plan which called for a "direct attack" on poverty:

In elaborating our strategy of development in earlier Plan documents we seem to have assumed that a fast rate of growth of national income will create more and fuller employment and also produce higher living standards for the poor. We also seem to have assumed that for reduction of disparities in income and wealth the scope of redistributive policies is surely limited. However the economy has now reached a stage where larger availability of resources makes it possible to launch a direct attack

on unemployment, underemployment and poverty and also assume
adequate growth.

The economic argument that favored the new strategy was that two
decades of growth had made it possible to make a frontal attack on poverty. There were political compulsions also. In a democratic society
based on universal adult franchise, a pattern of growth visible to all but
not accessible to the majority would not long be tenable. Hence "banish
poverty" became the political slogan of the parliamentary elections of
1971 as well as the thrust of the Fifth Five Year Plan launched immediately after.

What the Fifth Plan proposed for its direct attack on poverty was a
macro-strategy to accelerate growth and to redistribute incomes from
the top three deciles of the population to the bottom three deciles, by
imposing restrictions on the level of consumption of the top groups. A
model was produced showing the feasibility of transferring resources
to the poor by correspondingly imposing restrictions on the consumption of the top groups, but steps necessary to implement the strategy
were not worked out. Thus as the Fifth Plan period closed it was still
being said that although the growth rate was satisfactory, no dent had
been made in the problem of mass poverty. A further shift in strategy
was necessary.

That new strategy has come to be known as the "target group approach." In essence, it is an attempt specifically to identify weaker sections, for instance in terms of occupations and locations, and to target
special assistance aimed at raising standards of living. This micro-
strategy for directly reaching the poor was outlined in a Sixth Plan
preparatory document:

> The poorest sections belong to the families of landless labour, small and
> marginal farmers, rural artisans, scheduled castes, scheduled tribes and
> socially and economically backward classes. The household will remain
> the basic unit of poverty eradication in target group oriented
> programmes. Families differ in such vital respects as dependency ratios,
> asset holding, skills and even the ability to perform manual labour on
> public works. Hence each household below the poverty line will have to
> be assisted through an appropriate package of technologies, services and
> asset transfer programmes.

Programs for special groups such as small farmers and agricultural
laborers had been part of Indian planning at least from the Fourth Plan,
and the aborted (Sixth) Five Year Plan of 1978-83 had given such programs a prominent place. But it is the Sixth Five Year Plan of 1980-85
which projected the target group approach as a major strategy and emphasized it as the distributive justice component of the Plan. In view of
the proven inadequacy of the trickle-down effect of growth a strategy

of administrative intervention to reach the poorer sections directly has much to commend it. The specific programs under this strategy have included the supply of inputs and credit to small and marginal farmers and rural artisans, support for self-employment activities of petty traders and repairmen in both rural and urban areas, employment guarantee schemes, and transfer of some income-yielding assets to agricultural laborers. Most recently attempts have been made to coordinate these beneficiary-oriented schemes through an Integrated Rural Development Program. A total of about Rs. 40 billion (out of a total public sector outlay of Rs. 975 billion) was set aside in the Sixth Plan for these welfare schemes, and there is no doubt that where carefully implemented they benefited many members of the target groups.

# III

The real question is to what extent the new approach has succeeded in resolving the paradoxes of planned development and whether, at least in the long run, it can be relied upon as the main instrument to bring the benefits of development to the vast majority, for whom thus far "development" has largely been an experience watched from a distance, sometimes with the hope that their own chance may come, but more often with mixed feelings of resignation, frustration, and anger.

The question has been and continues to be debated in India and the outcome remains unclear. Since the strategy is essentially an administrative scheme, the issues frequently discussed have to do with the adequacy of administrative machinery to implement the programs effectively, and with various forms of corruption that become possible in light of the large financial outlays that the programs involve. Thus it has been pointed out (and documented) that in many instances the program benefits have gone to those other than the specified target groups because of the ease with which outsiders can exploit the programs, either because loopholes in the administration or because of outright corrupt practices. Another criticism frequently heard is that bureaucrats are only concerned with fulfilling the financial targets—perhaps at the very end of the financial year to satisfy audit requirements — but are not bothered about the real components of the programs, such as the digging of wells or providing employment. Also, the lack of departmental coordination in implementation of programs (for instance, between the Departments of Agriculture and Public Works in irrigation projects) has been pointed out in a series of evaluation reports.

These and similar defects at the implementation level cannot be overlooked in any serious evaluation of the efficacy of the target approach. But to suggest that administrative lapses are the main problems, and that but for them the strategy would succeed in achieving its defined objectives, is to take too simplistic a view of the complex issues of production and distribution in an economy such as India's. To appreciate the paradoxes of planned development it is necessary to probe a little deeper into some aspects of the entire socioeconomic system.

The rationale of planned economic development can be traced back to the constitutional imperatives noted earlier. These ensure that citizens have adequate means of livelihood, that ownership and control of material resources are distributed so as to subserve the common good, and that the operation of the economic system does not result in a concentration of wealth. From time to time in India's planned economy specific guidelines and regulations are laid down to ensure that these broad socioeconomic objectives are achieved; but, of course, these guidelines and regulations arising from social urges do not work in a vacuum. They are embedded in and must be negotiated through the existing economic system, and India's economic system is based essentially on private property and organized primarily on market principles. Where resources are privately owned, unequally distributed, and used principally to add to the command over resources, decisions regarding what will be produced, how, and how the product will be shared among different sections, will depend largely on the given distribution of resources in the system.

A brief account of the structure of the Indian economy may help one to appreciate this operating pattern. It is generally known that India is primarily an agricultural country, but that almost 70 percent of the workforce is engaged in agriculture may not be so well known. According to the 1981 Census Report there has been a slight reduction in this percentage to around 67 percent. Even this marginal variation is significant because throughout the century the figure was persistently around if not above 70 percent. This reduction shows a fall in the proportion of cultivators (from 52.3 percent in 1961 to 41.5 percent in 1981), but an increase in the proportion of agricultural laborers (from 17.2 percent in 1961 to 25.2 percent in 1981). Most of these laborers are landless and are therefore dependent on wages from cultivators for their livelihood. Since agriculture is a seasonal activity, wage employment is a seasonal phenomenon, although some agricultural laborers take to nonagricultural employment, if it can be found, during off-seasons.

It is necessary to know the characteristics of the cultivators. Slightly over 40 percent own less than one acre of land; 35 percent own only one-half an acre or less. Many of them have to resort to wage employment from time to time to supplement their earnings. Fewer than 10 percent of the cultivators own more than 10 acres of land, but together they account for over 50 percent of all cultivated land, whereas 40 percent of the cultivators with less than one acre claim hardly two percent. Available evidence suggests that in recent years the category of these "marginal farmers" has been increasing. Thus, according to an official estimate, when the number of operational holdings increased by 14.8 percent between 1970-71 and 1975-76, the number of marginal holdings (below one hectare, i.e., 2.5 acres) increased by 23 percent.

Around 30 percent of the workforce is now engaged in non-agricultural operations, divided into manufacturing (about 11 percent); trade, transport and communications (12 percent); and the rest in "other services." Even within these groups anywhere between 60 and 80 percent of the workers are engaged in "informal" activities, using all their resources and ingenuity simply to eke out a living as petty traders, repair workers, and in a host of other miscellaneous services.

This is the economic reality within which efforts at planned development take place, and whose working is sought to be modified by administrative interventions based on broader sociopolitical considerations. Hence the success of the interventions depends upon the relative strength of the economic and political forces at work within the social system. Some concrete instances will illustrate the nature of the problem.

Foodgrain production in the country increased from about 50 million tons in the early 1950s to about 90 million tons by the mid-1950s, mainly as a result of the extension of the area under cultivation. In 1965-66 and 1966-67 foodgrain production declined to less than 75 million tons. It was against that background that India turned to the Green Revolution. This was based partly on the miracle seeds, but its main strategy was to change the input structure of Indian agriculture, particularly in foodgrain production. Traditional Indian agriculture relied primarily on that sector itself for seeds and other inputs; recourse to commercial agriculture and related commercial inputs was extremely limited. This pattern changed with the introduction of the high-yielding varieties program. Commercial fertilizers, pesticides, and water at appropriate times and in appropriate quantities became essential. Because this is a highly risk-prone practice, however, only larger farmers able to spare land for experimentation and with resources to purchase inputs could initially take advantage of the new varieties. Officially, the program was conceived as "selective but intensive." It was selective in three different ways. First, it was to concentrate on two foodgrains, initially wheat and then rice, giving very low priority to a variety of other cereals grown and consumed in different parts of the country. Second, it was to be geographically concentrated in the Punjab-Haryana wheat belt and in some of the southern rice bowls. And third, effort was to be concentrated on farmers who were in a position to take immediate advantage of the new schemes. The assumption was that if foodgrain production could be increased, the increase would reach over the country to different sections of society.

Each one of these selective aspects had different social consequences than the ones anticipated. First, foodgrain production in 1950-51 of 50.8 million tons consisted of 20.5 million tons of rice, 6.4 million tons of wheat, and 15.5 million tons of other cereals (the rest being pulses which are included in the foodgrain aggregate). In 1966-67, on the eve of the Green Revolution, the production pattern was 30.4 million tons of rice, 11.3 million tons of wheat, and 24.1 million tons of other cereals. In the record year of 1983-84, the share of rice was over 53 million tons and of wheat nearly 60 million tons, with the production of other cereals being less than 30 million tons. It is thus evident that the Green Revolution was a wheat and rice revolution. Other cereals produced in different parts of the country and consumed locally, largely by the poorer families, have remained stagnant. The increased production of wheat and rice has led to the elimination of imports, except marginally, and to an improved subsidized public distribution system (through a policy of procurement) in the urban areas. Nevertheless, it is doubtful whether there has been any increase in the per capita availability of foodgrains in the rural areas.

Second, since the price of foodgrains is determined to a large extent by the government's procurement price, which is based on the cost of production, and since the cost of commercialized food production has gone up, foodgrain prices have increased despite major increases in production. Thus, the index of food prices (base 1960) increased from 195 in 1970-71 to 630 in December 1983. The continuing increase in food prices has had an adverse impact on the real earnings of agricultural laborers. According to an official estimate, at the all-India level the average daily real earnings of men belonging to agricultural labor households in 1974-75 was only 88 percent of what it was in 1964-65. Although no comparable figures have become available for a later period for the country as a whole, the situation cannot have improved much since then. In fact, since the rate of inflation increased in the decade after 1974-75, the chances are that the position of agricultural laborers has further deteriorated.

Third, many smaller farmers have found it difficult to continue as cultivators because of increasing costs of production, even though special credit schemes have been designed to help them.

Fourth, in many parts of the country subsidized private sources of irrigation (tube wells, for instance) have come to play a major role in agriculture. These subsidies are mainly taken advantage of by larger farmers who are able to benefit from a variety of credit-cum-subsidy schemes. The availability of assured water on one's own land greatly enhances its value, and makes cultivation extremely profitable for farmers who have land, sources of water, and access to farm implements and credit. They can even sell water to their smaller neighbors — one-third of the total output in kind as "water rent" is not now uncommon in some parts of the country — and can shift land to the cultivation of commercially more profitable crops such as sugarcane when a continuing water supply is assured.

Thus, while output at the national level is increasing, in many instances that process of "growth" confers benefits on some and simultaneously imposes burdens on others. In a period of rising prices, agricultural employers find it profitable to give up the traditional practice of payment in kind in favor of the more modern method of payment in cash. Under a growing regime of commercialization many other traditional claims of the weaker sections also erode.

The problem is not confined to the agricultural sector. When "growth" is evaluated in value terms and the values are determined by market forces backed by resource power, those who have limited saleable resources stand to fall behind. One of the most glaring instances of this phenomenon has been the sharp increase in the price of shrimp and other seafood as a result of the development of an export market. The entry of big commercial concerns into fishing has led to the displacement and deprivation of poorer traditional fisherfolk. The hardships imposed on handloom workers (who account for a significant proportion of non-agricultural labor) as a result of the phenomenal growth of the powerloom sector, and on those who have done hand printing of textiles and now confront large-scale mechanization, have received considerable public attention.

The basic problem may now be summarized. Growth is not simply a phenomenon of increasing output. In a socioeconomic framework in which growth is propelled by unequal resource power, it is a rather complicated process which tends to confer additional advantages on those who already have that power; but it also tends to deprive those with little resource power of any new real entitlements. This has been the paradox of growth in the Indian context.

Planned development has sought to ameliorate some of this effect by using political power to counter some of the natural proclivities of the growth process. The target group approach is one such effort to utilize political power to redistribute some resources in favor of those who do not have resource power, within a system where production and distribution turn on an existing unequal distribution of resources. The attempt is to moderate the functioning of resource power, but within the broader social framework the situation is not one in which two opposing powers confront each other in a test of relative strength: political and administrative power may seek to moderate resource power, but resource power may often influence or prevail over political power. That is one of the reasons for postponing, if not abandoning, the emphasis on structural and institutional changes, and for the increasing reliance on more "pragmatic" considerations of technological progress to increase production along with special programs of support to the poor. But it is doubtful that the rate at which resources are being diverted to the poor is adequate to compensate for the erosion taking place in their economic condition as a result of the "normal" working of the system. Some of the basic aspects of that system set limits to the extent of public compensation that may be contemplated. So the paradox of planned development remains.

# IV

What does the future hold in store? The present indications are that the target group approach will continue. *The Approach to the Seventh Five Year Plan* document says that "the package of poverty alleviation programmes will continue at an accelerated pace in the Seventh Plan . . . . The tendency to view poverty alleviation activities in isolation has to be given up, and effective linkages have to be forged with other developmental activities in the rural areas to ensure that the flow of benefits from all these schemes converge on the poverty-stricken group as a package." The *Approach* document, in fact, goes further. It calls for redistributive land reforms to be integrated directly with the anti-poverty package of programs and goes on to say:

> The present individual approach to the poverty alleviation activities needs to be substituted by group ventures and collective action to protect the beneficiaries from the adverse operation of market forces whether on supply of inputs or on the sale of their produce. In the ultimate analysis, the objective of removal of poverty can be fulfilled in the measure in which the poor themselves become conscious, improve their education and capabilities and become organized and assert themselves.

In brief, the official policy is to continue the package of anti-poverty packages, to streamline the administration to prevent leakages, to reinforce it with measures of asset redistribution, and to expect the poor to organize and assert themselves.

The feasibility of each of these must be examined to see whether the paradox of planned development is likely to be resolved in the remaining years of this century. That the package of anti-poverty programs will continue in coming years is fairly certain. The target group approach is an almost unavoidable strategy in a political system based on universal adult franchise. Where a substantial section of voters is largely excluded from the benefits of an economic activity, political steps must be taken to ensure that they are not totally excluded. Because many voters are potential beneficiaries of special programs, the designing and advertising of these become a major component of political activity. The "visibility" of the target group strategy — that something is being done for every section of society however selective the result may be within that section — gives it a special political utility that no government or political party is likely to give up.

Soon one comes again to the paradox. The logic of the program indicates that no major redistribution of income can be sustained without some redistribution of assets, hence the recognition that redistributive land reforms and other kinds of asset transfers will have to be incorporated into the program if the poor are to have access to schemes organized on their behalf. Yet, stimulated economic growth makes assets more valuable to those who have them, thus facilitating a further accumulation of assets. The logic of the economic system prevents any significant change in the ownership pattern of assets, especially land, and the history of land reform measures is good evidence of this. There was first a diluting of the kind of land reform measures required to effect real redistribution; then land reform legislation was brought in "with loopholes so large that an elephant could comfortably walk through them," as a perceptive observer put it; and then there was tardy implementation (if not non-implementation) of the statutes. This does not mean that strong economic interests totally oppose some of the minor asset transfers attempted by the anti-poverty measures, such as those of milk animals or sewing machines to selected target groups. On the contrary, in the hope that these token measures may become substitutes for the basic asset redistributions called for by the social objectives, the anti-poverty programs receive support from powerful economic interests. Thus, both political and economic expediency lend support to the kind of programs presently in place and they are likely to be continued.

Whether they will remove poverty or even substantially reduce it remains a debatable point. A crucial factor, as the *Approach* document recognizes, is the extent to which the poor will organize and assert themselves. That, of course, is a political question, and will remain a major political question for the rest of the century.

# NOTES

1. Hollis Chenery and others, *Redistribution with Growth*, Oxford, Oxford University Press, 1974.

Chapter Eleven

# Environmental Protection and Economic Development In India

SUSAN G. HADDEN

Environmental protection has been a policy of affluence. In the mid-1960s, after deadly smogs in Los Angeles and kills of millions of fish in polluted waters, the United States began to act forcefully to preserve and restore its natural resources in order to offset the depredations of industrial development. By the year 2000, India's population is expected to exceed one billion people. Without increased industrial development, more and more of those people will live in poverty. Prime Minister Indira Gandhi was well aware of the contradictions of industrial development:

> The rich countries may look upon development as the cause of environmental destruction, but to us it is one of the primary means of improving the environment of living, of providing food, water, sanitation and shelter, of making the deserts green and the mountains habitable . . . . We do not want to impoverish environment any further, [but] we cannot forget the grim poverty of large numbers of people . . . . When they themselves feel deprived, how can we urge the preservation of animals? How can we speak to those who live in villages and in slums about keeping the oceans, rivers and the air clean when their own lives are contaminated at the source? Environment cannot be improved in conditions of poverty. Nor can poverty be eradicated without the aid of science and technology.[1]

The purpose of this essay is to consider the effects on India's poor of expending national resources on environmental protection programs. Its thesis is exactly the contrary of Mrs. Gandhi's, that environmental protection is a luxury. It argues, instead, that while the poor may bear more of the short-run costs of environmental protection (and the evidence is not at all clear even on that point), they certainly bear more of the long-run costs of not protecting the environment. The "environment" comprises many resources, including air, water, and soil, that are critical to economic development. Exhausting these or reducing their quality inhibits achievement of the very goal — economic growth — in whose name they are being used. The slowing of economic growth hurts the poor; at the same time, it is they who are most directly harmed by polluted resources since they cannot buy safety.

## State of India's Environment

The causes of degeneration of the environment in developing nations such as India can be divided for analytical purposes into two categories: stresses from lack of development and stresses from development. This differentiation highlights the difficulties of formulating effective public policies in areas where both the status quo and alterations to it are likely to have adverse environmental effects. Others have called this duality "resource exhaustion" and "resource degradation."[2]

Stresses on the environment from a lack of development arise when people use more resources than they can restore. Among the most serious problems of this kind in India are:

(1) *Increasing cultivation of marginal lands* as population increases. Between 1970 and 1985, about 40 million additional hectares (one hectare equals 2.47 acres) were brought under cultivation, an increase of nearly 40 percent.[3] Another indicator of marginal land cultivation is that the area subject to floods has doubled from 20 to nearly 40 million hectares in the last decade.[4]

(2) *Cutting trees for firewood* faster than trees can grow. Between 1951 and 1972, India lost some 155,000 hectares per year of forest area; nearly 70 percent of rural and 46 percent of urban households used firewood as the primary energy source. Between 1962 and 1980, although firewood declined as a proportion of total energy used, the amount used increased from 110 to 163 million coal-ton replacements, or a 45 percent increase. The resulting soil erosion not only wastes an agricultural resource, but contributes to the great amount of dust, amounting in India's windy season to 500 micrograms of dust per cubic meter of air (compared to the permissible limit in the United States of 75 micrograms).[5]

(3) *Water pollution from human wastes* not disposed of in sewers and treated. Of India's 3,119 towns and cities, only 209 have partial and only eight have full sewerage and sewage treatment facilities.[6]

(4) *Air pollution from cooking fuels.* Nearly half the energy consumed in India is used in the household sector, largely for cooking. Even in cities, most families cook with stoves that use coal products or firewood and whose efficiencies average around 15 percent. Oil stoves, used by one-third of urban families, are equally inefficient.[7]

(5) *Loss of species and unique habitats.* Although of great importance, this topic is outside the scope of this essay.

At the same time, India faces problems of environmental pollution associated with economic development, including:

(1) *Air pollution from automobiles, factories, and power plants.* In Delhi, the number of automobiles increased by more than 500 percent from 1961 to 1978 while bicycle rides as a proportion of all trips in the city decreased from 36 percent to 20 percent between 1957 and 1981.[8]

(2) *Water pollution from production and use* of industrial products. Production has grown rapidly in such polluting industries as cement, fertilizer, and paper. Production of sulphuric acid increased nearly 900 percent from 1960 to 1981, and production of soda ash sextupled in the same period.[9] Fertilizer, the use of which has increased even more

—rapidly, often runs off into surface and ground waters and contaminates them.[10]

(3) *Degradation of agricultural resources* from introduction of "advanced" technologies. The introduction of high-yielding crop varieties has resulted in loss of genotypes, thus increasing the tendency to monoculture and increasing the susceptibility to disease. High-yielding varieties deplete soil nutrients more quickly and these are not being fully replaced. In 1980-81, about 18 million tons of nutrients were removed from the soil by foodgrain crops, but only 5.5 million tons of fertilizer were applied.[11] The most noticeable problems are those associated with irrigation, including salinization and waterlogging. At present, some seven million hectares out of the 143 million cultivated are saline, with another six million hectares waterlogged, both conditions largely resulting from improperly executed surface irrigation projects.[12]

(4) Reduction in human health and agricultural productive capacity from *increased use of pesticides.* In the seven years between 1975 and 1982, India's production of pesticides increased more than 250 percent; their consumption increased even faster through imports. If United States patterns are followed, rice will receive especially heavy doses of herbicides, residues of which may affect subsequent production.[13] The use of DDT to control malaria has adversely affected wildlife and edible fish and its concentrations are magnified in the food chain. In 1973, subjects in India and Pakistan showed the highest parts of DDT per million (25) in their blood of those studied throughout the world.[14]

India's size and environmental diversity mean that no single figure will describe conditions throughout the country. Also, India lacks the concrete data, especially time-series data, needed to measure changes taking place in India's environment. Existing data "snapshots" suggest that there are indeed serious problems of both resource exhaustion and resource deterioration.[15]

Table 1 lists environmental pollutants commonly associated with the manufacture of products important in India's economy. Table 2 presents production data for these industries over the last three decades, along with projections of future development. The 1984-85 projections are those made by the Planning Commission at the outset of the Sixth Five Year Plan and the 1990 projections were calculated using regressions on production beginning in 1965. The data on unregulated output of certain pollutants per unit of production were obtained by the United States Environmental Protection Agency (EPA) in the early 1970s as the basis for developing pollution standards. In the decade or more since these data were obtained many production technologies have changed significantly, so that the figures may be high or unrepresentative of the

TABLE 1
## COMMON POLLUTANTS

| Pollutant | Polluted Medium(s) | Industrial sources | Environmental Effects |
|---|---|---|---|
| $SO_x$ (oxides of sulfur) | Air | Burning coal and oil (especially electric power) | Acute and chronic leaf injury; irritate upper respiratory tract; corrode metals; disintegrate paper and textiles |
| Particulates | Air, water | Steel, textiles, burning coal, fertilizer, cement, paper | Speed chemical reactions; corrode metals; lung problems (humans and animals); require polluted medium to be cleaned for industrial (or human) use |
| CO (carbon monoxide) | Air | Internal combustion engines | Impairs mental processes; headaches |
| $NO_x$ (Nitrogen oxides | Air | Steel, fertilizer, paper, textiles | Leaf damage; irritate eyes and nose; corrode metal; stunt plant growth. In sunlight—photochemical oxidants, including ozone |
| Heavy metals | Air, water | Steel | Acutely toxic at high concentrations; chronic health effects including carcinogenicity at lower concentrations. Lead—decreased mental capacity |
| Toxic organics | Air, water | Steel, pesticides, paper, textiles, plastics | Acutely toxic at high concentrations. Long-term health effects at very low concentrations, including carcinogenicity, mutagenicity, teratogenicity |
| BOD (Biochemical oxygen demand) | Water | Steel, textiles, paper, fertilizer, cement | Decreased utility of water for animals; eutrophication of bodies of water |

TABLE 2

# PRODUCTION OF SELECTED INDUSTRIES AND POLLUTANTS

| Industry | 1955-56 | 1965-66 | 1975-76 | 1982-83 | Target 1989-90 | Projections 1982-83 – 1989-90 | |
|---|---|---|---|---|---|---|---|
| Steel million tons | 1.3 | 4.5 | 5.9 | 9.8 | 18.4 | 15.2 | 20.8 |
| Cement million tons | 4.7 | 10.8 | 18.6 | 27.6 | | 53.4 | 65 |
| Fertilizer thousand tons | .92 | 345 | 1,855 | 4,700 | 5,400 | 8,279 | 11,400 |
| Synthetic textiles million meters | | 66.3 | | | | | |
| Pulp & paper thousand tons | 190 | 558 | 892 | 1,151[1] | | 2,300 | 3,000 |
| Cotton textiles million meters | 6,260 | 7,440 | 8,319 | 9,638[1] | | 13,000 | 26,200 |
| Petrochemicals, plastics thousand tons | 3,685 | 9,611 | 23,336 | 27,183[1] | | 57,900 | |
| Aluminum thousand tons | 7.4 | 62.1 | 187.3 | 205.2 | | 309.4 | 700 |
| Lead thousand tons | | | 5.1 | 11.4[2] | | 28.0 | 75 |
| Coal million tons | 39 | 70 | 103 | 133 | | 215 | 345 |
| Pesticides million tons | | | 64.7 | 160[2] | | | 1,140 |

TABLE 2
# PRODUCTION OF SELECTED INDUSTRIES AND POLLUTANTS, *Cont.*

| Industry | Pollutants | Unrestricted Pollutant Output | Annual Increase in Production 1982-83–1989-90 | Annual New Pollutant Burden |
|---|---|---|---|---|
| Steel | Particulates | 150 lb./ton (air) (blast furnaces) | .075 million ton | 80,000 tons |
| | Toxic metals | 10,000 lb./year/ factory | | |
| Cement | Particulates | 6 lb./ton (water) 301 lb./ton (air) | 3.225 million tons | 9,675 tons 48,500 tons |
| | $SO_x$ | 21.7 lb./ton (air) | | 35,000 tons |
| Fertilizer | $NO_x$ | 6,125 lb./ton (air) | 87.5 thousand tons | 5.5 tons |
| | Particulates | 12.7 lb./ton | | 5,500 tons |
| | Ammonia | 1,670 l./kkg. | | 146,000 liters |
| Synthetic textiles | Particulates | 7-35 lb./ton | | |
| Pulp & paper | Particulates | 89 kg./kkg. (water) 198 lb./ton (air) | 128 thousand tons | 11,392 kg. 12,000 tons |
| | $SO_x$ | 5 lb./ton | | 320 tons |
| | CO | 70 lb./ton | | 4,500 tons |
| | BODS | 7 kg./kkg. | | 450 tons |
| Cotton textiles | Sulfides | 154 ppm. (air) | 429 million meters | |
| | Chromium | 239 ppm. (air) | | |
| | Phenol | 52 ppm. (air) | | |

*Sources:* 1984-85 Projections: Mohd Fazal, *New Trends in the Indian Economy.* Other Projections: Sixth Plan. Unrestricted output: Ranked Input-Output Data Used to Determine Impact . . . , April 1977. Prepared for U.S. EPA by Research Corporation of New England.

[1]1980-81

[2]1979-80

Indian case. In the absence of better data, however, the last column multiplies expected annual increases in production (1982-90) by per-unit production of pollutant, to give some notion of the annual increase in the pollutant burden India would face from these few industries alone.

Increases in population and increases in per capita GNP create larger demands upon resources. Steel consumption in the United States rose from about 0.15 tons per person per year in 1900, when per capita GNP was $1,000, to 0.70 tons per person per year in 1969, when per capita GNP was $3,500 — nearly a 500 percent increase as against a per capita GNP increase of only 350 percent. Copper consumption per capita rose even more quickly.[16] A significant proportion of the increases in production reflected in Table 2 is due to rising income, but some increases reflect increased demand resulting from population increase. If each person in India directly or indirectly requires 0.01 ton of steel, one-tenth of the 1900 United States rate, the projected increase in population of 200 million people between 1986 and 2001 will result in a demand for two million additional tons of steel by 2000.[17] Together, the tables show the enormous burden placed on the Indian environment by a combination of rapid population growth and rapid industrialization.

## Distributive Effects of Environmental Protection

The widely accepted argument put forward by Mrs. Gandhi suggests that environmental protection conflicts with development, and especially with the improvement of the lot of the poor. In fact, it is the poor who suffer most from a polluted environment. This is true not only for those kinds of environmental degradation that are facets of poverty itself, such as the lack of firewood or the presence of raw sewage in water used for drinking and washing, but also for the kinds of pollution associated with industrialization and economic development.

A graphic example of how the poor suffer the effects of resource exhaustion is found in the case of firewood gatherers in the hills. A person must walk for half a day or more to obtain wood for cooking, effectively devoting his or her entire labor to this single task.[18] Similarly, the poor have less access to safe drinking water and use less water of any kind. An average of 20 or so liters of water per person per day is available in rural areas as opposed to nearly 300 liters in developed urban areas.[19] The quality of the water is likely to be lower for the poor, especially those in urban areas who use untreated water containing effluents from the cities' sewage systems.

Air pollution arises from poverty and from industrialization. Users of fire and charcoal fires are affected by pollutants from imperfectly oxidized products. Women cooking indoors inhale carcinogens equivalent to those from smoking 20 packages of cigarettes a day.[20] Lung and upper respiratory problems are endemic among families using such fuels. In the United States, the poor also suffer more industrial air pollution; and, even if that pollution is controlled, the poor benefit less than the wealthy.[21] These effects occur because the poor often work in polluted factories and because they live in more polluted areas where low land values make housing affordable.[22] Similarly disproportionate effects on the poor can be documented for water pollution, soil quality, toxic waste dumps, and lead exposure. Thus, to argue that environmental protection will divert resources that would otherwise help the poor through productive investment is to misunderstand how the costs of development are presently distributed. In addition, evidence from western countries reviewed in the following paragraphs suggests that few resources are diverted by a strong program of environmental protection.

When environmental protection first gained widespread public attention in the West, opponents argued that raising the cost of production would increase prices, drive down demand, and reduce employment.[23] Data from western countries do not confirm this hypothesis. A study by the OECD found few effects on employment, although some sectoral problems arose when strong pollution controls were imposed.[24] A later study of United States firms found little relationship between increased pollution standards and unemployment, although again effects were felt in some sectors. Although large manufacturers of food and chemical products sometimes threatened to relocate plants to countries with lower standards, only four out of a sample of approximately 70 actually did so. There was some relocation within the United States, causing local unemployment but little net change.[25]

Finally, the EPA itself identified a maximum of 153 plant closings affecting 32,000 workers in the decade from 1971 to 1981 that might be attributed to costs of environmental protection. These workers made up 0.003 percent of the workforce. At the same time, about 600 new companies were created to manufacture and install pollution-related equipment or to provide technical services concerning pollution reduction.[26] Direct employment in pollution control activities increased by about 360,000 in federal, state, and local governments, 283,000 in industry, and 21,000 in educational institutions.[27] Other analysts found that pollution control expenditures in all sectors of the economy generated 1.1 million new jobs.[28]

For India, the primary employment effects will occur if foreign investors choose other countries for their factories to avoid stringent environmental controls. At present other factors, including investment incentives, tax rates, local participation requirements and so on, far outweigh the effects of environmental standards as criteria for new factory locations. Internal changes in employment due to imposition of environmental standards will be across sectors, as in the United States, and with a net employment gain. Since many environmental protection activities are labor intensive, proportionately more jobs may be generated in the Indian economy, with its relatively cheap labor, than were generated in the West.

Data on the overall costs of environmental protection support the contention that it is compatible with continued growth. Studies conducted in the United States and western Europe in the late 1970s found that investment in pollution control constituted about one percent of GNP, ranging from 0.2 percent to two percent.[29] These studies do not include offsetting benefits from the absence of pollution. More important for long-run development than direct monetary outlays is whether installation of environmental controls reduces production efficiency. One study concluded that productivity may be decreased by about one percent if business bears the full burden of environmental costs, and less if the burden is borne in part by government or consumers.[30]

Offsetting these rather small costs are some benefits of environmental protection that actually save resources which can then be funnelled to government programs for the poor; one especially important source of savings comes from health benefits. An EPA study conducted in 1974 found that air pollution alone contributed $4.6 billion of loss in health, $1.7 billion in losses to materials, $0.2 billion in losses to vegetation, and $5.8 billion in losses because of soiling or aesthetics.[31] If the costs of pollution control are balanced against the benefits of reducing these kinds of costs, net production may well increase.

The argument so far can be summarized as follows: the poor are most seriously affected by the kinds of pollution that result from resource exhaustion. These kinds of pollution can be overcome only by economic growth and development, which in turn must rely at least in part upon industrialization. Unfortunately, the poor also bear a large proportion of the direct and indirect costs of the environmental pollution caused by industrialization. Investment in environmental protection does not, however, appreciably reduce the speed of economic growth. It is therefore incorrect to assert that industrial development and environmental protection conflict; both can be achieved. It is not expensive to include pollution abatement mechanisms in new factories; retrofitting is significantly more expensive but costs should still be offset by the benefits of not having to clean up the environment later and retrofit the added factories built in the interim. Those who argue that India, and especially India's poor, cannot afford environmental protection yet, are probably only trying to find arguments to justify opposition to environmental protection based on other grounds.

One issue rarely raised in western studies concerns the balance between environment and development inherent in adoption of modern agricultural techniques. The productivity of the Green Revolution has allowed economic growth to occur. Insofar as economic growth is the primary means of assisting the poor, continuing use of modern agricultural techniques is critical. Nevertheless, as in industry, the poor bear more risks from these new techniques. Among these are: the effects of a monoculture of high-yielding varieties, since the poor are less able to sustain the complete losses that are associated with crop problems if only one variety is raised; the increased burdens new varieties place on the soil, since the poor are less likely to be able fully to replace the nutrients; the increased likelihood of erosion and nutrient loss on marginal lands, which the poor are more likely to be cultivating; and the increased exposure to pesticides, which are usually applied by agricultural laborers who are often illiterate and rarely trained in application techniques. Environmental protection policies are unlikely to address these issues, and are unlikely to affect them should they try, since agriculture is decentralized. Education and careful monitoring of lands where modern farming is supported by national programs could help to mitigate some of these effects on the poor.

## Government Policies to Protect the Environment

India's government has not been inactive in the face of many of these environmental problems. Legislation has been enacted, pollution standards devised, and the Sixth and Seventh Plans make specific outlays for environmental protection. Numerous laws are intended, at least in part, to protect the environment. Two major national laws affect air and water. Because of constitutional restrictions, the Water (Prevention and Control of Pollution) Act of 1974 defines a limited role for the national government. It establishes a Central Water Pollution Board and suggests that the states establish such boards. Six states, including Tamil Nadu, Orissa, Mizoram, and Nagaland, have chosen not to do so.[32] The state boards are empowered to plan for prevention or abatement of pollution of streams and wells, to inspect sewage and industrial effluents, and to set effluent standards. Failure to comply is punishable by a jail term of three months and a fine of Rs. 5,000 or, for continuing offenses, Rs. 1,000 per day. The law is limited in many ways: it covers only streams and wells and does not include ground water; state boards are not able to close offending establishments; and penalties, which are minimal for large companies, are difficult to impose. By 1979 only 28 prosecutions had been initiated by all the state boards, and no convictions had been obtained.[33]

The Air (Prevention and Control of Pollution) Act of 1981 is the most fully central of the environmental protection laws. Since it has national scope, it requires states without water pollution control boards to establish boards to oversee air pollution. States with water boards may add air pollution oversight to their existing duties. As under the water act, the Central Board oversees planning for pollution control and coordinates state activities, sets pollution standards, conducts a media education program, and oversees a training program for inspectors. State boards advise their governments on specific proposed industrial projects and help set and enforce pollution standards, especially by specifying the kinds of pollution control devices to be installed. States may take samples and use them as the basis for prosecution; as under the water act, fines are not heavy and have seldom been imposed.

Table 3 describes some Indian Standards Institute standards for air and water pollution and compares them, where appropriate, to standards adopted by the EPA. Several important differences should be noted. First, EPA has promulgated its standards as rules, so that existing standards have been subjected to public notice and comment. ISI standards are developed primarily by technical personnel and have been adopted by reference as standards at the central and some state levels. Second, EPA's standards for water pollution differ for every industry, every sector, and, in some instances, even for every factory. ISI's water standards are much less complex. They are defined in terms of two crosscutting dichotomies: industrial or non-industrial; inland surface water or sewage. On the whole, the EPA standards allow average effluent levels higher than those specified in the more general Indian standards.

India's air standards are more restrictive than the United States' standards in the case of sulphur dioxide, but less restrictive on suspended particulates, presumably because of the amount of air dust which cannot be controlled except by reforestation and other ecological means. India's air standards do not cover vehicles which, because of their age and improper maintenance, are heavy contributors to air pollution in India's cities. Another important difference is that EPA standards were developed for regions. For the last several years, manufacturers within those regions have been able to buy and sell pollution rights within these regions so long as the total pollution level is not exceeded. This is known as the "bubble" concept. There is not any impediment to the use of this concept in India, if appropriate calculations could be made, but it does not appear to have been encouraged.

TABLE 3
## POLLUTION CONTROL STANDARDS,
## UNITED STATES AND INDIA

| Pollutant | Medium | EPA | ISI |
|---|---|---|---|
| Particulates | Air[1] | 75 $\mu$g/m$^3$ (annual mean) 9 ppm max. 8-hour concentration | 150 $\mu$g/m$^3$ |
| S0$_2$ | Air[1] | 80 $\mu$g/m$^3$ (annual mean) | 60 $\mu$g/m$^3$ |
| C0 | Air | 10 mg/m$^3$ (9 ppm) max. 8-hour concentration | |
| N0$_2$ | Air | 100 $\mu$g/m$^3$ (.05 ppm) (annual mean) | No standard yet established |
| Lead | Air | 1.5 $\mu$g/m$^3$ (3/mo. mean) | |
| TSS (solids) | Water[2] | 10-700 ppm | 100/600 |
| BOD | Water[2] | 300-1200 ppm | 30/500 |
| pH | Water | 6-9.9 | 5.5-9 |
| Fluoride | Water | 25 g/liter | 2.0 mg/liter |
| Toxic metals | Air | 100 g/m$^3$ (.005 ppm) | |

[1] Primary standards.
[2] Water standards differ between each industry; this is the general range.
*Note:* ISI water standards differ between industrial and other effluents. Standards given here are for industrial, distinguished between inland surface water/sewers. There are additional water standards for a variety of substances in both countries.
*Source:* EPA Standards: appropriate federal regulations in 42 CFR.
ISI standards: *Environment 1982*, pp. 19 (water); 74 (air).


The Sixth Plan was the first to include direct expenditures for environmental protection. These amounted to a total of Rs. 40 crores (one crore equals 10 million) out of a plan outlay of some 47,000 crores, or less than one-tenth of one percent. Much of this money is for administrative and research activities; Rs. 5 crores is for training and education programs.[34] Additional environment-protecting expenditures in the

Plan are for forestry, flood control, renewable energy, and sanitary water supplies; actual expenditure figures are not available in the Plan document.

Legislation and financial outlays are not always adequate responses to problems. Environmental protection in India faces many impediments, including the lack of a cohesive set of interest groups focused on the problem. Three factors that have limited the effectiveness of environmental protection so far are India's federal structure, failure to consider environmental aspects of other plan outlays, and difficulties in administering and implementing environmental policy.

India's federal structure is an important determinant of the way in which public policy is formulated and executed. The states have long had jurisdiction over the ownership and use of natural resources such as land and water; ensuring a consistent national policy on these and similar environmental matters has been very difficult. Forests, a state subject as a natural resource, were made a concurrent subject in 1976, paving the way for an as-yet-unformulated national forest policy.[35] Similarly, water is a state subject; in order to formulate national policy, the national government had to obtain approval from at least two state legislatures. The Water Act was adopted in 1974 after some five years of parliamentary maneuvering; it is applicable only in federal jurisdictions and in those states that have passed enabling resolutions. Implementation of laws continues to rest with the states.

Although the Sixth Plan includes outlays for environmental protection, there is a striking absence of consideration of environmental effects of other aspects of the Plan. If environmental consciousness is truly to be raised, public expenditures on steel, coal, and other polluting industries should give incentives to retrofit existing plants and minimize pollution by new ones. A similar disregard for the implications of those aspects of the Plan not explicitly designated as "environmental" is found in the list of industries reserved to the small-scale sector, many of which have highly toxic wastes. Among these are asbestos pipes and fittings, glass manufacture, a wide range of organic and other chemicals, plastic-fabricating activities, production of primary paper and leather goods, and extraction of seed oils.[36] Experience in the United States has shown that it is the small-scale sector which is least likely to comply with environmental regulations and where enforcement is most difficult and expensive. Not only does reserving these activities to the small-scale sector virtually ensure that wastes will be inadequately treated, but the very serious health effects that can accrue to workers in many of these industries are, as a matter of public policy, reserved to the poor members of the population.

All governments are limited in their capacity to enforce environmental regulations. Regulated industries often oppose standards, regulatory staffs are limited in size, data needed to support enforcement actions are complex and difficult to obtain, and responsibility for particular problems is hard to determine. India faces all these problems. A quick perusal of the pages of *Commerce* (Bombay) will show that industry complains noisily about environmental standards. India faces severe problems because of the disparity between the size of regulatory staffs and the number of producers who must be regulated. State water boards, for example, must grant "consents" or discharge permits. An indication of the magnitude of the task can be obtained from Maharashtra's board, which granted about 4,400 consents to private firms and 82 to municipal councils between 1975 and 1981. These covered about 85 percent and 55 percent, respectively, of the total discharges from the two sources, but encompassed only about one-fourth of the industries that ultimately require permits.[37] Following the accidental release of a toxic chemical used in manufacturing a pesticide at Bhopal, Madhya Pradesh, a reporter found that each inspector of occupational safety in that state was responsible for more than 150 factories.[38] The inspectors had to rely on the managers of the factories to provide them with testing equipment and had to use public transportation to reach factories to be inspected. Fines are minimal, as low as two rupees per day per infraction.

Lack of resources characterizes environmental protection programs in all nations. Vigorous enforcement of penalties for infractions detected is one of the most important incentives for compliance. Low fines, the failure to support inspectors, and establishment of overly complex procedures all suggest that authorities are not really commited to environmental protection. These implementation problems are probably the most serious impediment to effective pollution control in India.

## Policy Responses for Environmental Protection

One means of overcoming difficulties in implementation is to design policies with which people want to comply. Such incentives may be built into policies in a variety of ways. One is to design policies that give benefits. Tax benefits, subsidies, and effluent charges are popular means, because they create conditions in which it is in the actors' own interests to behave in environmentally sound ways.[39] The success of these methods depends upon an effective tax system and adequate data collection, both lacking in India.

Not all important policies lend themselves to these compliance methods. The following critical components of a successful environmental policy in India will require both incentives and direct enforcement:

(1) *Restoration of lost soil nutrients.* While use of commercial fertilizer will continue to grow, the environmental problems associated with its manufacture and the inability of farmers to pay for sufficient fertilizer to maintain the soil, suggest the need to look for other means of restoring or preserving soil nutrients. Obvious but underutilized sources in India include, in ascending order of their potential contribution: urban sewage; animal dung; and farm and food industry wastes; the last of which alone could yield more nitrogen, phosphorus, and potassium than is presently consumed in commercial fertilizers in all of India.[40] Technologies to recycle these wastes are already available, although some must be operated on a large scale to be economically viable. Policies to encourage use of these resources include providing incentives to industry to recycle organic waste, provision of appropriate small-scale technology to villages, and price reductions on fertilizer using recycled organic materials. In addition, pressures to use dung as fuel rather than for fertilizer must be relieved by a coordinated fuel policy.

(2) *Replacement of forests.* Reforestation stabilizes eroding soils, provides a renewable source of fuel and fodder, and serves industrial and recreation needs. Unfortunately, pressures on forests will not be relieved if villagers require additional land for cultivation; appropriate policies entail subsidizing owners of tree plantations until they can begin making money from their slow-growing crop, developing alternative cooking fuel sources, training a new set of forest officials to emphasize preservation rather than exploitation, and providing alternative employment. The projected Sixth Plan outlay for forestry, including research, establishment of new plantations, and education programs, was Rs. 105 crores at the central level and, consonant with their primary role in this area, Rs. 560 crores at the state level. Ensuring that alternative cooking fuel is available has human health benefits in addition to preserving forests; at present, low fuel availability means that the poor cook their food imperfectly, which fails to kill germs, does not oxidize certain pesticide residues, and makes the food difficult to digest.

(3) *Minimizing dumping of human wastes* into water. Programs to keep waste out of drinking water would reduce the enormous costs (Rs. 700 crores annually) for treating water-borne disease, would increase the utility of aquatic foods, and would provide organic waste for use as fertilizer. India has long had a policy of trying to make rural water supplies safe. Rs. 262 crores was expended between 1974 and 1978 on rural water supplies; annual expenditures thereafter have been well

over Rs. 100 crores.[41] These efforts concentrate on provision of wells. Surface water, however, suffers adverse effects from the runoff of organic wastes. Construction of urban water and sewer systems would alleviate a major portion of this problem; construction of rural sanitation facilities would also help. These projects could be undertaken as public works, providing cash income for the poor as well as long-term health benefits.

(4) *Control of population growth.* Population pressures contribute strongly to the use of inappropriate land for farming, overuse of wood for fuel, and to the lack of resources for such amenities as urban sewage collection and treatment systems.

Because the components of the environment are so interdependent, and because they in turn are such essential ingredients of economic development, it is often difficult to determine the appropriate balance of policies. An aggressive afforestation policy would take some land out of production and would entail increasing the productivity of remaining land. The most dramatic increases in land productivity have been achieved by the use of modern agricultural inputs such as fertilizer, pesticides, and high-yielding varieties; the environmental dangers of these methods were discussed above. At the same time, reducing the amount of land under production will drive more people to seek employment in the industrial sector, which will further pollute the environment. Since the marginal lands to be reforested are likely to be worked by poorer farmers, the effects of such a policy will fall directly on them; if employment in industry is not available, they will pay very heavily.

There are few painless solutions to this complex of problems; however, this is not reason to postpone effort. Any political difficulties that arise from the distributive effects of environmental protection can be ameliorated, perhaps by direct grants. Conversely, the failure to protect the environment now will be enormously costly later and environmental burdens will continue to fall most heavily on the poor.

## Conclusion

India will have severe problems implementing environmental protection policies. Although some of these are due to lack of resources (devices to measure pollution, trained inspectors applying appropriate standards), more appear to be attributable to lack of political initiatives. Ground water pollution and toxic substances in the environment are rarely considered. The purely hortatory nature of much of the government's interest in the environment is made clear by its continued investment in polluting industries and by its failure to send appropriate financial signals to the states, which are expected to bear most of the burden of regulating air and water pollution.

It would be easy to argue that the lack of information about the most elementary basis for such policies — how much forest is being lost each year or the costs of requiring factories to reduce air pollution — prevents their formulation. The government appears to be sensitive to this criticism, since it puts a significant proportion of resources for environmental matters into research. Calls for further research, however, are frequently an excuse for postponing unpleasant decisions. In the case of the environment, delay often increases the costs of implementing policies. Not only is the degree of environmental degradation to be reversed greater, but the opponents of reform have had more time to gather their forces.

The experience of the United States suggests that even a very strong central effort will be resisted by many states and most industries. The powers so far available to and exercised by the national government in India do not begin to compare with those granted to the EPA. A coalition of industry and the poor, arguing that environmental protection is a luxury that India cannot yet afford, could easily stall progress. The remainder of the century must be devoted to formulating and effectively implementing policies that provide desired economic growth and ensure the availability of resources for economic development in the next century. New Delhi must act immediately to deploy resources that will induce the states to enforce existing environmental protection acts and encourage them to adopt new strategies, such as siting licenses for industrial projects. Training of environmental specialists and providing appropriate status and emoluments for them are other critical components of a serious program.

Perhaps the most important feature of a successful effort to protect the environment is to ensure that people themselves understand the extent to which they stand to lose from environmental degradation: in losses of health and livelihood, in reduced industrial productivity, and, most especially, in reduced agricultural productivity and a still greater impoverishment of the lives of the very poor. If there is such understanding, India could be a model for other developing nations as they grow increasingly aware of environmental problems and the need to plan their future environments.

## NOTES

1. Indira Gandhi, address to the United Nations Conference on Human Environment in Stockholm, June 14, 1972, reported in *The Times of India* (New Delhi), June 15, 1972, p. 1.

2. Charles Pearson and Anthony Pryor, *Environment: North and South, An Economic Interpretation*, New York, Wiley-Interscience, 1978, ch. 1.

3. Desh Bandhu, editor, *Environmental Management*, Delhi, Indian Environmental Society, 1981, p. 39, quoting National Commission on Agriculture, 1976.

4. Centre for Science and Environment, *The State of India's Environment 1982: A Citizens' Report*, Delhi, Centre for Science and Environment, 1982, p. 2. Hereafter, this work will be called *Environment 1982*.

5. *Environment 1982*, pp. 33, 149; L. C. Sharma, "Fuel Crisis in India," *Commerce*, November 1, 1982, p. 832; V. V. Shirvaikar, "Role of Industry in Air Pollution Control," *Commerce*, October 17, 1981, p. 17.

6. *Sixth Plan*, p. 400.

7. For similar experience in China, see Vaclav Smil, "Environmental Degradation in China," *Asian Survey*, August 1980, pp. 777-778. Smil documents the existence of chronic respiratory disease as a result of lump coal use. Also see All-India Congress Committee (I), "Energy Policy," AICC Science and Technology Series 1, n.d., p. 31, where thermal efficiency at Delhi of major energy sources for cooking and price per kilogram are given as follows:

| | | |
|---|---|---|
| LPG | 58% | Rs. 2.33 |
| Kerosene | 45 | 1.70 |
| Soft coke | 22 | .28 |
| Firewood | 18 | .35 |
| Dung | 11 | .00 |

8. *Environment 1982*, p. 101.

9. "Statistical Profile," *Commerce*, November 13, 1982, p. 34.

10. *India Abroad*, September 14, 1984, p. 17.

11. *Environment 1982*, p. 10.

12. *Environment 1982*, p. 7. The Tiwari Committee (Committee for Recommending Legislative Measures . . . for Ensuring Environmental Protection), p. 13, quoting a 1972 study showing that 4.5 million hectares were saline and six million waterlogged.

13. Pearson and Pryor, *op. cit.*, p. 311, show that while rice constitutes one percent of total U.S. cropped acreage, it receives four percent

of herbicide use. Cotton, also an important crop in India, accounts for three percent of the U.S. cropped area, but 33 percent of insecticide use.

14. USAID study reported in Pearson and Pryor, *op. cit.*, p. 316. The U.S. figure was 9.5; Holland was the lowest at 2.0. Similar results are found in Wayland J. Hayes, Jr., "Monitoring Food and People for Pesticide Content," in *Scientific Aspects of Pest Control*, Washington, D.C., National Academy of Sciences, 1966. Hayes reports 26 ppm in body fat in Delhi, 1964; 12.7 ppm in southern U.S. in 1961; a U.S. average of 7.6 in 1964; and 10 ppm in the U.S. in 1942 and France in 1961. Quoted in Donella H. Meadows *et al.*, *The Limits to Growth*, second edition, New York, Universe Books, 1974, p. 85.

15. Arun C. Vakil, *Economic Aspects of Environmental Pollution in India: An Exploratory Study*, Bombay, India, Arun C. Vakil, 1984 provides a similar if longer compendium of data.

16. *Limits to Growth*, p. 111.

17. These projections in *Statistical Outline of India 1984*, Bombay, Tata Services Limited, 1984, p. 35. The 1986 population will be 758 million; the low estimate for 2001 is 959 million while the high estimate is 1,052 million.

18. On firewood, see Erik Eckholm, "Trek Through Nepal," *The New York Times* (National Edition), February 14, 1984, pp. 17, 20; accounts of the *chipko andolan* (the movement to hug trees) such as the one described in *Environment 1982*, pp. 42-43; and the fascinating data in Centre for the Application of Science and Technology to Rural Areas, *Rural Energy Consumption Patterns: A Field Study*, Bangalore, Indian Institute of Science, 1982. These data show that 47,000 hours a year is spent by 53 families in gathering firewood; each household makes an average of 172 trips a year to gather wood and each trip averages over 8.5 kilometers roundtrip.

19. Anne U. White, "Water Supply and Income Distribution in Developing Countries," in *Economic Development, Poverty, and Income Distribution*, edited by William Loehr and John P. Powelson, Boulder, Colorado, Westview Press, 1977, pp. 267-88, esp. p. 270. Even development may hurt the poor; White notes (p. 275) that while the proportion of people with access to safe water in cities rose slightly overall, it decreased from 27 to 14 percent for those with standpipe service and increased from 60 to 67 percent for those with in-house connections.

20. Quoted in Eckholm, *The New York Times, op. cit.*

21. David Harrison and Daniel L. Rubinfeld, "Distribution of Benefits from Improvements in Urban Air Quality," *Review of Economics and Statistics*, November 1978, pp. 635-38.

22. For a review of the evidence on land value and air pollution, see A. Myrick Freeman III, *The Benefits of Environmental Improvement*,

Baltimore, Johns Hopkins University Press for Resources for the Future, 1979, esp. pp. 156-58. The most common finding is a negative relationship between increasing concentrations of air pollutants and land values.

23. It is important to remember that the costs of pollution were not lost in economies prior to the raising of the environmental conscience; rather, these costs were dumped on society at large rather than being placed on producers and, ultimately, consumers of products the manufacture of which created pollution. Forcing producers to bear the costs meant that society was no longer subsidizing consumption or production of these products. The employment argument was thus in some sense a red herring to create opposition to a policy that was actually trying to improve the market mechanism.

24. OECD, *Economic Implications of Pollution Control: A General Assessment*, Paris, OECD, 1974, p. 41.

25. Maureen Kallick and James Morgan, "Pollution Control and Employment," in Anthony Y. C. Koo *et al.*, *Environmental Repercussions on Trade and Investment*, East Lansing, Graduate School of Business Administration, Michigan State University, 1979, pp. 83, 91.

26. Studies reported in Richard Kazis and Richard Grossman, "Job-Taker or Job-Maker?" *Environment*, November 1982, pp. 12-20, 43.

27. Joseph P. Biniek, *The Status of Environmental Economics: An Update*, U.S. Congress, Senate, Committee on Environment and Public Works, 96th Congress, 1st Session, July 1979, Committee Print 96-6, quoting National Academy of Sciences, *Analytical Studies for the Environmental Protection Agency*, Vol. II, Washington, D.C., NAS, 1977. Hereafter, the secondary source is called by the name of its author, Biniek.

28. Kenneth Leung and Jeffrey A. Klein, "The Environmental Control Industry: An Analysis of Conditions and Prospects . . .," a report prepared for the Council on Environmental Quality, December 1975, quoted in Biniek, p. 90.

29. These studies are reviewed, and many reprinted, in Biniek.

30. Edward F. Denison, "Effects of Selected Changes in the Institutional and Human Environment upon Output per Unit of Input," *Survey of Current Business*, January 1978, pp. 21-42. The quotation is from Biniek's assessment, p. 40.

31. Thomas E. Waddell, *The Economic Damages of Air Pollution*, Washington, D.C., Environmental Protection Agency, May 1974, EPA 600/5-74-012, cited by Biniek, pp. 69-70.

32. *Environment 1982*, p. 82.

33. Dwivedi and Kishore, *op. cit.*

34. *Sixth Plan*, p. 351.

35. *Sixth Plan*, p. 136.

36. *Guide to New Industrial Policy of Government of India 1983-84*, New Delhi, Guide Publication, 1984, pp. 117-37.

37. D. N. Capoor, "Prevention of Water Pollution: Cooperation by Industry," *Commerce*, October 17, 1981.

38. Stuart Diamond, "Disaster in Bhopal," *New York Times*, January 31, 1985, p. 6.

39. For a guide to the early literature on this subject, see Fred Lee Smith, Jr., "Pollution Charges: The Practical Issues," in *Resource Conservation: Social and Economic Dimensions of Recycling*, edited by David W. Pearce and Ingo Walter, New York, New York University Press, 1977. For a forceful and persuasive argument, see Allen V. Kneese and Charles L. Schultze, *Pollution, Prices, and Policy*, Washington, D.C., Brookings Institution, 1975, esp. ch. 7.

40. *Ibid.*

41. *Sixth Plan*, p. 223.

Chapter Twelve

# Women in Contemporary India: The Quest For Equal Participation and Justice

GAIL MINAULT

In late 1974, the Indian national committee on the status of women published its report, *Towards Equality*.[1] In that report, the result of several years of research, were details concerning Indian women's rights in law, their opportunities for economic participation, their educational development, and political status. It was a remarkable document, unique in developing countries for its detail and sophistication, and—for a study enjoying government patronage—its admission that all was not well with the status of women in India. The report is a tribute to the openness of public discourse in India. It provides a benchmark by which future developments in Indian women's rights and status may be measured.

Any speculation about India's future would be incomplete without a look at the way economic and social changes affect the lives of Indian women. This essay will concentrate on two areas: women's participation in economic development and women's legal rights. It uses the 1974 report as a starting point and relies on recent research and activism by Indian women's organizations for the discussion of current trends. Such women's organizations, led by educated women but arising out of the needs of the poor and the less articulate, give evidence of the attempt to bridge class differences among Indian women. This is a vital need, given that economic development exacerbates class differentiation of the Indian women's movement, I am encouraged by this growing feminist consciousness in the face of otherwise discouraging statistics.[2] I see women's advocacy of women's rights becoming a more vibrant force in Indian society, and find an increasing tendency for women, regardless of class, to confront patriarchal authority, whether landlords, the police, or exploitative employers. Young women also are challenging the traditional power of their mothers-in-law.

## Women's Participation in Economic Development[3]

Economic development is often defined as a growth in per capita gross national product. Under such a definition, if India increases its agricultural and industrial production, all Indians (including women) benefit, and hence worrying about women's participation in economic development is — if not superfluous — at least a low priority. Of course, such a definition is too simple and mechanistic to encompass the highly complex human processes involved in economic development. As the earlier chapter by C. T. Kurien emphasizes, even with aggregate increases in production, the problem of distribution of the benefits of development remains. In India, the Green Revolution has brought self-sufficiency in foodgrain production — a tremendous achievement — but with high social costs. The increased marginalization of landless laborers and the need to find alternative sources of employment are facts with which economic planners have to grapple.

If the poor are being marginalized by economic development, so too are many, if not most, women workers. Women, in fact, are asymmetrically affected by economic development. Some women benefit greatly, but most do not, so that women workers have become the poorest of the poor. Many of the agricultural processes carried out manually by women are the first to be rendered obsolete by mechanization or by the more sophisticated processes required by high-yielding varieties and by market, as opposed to subsistence, production. Economic development that affects adversely half the agricultural population may raise the per capita GNP, while simultaneously increasing the probability of serious social and political upheaval. Clearly, more attention needs to be paid to the differential effects of development, not only in relation to class or regional disparities, but also in relation to the sexual division of labor.[4]

Looking at statistics on economic development provides abundant evidence that women are, with a few notable exceptions, adversely affected by economic development. The 1974 report found that women's economic participation had been declining since 1921, both in percentage of workers to total female population and in the percentage of women workers to the total labor force. In seeking an explanation for this, the report's authors mentioned the tendency not to count women as gainful workers because much of their labor was unpaid or household work, but felt that this was a statistically marginal explanation. A more plausible explanation, from the viewpoint of the authors, was the division between organized and unorganized sectors of the economy. The difference between these sectors is not functional (i.e., agricultural, industrial, or service) but rather is in terms of the organization of productive relations, the degree of public control and regulation, and the recognition of data collecting agencies.[5] In other words, since women are more likely to be found in the unorganized sector, they are less likely to earn even the minimum wage, to have any kind of job security, or to be counted in statistics. A recent report based on census data from 1961 to 1981 finds that women's workforce participation at the all-India level continues to decline, despite government programs for rural development, employment, and income generation.[6] It seems that this trend, well established during most of the twentieth century, will continue into the twenty-first.

Sectoral data yield no rosier a picture. According to the census of 1971, approximately 80 percent of women workers are in agriculture. The census classifies agricultural workers into two categories: cultivators and laborers. Even given the difficulty of defining these categories, a trend seems clear; there was a sharp decline in the number of women cultivators from over 18 million in 1951 to around nine million in 1971. There was an increase in women agriculture laborers from around 12 million in 1951 to over 15 million in 1971. This clearly indicates an increase in poverty and landlessness among rural women.[7] Among marginal rural households, women contribute one-half or more of the total family income by their labor. Hence, an increase in female poverty indicates an increase in overall rural poverty.

A later report analyzes changes in the employment of women agricultural laborers vis-à-vis men and finds that: (1) the numbers of agricultural laborers of both sexes has increased, but the increase is substantially more for females; (2) the average number of days of employment has decreased for both men and women laborers, but the number of days of employment was lower for women than for men; and, (3) the average real daily wage earnings of agricultural laborers have declined for both women and men but, with women earning lower wages and working, on the average, fewer days than men, the impact on women's earnings has been greater.[8] Women are less mobile than men, since child care falls almost exclusively to them; hence the decline in village or cottage industries, another trend, affects more heavily women's chances for alternative employment.

In non-agricultural occupations, women are found in greater numbers in the unorganized sector, as construction workers (taking their babies to the construction site, with all the dangers that entails), as *bidi* makers (working with the tobacco at home on a putting-out system), and as embroiderers (working on a piecework basis). The possibilities for exploitation of all kinds are rife in such situations and the chances for labor organization are minimal.

The 1974 report found that while total employment in industry in the organized sector had increased, women's share in industrial employment had declined, from 11.43 percent in 1951 to 9.1 percent in 1971. In plantation labor, however, women's employment increased slightly from 46 percent to 49 percent.[9] Some analysts attribute the decline in women's industrial employment to protective legislation and the need to provide maternity benefits, creches, and separate sanitary facilities for women workers. There is a requirement, for example, that an employer of 30 or more women employees provide a creche, which leads employers to hire only 29. This may indeed be a factor, but the 1974 report indicated that more significant in the decline of women's industrial employment was the nature of modern technologies. In industries where workers are displaced by mechanization, women workers are more likely to be displaced than men, since retraining programs are provided first for men and women are less likely to belong to the unions which demand such programs. This latter factor is as much a result of union apathy toward women's problems as it is employers' attitudes, although in both instances the prevailing attitude is that women are supplemental and men are primary earners. This takes no cognizance of rising numbers of female-headed and other households where women are the primary earners.[10]

In the service sector, the figures are more encouraging. Women's employment in clerical and administrative services and in the professions has risen over the last several decades. This improvement, however, affects a very small proportion of employed women at the top of the social and educational ladder. Women in menial services, such as cleaners, sweepers, and the like, have declined in numbers.[11] All of these statistics boil down to one thing: no matter how much more visible women may be in the workplace, most women workers are worse off now than they were several decades ago. Attitudes which relegate women to a secondary place in the labor force and assumptions about women's primary place being in the home persist, although vast evidence indicates the necessity of women's earnings for the survival of their families and the necessity of their labor for the maintenance of production levels, especially in agriculture.

The fact that poor women are not benefiting from economic development is abundantly clear and further recitation of dismal statistics would only reinforce such a conclusion. At the same time, educated women have benefited from improved economic opportunities in the expanding modern and professional sectors. This increased class differentiation among women indicates that poor women are marginalized because of social organization. Working class organizations do not address the specific problems of women in the unorganized sector; middle class women's organizations do not address the specific problems arising from the poverty and vulnerability of these poorest of the poor. What, then, can be done? Is there no way out of this dilemma? That would seem to be the case, save for two factors. The first is the tradition of women's political activism born of the Indian nationalist movement. There are women activists whose consciousness transcends narrow class interests. The second is the very vulnerability of women generally in India, regardless of class, which means that feminism has a very strong raison d'être. Women must make their own platform and fight for their economic, social, legal, and other rights, for they have no other choice. The very desperation of the situation of poor women in India is in some measure their strength. An examination of two organizations will illustrate this kind of political activism. These organizations arose out of the needs of poor women; educated women played guiding and facilitating roles in them, but the programs are dedicated to self-help.

One of the best known examples of an organization of poor women is the Self-Employed Women's Association (SEWA) of Ahmedabad.[12] This association, a union of over 5,000 poor workers — head loaders, ragpickers, junk dealers, vegetable vendors, and handcart pullers, among others — was started in 1972 and is headed by Ela Bhatt, a concerned Gandhian who was an official in the women's wing of the Ahmedabad Textile Labor Association (TLA). SEWA was eventually expelled by the TLA, but it continues to grow and provide a variety of services to its poor members. It has organized demonstrations for higher wages and improved working conditions, and has defended members against harassment by police and middlemen. These are part of SEWA's "struggle" or union-style activities, but it is also involved in developmental work; it provides a credit and savings bank, training programs, social security schemes, and production and marketing cooperatives.

The secret of SEWA's success is that it arose out of the felt needs of its members and they direct most of its activities. Ela Bhatt and her co-workers provide overall direction, but emphasize self-help as their guiding principle. For illiterate women to organize and direct a successful bank may seem impossible, but they have done so. One of the direst needs of small-scale sellers and home producers is for credit. The SEWA bank provides it and has a much better record of repayment than most. Training programs to improve production and design of bamboo products, block printing, embroidery, and so on, and marketing cooperatives to avoid exploitation by middlemen, have been organized. It has given its members more economic and social power both as individuals and as members of their families. The organization itself has drawn attention to the unorganized sector in the development process. SEWA arose out of its environment in Ahmedabad and has benefited from enlightened leadership as well as grassroots enthusiasm. Whether it can be successfully replicated elsewhere remains a question; there is a small SEWA in Delhi and one has been started in Chandigarh. SEWA points to the importance of organizations of, by, and for poor women, and of self-help organisms generally.

Another example of a grassroots organization of the poor is the Shramik Sanghatana among the Bhil tribals of Dhule district in Maharashtra.[13] Poverty and landlessness are problems among the tribals of the region. The Shramik Sanghatana arose in the early 1970s in response to attempted land grabs by the dominant Gujar caste, to force the government to cancel transfers of tribal lands, and to demand enforcement of minimum wages. The leaders of the Shramik Sanghatana were educated tribals who had previously been active in the Sarvodaya movement, a Gandhian offshoot, but who founded their own organization when they determined that Sarvodaya was insufficiently mass-based.

The Sanghatana established village-level committees of tribal agricultural laborers. In 1972, it organized an agitation by contract laborers to raise their annual pay from Rs. 100 to Rs. 150-200, and to raise the wages of day laborers from Rs. 2 to Rs. 4 for men and from Rs. 1.50 to Rs. 2.75 for women. They sought the abolition of *begar*, compulsory unpaid labor. At that time, the Shramik Sanghatana was an organization of the rural poor, without any particular emphasis on women's needs. As it developed, however, the Sanghatana organized tribal women, holding its first training camp for women in 1973, and urged the women to express their problems without shame, to discuss their experiences with women from other villages, to organize their own village committees, to attend night schools, and to work toward stopping the men's drinking, gambling, and wife-beating.

One particular incident is illustrative of the effects of such organization and consciousness-raising:

> A landlord in the village had the habit of throwing his garbage in front of an *adivasi* (tribal) woman's house. When she complained one day, he became enraged at her "impudence," grabbed her and dragged her twenty feet by the hair. He tore off her blouse, threw her on the ground, sat on her stomach and beat her severely.
>
> The Shramik Sanghatana activists sent the woman to the police to register a case against the landlord. The police told her that although the case was non-cognizable, they would investigate it, but they never did. The activists decided to take the woman to the surrounding villages so that other women would be incited to take action. When the woman and the activists reported the incident, women responded immediately. They decided on a date to take a *morcha* (procession) to the landlord's house.
>
> Two hundred to three hundred women from about twelve villages, and one hundred to one hundred and fifty men, whom the Shramik Sanghatana persuaded to remain in the background, collected on the appointed day. They appealed to the *sarpanch* (village headman) and the police *patil* (constable), who did nothing. The women surrounded the landlord's house, forced him to come out, and demanded that he recount the incident. They allowed him ten minutes to justify his actions, in the form of a public trial. When he could not, the women garlanded his neck with their *chappals* (sandals), blackened his face, and sat him on a donkey. They then paraded the landlord through the villages where the women beat him and abused him. The police arrested sixteen villagers that night. The activists were released on bail but told to report to the police station daily like criminals. Two hundred women came forward and

told the police they were prepared to be arrested, and one thousand people offered to pay the bail. The cases were eventually dropped.[14]

Such incidents are dramatic; they are indicative of the growing tendency on the part of women to resist violence, whether from the landlords or from the hands of their own men. As women become more militant, they often shame their men into standing up for their own rights. Resistance to the rape of tribal women becomes symbolic of resistance to tribal powerlessness.

## The Quest for Gender Justice

The quest for protection of women's economic roles and rights leads, almost by definition, to the quest for legal rights. This issue is linked to economic participation in very intimate ways. The escalation of violence against women has economic roots, not only among tribal populations seeking their rights to the land, but also among the middle and lower-middle classes. In these groups dowry has become one of the major sources of ready capital, thus increasing demands upon new daughters-in-law and their parents for higher payments. The increasing monetization of the marriage market, with the decline of traditional methods and networks for determining the eligibility of potential mates, means that demands for dowry are escalating, even in groups in the society where dowry was not traditionally demanded. The conversion of the custom of brideprice among tribals into dowry is one example. The result is a devaluation of women and increased pressure on young brides and their families for money they can ill afford.

The phenomenon of bride burning (or abetting suicide) is probably not new in India, but certainly the scale of the problem is new, as is the publicity the phenomenon has received lately. Before this, one read about the occasional accidental burning ("poor dear, she got too close to the kerosene stove in her new nylon sari"). Now, women's organizations in cities all over India have taken up the issue, pressuring the police to investigate more closely suspicious cases of "suicide" among recent brides and young married women, and demonstrating to call attention to such cases and waken public opinion to the problem.[15] The phenomenon of bride burning in the middle class is comparable in some ways to the problem of rape of tribal and landless women. It is indicative of the breakdown of traditional social relations and substitution of a cash nexus and shows the devaluation and powerlessness of women in such a system of economic relations.

Women's equal rights are guaranteed in the Indian constitution, but that does not mean that they are a fact. Equal rights may be enshrined in the law, but as Americans learned in their civil rights movement, rights must be demanded by those who are supposed to enjoy them. Hence, in seeking their rights, as in the organization of poor women to achieve economic benefits, the activism of women can play an increasingly significant role. Before 1947, Indian women were involved in the movement for national independence and Indian women's organizations such as the All-India Women's Conference (AIWC) pressured nationalist leaders for a reform of Hindu family laws.[16] In the 1940s, a committee headed by B. N. Rau recommended a new Hindu Code, but it was not until after independence that the Hindu Code was passed, piecemeal, in the 1950s. Hindu women received rights to inherit property, to adopt, and to a somewhat liberalized divorce. These were significant advances, especially for women in families with property and those in a position to understand their increased rights. For others, the revised Hindu Code has made little difference, since many women simply do not know what their rights are, and the patriarchal and patrilinear family system continues to discriminate against daughters.

Furthermore, there is no uniform civil code in India, so the reform of Hindu family law has had no effect on the rights of Muslim or Christian women. Divorce is still extremely difficult for a Christian woman. A Muslim woman, who may be divorced all too easily by her husband or be faced with a polygamous household, finds that divorce is much harder to obtain if she is the one who seeks it. In property law, however, Muslim women have always had the right to inherit, although only one-half the amount of their brothers. The Indian government, with its commitment to secularism, has found it politically impossible to reform Muslim personal law and has shied away from pressing for a uniform civil code. Unless Muslim women organize to demand a reform of Muslim personal law, and I do not think that will happen in the immediate future, the situation of disparate civil codes will doubtless persist.

In recent years there have been efforts to reform the law in two areas where women have organized to demand such revisions. In late 1983, Parliament passed the Criminal Law (Amendment) Act of 1980, otherwise known as the new rape law, which raises the minimum punishment for rape from two years to seven, shifts the onus of proof from the victim to the accused, raises penalties for custodial rape (by police officers, jail staff, and so on), bans the publication of the victim's name or whereabouts, and provides that rape trials be held in camera. This law was passed after three years of extensive debate and remains controversial. The impetus for the reform of the rape law came from the case of Mathura, a 15-year-old girl who was raped in 1972 while in police custody. The case went all the way to the Supreme Court, where the two accused were acquitted, since Mathura had allegedly not resisted the policemen. At this point, four law professors took up Mathura's case and wrote an open letter to the Chief Justice in which they attacked the Supreme Court's verdict and pointed to serious lacunae in the rape law.[17] This letter is today considered to be among the best examples of social action litigation by direct appeal, a technique used by legal reformers, and has helped arouse public opinion in favor of a revision of the rape law. A Parliamentary Select Committee was appointed which examined witnesses from women's organizations, lawyers, social workers, and police officials, ultimately resulting in the new law.[18]

Another result of the Mathura case occurred in Mathura's home state of Maharashtra, where Dr. Seema Sakhare, an educator and social activist, became so indignant at the Supreme Court's verdict that she founded the Platform Against Rape (Balatkar Virodhi Manch) in Nagpur in 1980. This organization helps the victims of rape to report the crime, helps the police in collecting evidence and in bringing the accused to trial, and helps counsel and rehabilitate the victims. The Platform Against Rape relies on the pressure of public opinion, on its reputation for dedication to truth and justice, and on its organizers' knowledge of the sinuosities of the law.[19] Throughout the debate over the rape law, it is clear that legal reformers and women's organizations alike gained much from their ability to arouse public opinion through the media. This is an important force in the *satyagraha* tradition of India politics, which, unfortunately, the new law — with its strictures on publicity — has seriously hampered.

The movement to amend the Dowry Prohibition Act of 1961 is another case where women's organizations have been able to mobilize public opinion in favor of greater justice for women. The escalating numbers of bride burnings or dowry deaths were mentioned above, together with the growing coverage that such incidents have received in the press. Women's organizations such as the Mahila Dakshata Samiti, run by Pramila Dandavate, an opposition Member of Parliament who has been an advocate of dowry law amendment, and Saheli of Delhi, an organization which has led demonstrations outside the houses of burn victims and has become a refuge for battered wives, have become more and more outspoken. Saheli recently conducted a study of police reports on 107 deaths by burning of women during a two-month period. It was found that although 83 post-mortems were conducted, the results were not mentioned in the case records. In the remaining 24 cases where post-mortems were not carried out, the procedure had been waived in 20 cases on the request of the family, including the husband. Saheli's report noted the obvious conflict of interest involved when a husband can decide on whether or not a post-mortem should be conducted in a case in which he might be a suspect. Saheli studied burn cases at a major hospital in Delhi and found that women were burned ten times more seriously than men, that more women died of burns as compared to men (62 versus 24 percent of their sample; indicating, I presume, that the remaining 14 percent were not fatalities), and that 58 percent of the women burned were in cotton or other natural fiber saris, challenging the "nylon sari theory" of serious "accidental" burns.[20]

Responding, albeit tardily, to public pressure to put teeth into the anti-dowry legislation (there have been no convictions in the 23 years since its passage), the government introduced an amendment to the Dowry Prohibition (Amendment) Act of 1984. It changed the definition of dowry slightly from property or valuables given "in consideration for the marriage" to "in connection with the marriage," made the receipt of dowry a cognizable offense, and raised the minimum punishment. Loopholes and exemptions still remain in the act, and the amendment as passed may be no more enforceable than its predecessor.[21] In this case, as with rape legislation, changing the law is only a small step in a movement toward changing public attitudes and practices. The law cannot provide a more equitable society, but it can buttress those forces working toward one.

Judicial review has resulted in historic verdicts in recent years that are significant for women's rights. The Code of Criminal Procedure of 1974 provides for the maintenance of divorcees and children unable to support themselves. The ex-husband is now liable to prosecution under criminal law, not civil law. Muslims sought exemption from this provision, since their personal law provides for a lump sum payment of dower (*mahr*) to the ex-wife in event of divorce. The Supreme Court decided in the Bai Tahira case that a Muslim divorcee is entitled to maintenance under provisions of the criminal code. This decision demonstrates that discrepancies among the civil codes of India may be rectified through judicial review, but this is a special case of the overlapping jurisdiction of civil and criminal codes, leaving room for judicial interpretation.[22]

In assessing legal changes in India in recent years, one must note in conclusion that the law has increasingly defined and limited areas of harassment of women and attempted to prohibit the most flagrant examples of violence against women's persons. There is, however, little evidence of a positive theory of women's rights or position, or of a role of women — other than a supporting one — in the nation's development.[23]

These are only a few examples of the kinds of results that various organizations, mobilizing women and the poor, and helping to enlighten public opinion concerning economic and social injustice, have been able to accomplish in recent years. If the aggregate statistics concerning women's economic participation are not optimistic, local grassroots organizations and individual efforts offer a more encouraging picture. If these actions involve more confrontation with governmental and familial authority, so be it. Social change is a painful process and no one deserves a change in status more than the dispossessed Indian woman. At the same time, it is important to realize that greater justice for women will involve greater justice for other dispossessed and powerless elements in Indian society. There is no purdah in the quest for justice.

## NOTES

The author is grateful to Rajeev Dhavan for his helpful critique of an earlier draft of this essay.

1. Committee on the Status of Women in India, *Towards Equality*, New Delhi, Government of India, Ministry of Education and Social Welfare, December 1974; see also *Status of Women in India: A Synopsis of the Report of the National Committee*, New Delhi, Allied Publishers for the Indian Council of Social Science Research, 1977, cited hereafter as *Synopsis*.

2. See, e.g., Gail Minault, "Introduction: The Extended Family as Metaphor and the Expansion of Women's Realm," in *The Extended Family: Women and Political Participation in India and Pakistan*, edited by Gail Minault, Delhi, Chanakya, and Columbia, Missouri, South Asia Books, 1981, pp. 3-18; Gail Minault, "At Odds or In Tune with the Family? Some Reflections on Women's Activism in India and America," *Indian Journal of American Studies*, July 1983, pp. 27-35; and Gail Minault, "Scholars and Activists: The Indian Association of Women's Studies Conference at Trivandrum," *Choice India*, August 1984, pp. 37-38.

3. For theoretical discussions of this topic, see Ester Boserup, *Women's Role in Economic Development*, New York, St. Martin's Press, 1970; and Lourdes Beneria and Gita Sen, "Accumulation, Reproduction, and Women's Role in Economic Development: Boserup Revisited," *Signs*, Winter 1981, pp. 279-928.

4. V. M. Dandekar, "Integration of Women in Economic Development," *Economic and Political Weekly*, October 30, 1982, pp. 1782-86; Hanna Papanek, "Class and Gender in Education-Employment Linkages: Selected Country Studies," Boston University, Center for Asian Development Studies, Discussion Paper 22, pp. 2-4. (I am grateful to Hanna Papanek for sharing with me this paper, forthcoming in *Comparative Education Review);* Indian Association of Women's Studies

Report of a Workshop on Women, Work, and Employment, presented at the Second National Conference on Women's Studies, University of Kerala, Trivandrum, April 1984 (paper in author's possession).

5. *Synopsis*, pp. 60-63.

6. Workshop Report on Women, Work, and Employment, Trivandrum, April 1984.

7. *Synopsis*, pp. 65-66.

8. Workshop Report on Women, Work, and Employment, Trivandrum, April 1984.

9. *Synopsis*, pp. 71-72.

10. *Ibid.*, p. 74; Workshop Report, April 1984.

11. *Synopsis*, pp. 75-76; Hanna Papanek, "Class and Gender in Education-Employment Linkages."

12. This account of SEWA is based upon Devaki Jain, "Street Vendors of Ahmedabad," in her *Women's Quest for Power*, New Delhi, Vikas, 1980, pp. 20-76; Jennifer Sebstad, *Struggle and Development Among Self Employed Women: A Report on the Self Employed Women's Association, Ahmedabad, India*, Washington D.C., Agency for International Development, 1982; and on an interview with Ela Bhatt and visit to SEWA's headquarters in Ahmedabad, July 18, 1983.

13. I am indebted for this account to the work of Amrita Basu, "Two Faces of Protest: Alternative Forms of Women's Mobilization in West Bengal and Maharashtra," in Minault, *The Extended Family, op. cit.*, pp. 217-262; see also Gail Omvedt, *We Will Smash This Prison! Indian Women in Struggle*, London, Zed, and Delhi, Orient Longmans, 1979, pp. 91-97.

14. Basu, "Two Faces of Protest," pp. 242-243.

15. *How* (New Delhi), March 1983, Special Issue on the Dowry Problem; "Indian Women Speak Out Against Dowry," in *Third World, Second Sex*, edited by Miranda Davies, London, Zed, 1983, pp. 201-213.

16. For a detailed account of the activities of Indian women's organizations in working for the reform of the Hindu Code, see Geraldine Forbes, "In Pursuit of Justice: Women's Organisations and Legal Reform," *Samya Shakti*, I, 2, 1984, pp. 33-54.

17. Lotika Sarkar, Upendra Baxi, Vasudha Dhagamvar, and Raghunath Kelkar.

18. This account is based largely on Sunil Sethi, "Rape: Controversial Code," *India Today*, December 31, 1983, pp. 134-35; see also Upendra Baxi, "Taking Suffering Seriously: Social Action Litigation in the Supreme Court of India," *Delhi Law Review*, 1979-80, pp. 91-116.

19. Seema Sakhare, "Platform Against Rape," paper presented at the Second National Conference on Women's Studies, University of

Kerala, Trivandrum, April 1984 (paper in author's possession); "The Anti-Rape Movement in India," and "The War Against Rape: A Report from Karimnagar," *Third World, Second Sex, op. cit.*, pp. 179-186, 197-201.

20. Sumit Mehra, "Dowry Law: Debating the Delay," *India Today*, April 15, 1984, p. 39.

21. "The Dowry (Prohibition) Act, 1961: The Struggle for an Amendment," *Samya Shakti*, I, 2, 1984, pp. 131-134.

22. Lucy Carroll, "Muslim Family Law in South Asia: Important Decisions Regarding Maintenance for Wives and Ex-Wives," *Islamic and Comparative Law Quarterly* (New Delhi), I, 2, 1981, pp. 95-113.

23. I am indebted for this observation to Rajeev Dhavan; see, Upendra Baxi, "Patriarchy, Law and State: Some Preliminary Notes," paper presented at a Workshop on Women and the Law, Second National Conference on Women's Studies, Trivandrum, April 1984.